The Simple
Mediterranean Diet
Cookbook
For Beginners

2000 Days Quick, Nutritious & Mouthwatering Recipes Book for Body Management | No-Stress 30-Day Meal Plan for a Better You

Kelsey G. Hodgson

Table of Contents

INTRODUCTION

Welcome to the enticing world of Mediterranean cuisine! I am thrilled to introduce you to a delicious and healthy way of eating that has been enjoyed by generations of people living in the Mediterranean region. The Mediterranean diet is not just a diet but a way of life that emphasizes fresh, whole foods, and simple preparation methods. It has been shown to have numerous health benefits, including reducing the risk of heart disease, stroke, and certain types of cancer, as well as improving overall health and longevity.

In this cookbook, I have gathered some of the most delicious and authentic Mediterranean recipes that will take your taste buds on a journey through the sun-drenched lands of Greece, Italy, Spain, and beyond. From vibrant salads to hearty stews, each recipe is designed to showcase the unique flavors and health benefits of this in-credible way of eating.

Whether you are a seasoned cook or a beginner in the kitchen, this cookbook will inspire you to create de-licious and nutritious meals that your family and friends will love. So let's start cooking and discover the joys of the Mediterranean diet together!

Mediterranean Diet 101

Imagine you are sitting in a Mediterranean restau-rant, surrounded by the warm breeze and the sounds of the sea. The waiter brings a colorful array of dishes to your table, each one bursting with flavor and freshness. You take a bite of the grilled fish, seasoned with olive oil and fragrant herbs, and savor the delicate texture and taste. As you continue your meal, you taste the vibrant salads, loaded with crisp vegetables and drizzled with tangy dressing. You feel satisfied and energized, knowing that you are nourishing your body with the healthiest and most delicious foods that the Mediterranean region has to offer. This is the essence of the Mediterranean diet, a way of eating that will transport you to a land of sunshine, vitality, and pleasure.

What's Mediterranean Diet?

The Mediterranean diet is a dietary pattern that is primarily based on the traditional eating habits of countries surrounding the Mediterranean Sea. The diet emphasizes the consumption of plant-based foods, including fruits, vegetables, legumes, nuts, and whole grains. It also includes moderate consumption of fish and seafood, and low to moderate amounts of dairy products, poultry, and eggs. Red meat is consumed in small quantities or avoided altogether. Additionally, the diet places an emphasis on the use of healthy fats, such as olive oil, and limited intake of saturated and trans fats, as well as processed and refined foods.

This dietary pattern has been associated with a number of health benefits, including reduced risk of cardiovascular disease, diabetes, certain types of cancer, and neurodegenerative diseases. These health benefits are attributed to the high intake of fruits, vegetables, and whole grains, which provide a range of essential vitamins, minerals, and phytonutrients. Furthermore, the consumption of healthy fats, such as olive oil and nuts, has been shown to have a beneficial effect on lipid profiles and cardiovascular health.

The Mediterranean diet has been identified as a sustainable and healthy dietary pattern that is suitable for all age groups and can be easily incorporated into various cultures and cuisines. Despite its numerous benefits, adherence to the Mediterranean diet has been found to vary across different populations and geographical regions. In order to promote the Mediterranean diet, further research and educational efforts are needed to raise awareness about the health benefits of this dietary pattern and to encourage individuals to adopt healthy eating habits.

Mediterranean Diet History and Trend

The Mediterranean diet has been recognized as a dietary pattern that is associated with numerous health benefits. However, the history of this dietary pattern dates back to ancient times. In ancient Greece, Hippocrates, the father of modern medicine, emphasized the importance of nutrition and the use of food as a form of medicine. Similarly, in ancient Rome, the philosopher Pliny the Elder promoted the consumption of fruits and vegetables as a means of maintaining good health.

The modern concept of the Mediterranean diet was first introduced in the 1960s, when researchers observed that populations living in the Mediterranean region had lower rates of chronic diseases, such as cardiovascular disease and cancer, compared to other populations. Subsequent research identified the dietary patterns of these populations, which included high consumption of plant-based foods, such as fruits, vegetables, whole grains, legumes, nuts, and seeds, as well as moderate consumption of fish and seafood, and low to moderate amounts of dairy products, poultry, and eggs. The diet also placed an emphasis on the use of healthy fats, such as olive oil, and limited intake of saturated and trans fats, as well as processed and refined foods.

In recent years, the Mediterranean diet has gained popularity as a healthy and sustainable dietary pattern that is associated with numerous health benefits. In 2010, the United Nations Educational, Scientific and Cultural Organization (UNESCO) recognized the Mediterranean diet as an intangible cultural heritage of humanity. This recognition highlights the cultural significance of the Mediterranean diet and its importance as a part of the cultural heritage of the Mediterranean region.

The current trend towards plant-based diets and sustainable eating habits has further increased the popularity of the Mediterranean diet. Studies have shown that the Mediterranean diet is not only beneficial for health but also has a positive impact on the environment. The emphasis on plant-based foods and sustainable agriculture practices in the Mediterranean diet aligns with the principles of a sustainable food system.

The Healthy Mediterranean Diet Pyramid

The Mediterranean diet pyramid is a visual representation of the traditional Mediterranean dietary pattern, which is based on the eating habits of countries surrounding the Mediterranean Sea. The pyramid emphasizes the consumption of whole, minimally processed plant-based foods, such as fruits, vegetables, legumes, whole grains, and nuts, as the foundation of the diet. It also includes moderate consumption of fish and seafood, and low to moderate amounts of dairy products, poultry, and eggs. Red meat and sweets are consumed in small quantities or avoided altogether. Additionally, the pyramid emphasizes the use of healthy fats, such as olive oil, and limited intake of saturated and trans fats, as well as processed and refined foods.

The Mediterranean diet pyramid is divided into different tiers, with the foundation tier being the largest and the top tier being the smallest. The foundation tier emphasizes the importance of daily physical activity, as well as the consumption of whole plant-based foods, such as fruits, vegetables, whole grains, and legumes. The next tier includes the consumption of healthy fats, such as

olive oil, nuts, and seeds. The third tier includes the consumption of fish and seafood, as well as low to moderate amounts of dairy products, poultry, and eggs. The fourth tier includes the consumption of red meat in small quantities or avoided altogether, as well as the use of herbs and spices to flavor foods instead of salt. The top tier emphasizes the importance of limiting intake of sweets and processed foods.

The Mediterranean diet pyramid is designed to promote healthy eating habits and to reduce the risk of chronic diseases, such as cardiovascular disease, diabetes, and certain types of cancer. The emphasis on whole, minimally processed plant-based foods, as well as the use of healthy fats and limited intake of saturated and trans fats, is believed to contribute to the health benefits of the Mediterranean dietary pattern.

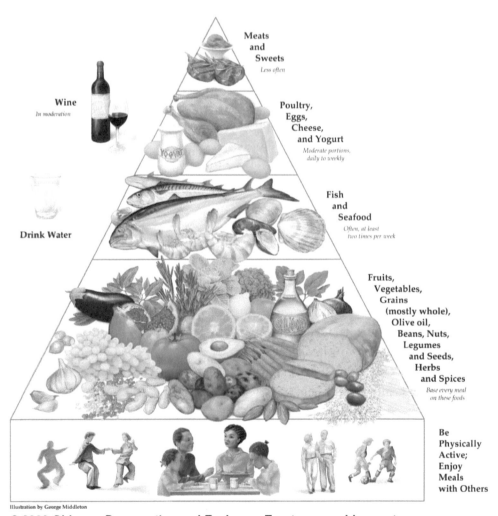

Mediterranean Diet Pyramid
A contemporary approach to delicious, healthy eating

Meats and Sweets
Less often

Wine
In moderation

Poultry, Eggs, Cheese, and Yogurt
Moderate portions, daily to weekly

Fish and Seafood
Often, at least two times per week

Drink Water

Fruits, Vegetables, Grains (mostly whole), Olive oil, Beans, Nuts, Legumes and Seeds, Herbs and Spices
Base every meal on these foods

Be Physically Active; Enjoy Meals with Others

Illustration by George Middleton

The Amazing Mediterranean Culture

The Mediterranean region is home to a diverse and rich culinary culture that has been shaped by centuries of cultural exchange and agricultural practices. Healthy eating is deeply ingrained in the Mediterranean living culture, which emphasizes the consumption of whole, minimally processed plant-based foods, as well as the use of healthy fats, such as olive oil, and limited intake of saturated and trans fats, as well as processed and refined foods.

One of the key features of the Mediterranean living culture related to healthy eating is the emphasis on fresh, seasonal, and locally sourced ingredients. The Mediterranean region is blessed with a wide variety of fruits, vegetables, herbs, and spices, which are used to flavor dishes and provide important nutrients. Traditional Mediterranean dishes often feature a variety of colorful vegetables, such as eggplant, tomatoes, peppers, and zucchini, as well as leafy greens, such as spinach, kale, and chard. Whole grains, such as bulgur, couscous, and barley, are also commonly consumed.

Another important feature of the Mediterranean living culture related to healthy eating is the emphasis on social eating and the importance of family and community meals. Traditional Mediterranean meals are often shared with family and friends, and the act of preparing and sharing meals is seen as a way of fostering social bonds and promoting overall health and well-being. In addition, the Mediterranean living culture encourages a slower, more relaxed approach to eating, with meals often enjoyed over several courses and extended periods of time.

Physical activity is also an important part of the Mediterranean living culture related to healthy eating. Many traditional Mediterranean communities engage in regular physical activity, such as walking, gardening, and dancing, which helps to promote overall health and well-being. The Mediterranean lifestyle also emphasizes the importance of stress management, with activities such as yoga, meditation, and socializing playing a key role in maintaining mental and emotional health.

The Benefits of Mediterranean Diet

The Mediterranean diet is widely recognized for its numerous health benefits. Here are some key advantages of adopting a Mediterranean-style eating pattern:

✧ **Heart health:** The Mediterranean diet is associated with a reduced risk of heart disease. It emphasizes the consumption of heart-healthy foods such as fruits, vegetables, whole grains, nuts, legumes, and fish, while limiting red meat and sweets. The moderate consumption of monounsaturated fats from olive oil, a key component of the Mediterranean diet, has been linked to lower rates of heart disease and improved cholesterol levels.

✧ **Weight management:** The Mediterranean diet promotes a balanced and wholesome approach to eating, with an emphasis on whole foods and portion control. It includes a variety of nutrient-dense foods while limiting processed and sugary foods, which can help with weight management and weight loss. The Mediterranean diet is also associated with a lower risk of obesity and abdominal obesity, which are risk factors for various chronic diseases.

✧ **Diabetes prevention:** Studies have shown that the Mediterranean diet can help prevent type 2 diabetes. Its emphasis on whole grains, legumes, fruits, vegetables, nuts, and healthy fats, and its moderate consumption of fish and dairy products can help regulate blood sugar levels and improve insulin sensitivity.

✧ **Cognitive function:** The Mediterranean diet has been associated with better cognitive function and a reduced risk of cognitive decline and neurodegenerative diseases such as Alzheimer's disease. The high intake of antioxidants from fruits, vegetables, and olive oil, as well as the beneficial fats from fish and nuts, may contribute to these cognitive benefits.

✧ **Cancer prevention:** The Mediterranean diet has been linked to a reduced risk of certain types of cancer, including breast, colorectal, and prostate cancers. The abundant intake of plant-based foods, which are rich in fiber, antioxidants, and phytochemicals, may play a role in cancer prevention.

✧ **Longevity:** Studies have shown that adherence to the Mediterranean diet is associated with increased lifespan and reduced mortality rates. The Mediterranean diet's focus on whole, nutrient-dense foods, along with its emphasis on social connections during meals and an active lifestyle, may contribute to overall longevity and well-being.

✧ **Nutritional balance:** The Mediterranean diet provides a well-rounded and balanced approach to nutrition, with a wide variety of foods that supply essential nutrients such as fiber, vitamins, minerals, and healthy fats. It encourages a diverse and colorful array of fruits and vegetables, which can help ensure a nutrient-rich diet.

Important Mediterranean Ingredients

The Mediterranean diet is a plant-based dietary pattern that emphasizes the consumption of whole, minimally processed plant-based foods, as well as the use of healthy fats and limited intake of saturated and trans fats, as well as processed and refined foods. Some important ingredients that are commonly used in the Mediterranean diet include:

1. Olive oil: Olive oil is a key ingredient in the Mediterranean diet and a staple in the culinary culture of the Mediterranean region. It is derived from the fruit of the olive tree and is rich in monounsaturated fatty acids, which are beneficial for heart health. Olive oil also contains high levels of antioxidants, such as polyphenols, which have been linked to numerous health benefits, including reduced risk of chronic diseases such as cancer and Alzheimer's disease.

Olive oil is commonly used in the Mediterranean diet as a healthy fat source in cooking, salad dressings, and as a condiment. It is used in place of saturated and trans fats, such as butter and margarine, which are linked to increased risk of chronic diseases. The use of olive oil in the Mediterranean diet is also associated with a reduced risk of cardiovascular disease, as it has been shown to reduce levels of LDL or "bad" cholesterol and increase levels of HDL or "good" cholesterol.

Olive oil is produced in many countries around the world, but the quality and flavor of olive oil can vary depending on the type of olive, growing conditions, and production methods. Extra-virgin olive oil, which is made from the first cold pressing of the olives and has the highest levels of antioxidants and flavor, is preferred in the Mediterranean diet. It is also important to note that olive oil is a calorie-dense food, and excessive consumption can contribute to weight gain and other health problems.

2. Fruits and vegetables: Fruits and vegetables are an essential component of the Mediterranean diet, a dietary pattern that is associated with numerous health benefits. The Mediterranean region is blessed with a wide variety of fruits and vegetables, which are consumed in abundance and feature prominently in traditional Mediterranean cuisine. The consumption of fruits and vegetables is central to the Mediterranean diet, with recommendations to consume at least five servings of these foods per day.

Fruits and vegetables are an important source of vitamins, minerals, fiber, and antioxidants, all of which play critical roles in maintaining health and preventing chronic diseases. Commonly consumed fruits in the Mediterranean region include citrus fruits, such as oranges and lemons, as well as stone fruits, such as peaches and apricots. Berries, such as strawberries and raspberries, are also popular, as are melons, figs, and grapes. Vegetables that are commonly consumed in the Mediterranean diet include tomatoes, eggplant, zucchini, peppers, leafy greens, and root vegetables, such as carrots and beets.

One of the key features of the Mediterranean diet is the emphasis on seasonal and locally sourced produce. This means that the fruits and vegetables consumed in the Mediterranean region vary depending on the time of year and the region in which they are grown. The consumption of seasonal produce is believed to provide important nutrients and antioxidants that are beneficial for health.

In addition to providing important nutrients and fiber, fruits and vegetables are also low in calories and can help promote weight loss and weight management. The high fiber content of fruits and vegetables can help to increase feelings of fullness and reduce the intake of high-calorie, low-nutrient foods.

Overall, the consumption of fruits and vegetables is a critical component of the Mediterranean diet, providing important nutrients and antioxidants, promoting weight management, and reducing the risk of chronic diseases. The emphasis on seasonal and locally sourced produce in the Mediterranean region is a valuable model for promoting healthy eating habits and overall well-being.

3. Legumes: Legumes are an important component of the Mediterranean diet and are commonly consumed in the region in a variety of dishes. Legumes are plant-based foods that are high in protein, fiber, and a range of important vitamins and minerals. Examples of legumes commonly used in the Mediterranean diet include chickpeas, lentils, beans, and peas.

Legumes have a long history of use in the Mediterranean region, dating back to ancient times. In many Mediterranean cultures, legumes were a staple food source due to their affordability, high nutrient density, and versatility in cooking. In addition to being used in soups, stews, and salads, legumes were often ground into flour to make bread, or roasted and ground to make coffee substitutes.

One of the key benefits of legumes as an ingredient in the Mediterranean diet is their high protein content. For individuals who follow a plant-based diet or have limited access to animal-based protein sources, legumes can be an important source of protein. In addition, legumes are high in dietary fiber, which can help to promote digestive health and reduce the risk of chronic diseases such as heart disease and diabetes.

Legumes are also a good source of a variety of important vitamins and minerals, including iron, magnesium, potassium, and folate. These nutrients are important for maintaining optimal health and preventing nutrient deficiencies.

In the Mediterranean diet, legumes are often prepared in a variety of ways, including as soups, stews, dips, and salads. For example, chickpeas are commonly used in hummus, a popular dip made with tahini, olive oil, and lemon juice. Lentils are often used in salads or soups, such as the classic French dish, lentil soup. Beans are commonly used in stews, such as the Spanish dish, fabada asturiana, which is made with white beans, chorizo, and other ingredients.

4. Whole grains: Whole grains are an important component of the Mediterranean diet and are widely used in the region's cuisine. Whole grains are grains that have not been refined, meaning that they contain all of their original nutrients, including fiber, vitamins, and minerals. Commonly used whole grains in the Mediterranean diet include wheat, barley, oats, and rye, among others.

Whole grains provide numerous health benefits, including reduced risk of heart disease, stroke, and type 2 diabetes. This is due in part to their high fiber content, which helps to reduce cholesterol levels and improve blood sugar control. Additionally, whole grains are a good source of important vitamins and minerals, including B vitamins, iron, and zinc.

In the Mediterranean region, whole grains are often used to make bread, pasta, and couscous, among other dishes. Whole grain breads are a staple of many Mediterranean diets and are often made using traditional methods, such as sourdough fermentation. Whole grain pasta is also popular, particularly in Italy, where it is often served with a variety of fresh vegetables and herbs.

One popular Mediterranean dish that features whole grains is tabbouleh, a salad made with bulgur wheat, parsley, mint, tomatoes, and onions, dressed with lemon juice and olive oil. Another common dish is pilaf, which is made with rice or other whole grains, mixed with vegetables and spices, and often served as a side dish or a main course.

5. Nuts and seeds: Nuts and seeds are an important component of the Mediterranean diet, which is a plant-based dietary pattern that emphasizes the consumption of whole, minimally processed plant-based foods. Nuts and seeds are rich in healthy fats, protein, fiber, vitamins, and minerals, making them a nutritious addition to any diet.

In the Mediterranean region, nuts and seeds have been consumed for centuries, and are commonly used as a snack or added to dishes such as salads, yogurt, and baked goods. Almonds, walnuts, and pistachios are some of the most commonly consumed nuts in the Mediterranean region, while sesame seeds, pumpkin seeds, and flaxseeds are commonly used in dishes such as hummus, tabbouleh, and bread.

Nuts and seeds are rich in monounsaturated and polyunsaturated fats, which have been linked to numerous health benefits, including a reduced risk of heart disease and improved cholesterol levels. They are also a good source of plant-based protein, making them a great addition to a vegetarian or vegan diet. In addition, nuts and seeds are rich in fiber, which can help to promote healthy digestion and prevent chronic diseases such as diabetes and obesity.

While nuts and seeds are a healthy addition to any

diet, it is important to consume them in moderation, as they are also high in calories. A small handful of nuts or seeds per day is a good way to incorporate them into a healthy diet without consuming too many calories.

6. Fish and seafood: Fish and seafood are important ingredients in the Mediterranean diet and are consumed in moderation as a source of protein, omega-3 fatty acids, and other nutrients. The Mediterranean region is surrounded by the Mediterranean Sea, the Adriatic Sea, and the Aegean Sea, which provide an abundant supply of fish and seafood. The Mediterranean diet emphasizes the consumption of fatty fish, such as salmon, sardines, and mackerel, which are rich in omega-3 fatty acids, a type of polyunsaturated fat that has been associated with numerous health benefits.

Seafood stews, such as bouillabaisse and cioppino, are also common in the Mediterranean region and are typically made with a variety of fish, shellfish, and vegetables.

The consumption of fish and seafood in the Mediterranean diet is associated with numerous health benefits. Omega-3 fatty acids found in fish have been linked to a reduced risk of heart disease, stroke, and dementia. Fish is also a good source of protein, which is essential for building and repairing tissues in the body. In addition, the consumption of fish and seafood is associated with a reduced risk of depression and improved cognitive function in older adults.

However, it is important to note that overfishing and unsustainable fishing practices have led to declines in fish populations and damage to marine ecosystems in the Mediterranean region. To ensure the sustainability of fish and seafood consumption, it is recommended to choose wild-caught, sustainable options and limit consumption of certain species that are overfished or harvested using unsustainable methods.

7. Herbs and spices: Herbs and spices are an essential part of the Mediterranean diet, and are used to add flavor and complexity to dishes, while also providing important health benefits. The Mediterranean region is home to a diverse range of herbs and spices, which are used to flavor everything from soups and stews, to meats, vegetables, and salads.

Some of the most commonly used herbs and spices in the Mediterranean diet include garlic, basil, oregano, thyme, rosemary, parsley, sage, and bay leaves. These herbs and spices are rich in antioxidants, vitamins, and minerals, and have been linked to numerous health benefits, including reducing inflammation, improving digestion, and boosting immune function.

Garlic, for example, is a potent anti-inflammatory and antibacterial herb that is used in many Mediterranean dishes, such as roasted meats and tomato-based sauces. Basil, a fragrant herb with a sweet and slightly peppery flavor, is often used in salads, pesto, and tomato-based dishes. Oregano, a pungent herb with a slightly bitter taste, is commonly used in Mediterranean cooking to flavor meats, tomato sauces, and soups.

Rosemary, another fragrant herb with a slightly piney taste, is often used to flavor meats and vegetables, as well as in marinades and dressings. Parsley, a mild and slightly bitter herb, is commonly used as a garnish, as well as in salads, soups, and stews. Sage, a herb with a strong, slightly peppery taste, is often used to flavor meats and sausages, as well as in stuffing and dressings. Bay leaves, which have a subtle and slightly floral flavor, are often used to flavor soups, stews, and sauces.

30-Day Meal Plan

DAYS	BREAKFAST	LUNCH	DINNER	SNACK/DESSERT
1	Gluten-Free Granola Cereal	Moroccan Vegetables and Chickpeas	Roasted Ratatouille Pasta	Crispy Apple Phyllo Tart
2	Greek Yogurt and Berries	Sun-Dried Tomato Rice	Orzo-Stuffed Tomatoes	Dried Fruit Compote
3	Heart-Healthy Hazelnut-Collagen Shake	Creamy Thyme Polenta	Balsamic Marinated Tofu with Basil and Oregano	Chocolate Pudding
4	Golden Egg Skillet	Greek Baked Beans	Greek Frittata with Tomato-Olive Salad	Strawberry Ricotta Parfaits
5	Berry Baked Oatmeal	Buckwheat Bake with Root Vegetables	Broccoli-Cheese Fritters	Banana Cream Pie Parfaits
6	Baked Ricotta with Pears	Fava Beans with Ground Meat	Quinoa with Almonds and Cranberries	Blueberry Compote
7	Egg and Pepper Pita	Mediterranean "Fried" Rice	Herbed Ricotta–Stuffed Mushrooms	Cinnamon-Stewed Dried Plums with Greek Yogurt
8	Harissa Shakshuka with Bell Peppers and Tomatoes	Rice and Lentils	Moroccan Vegetable Tagine	Crunchy Sesame Cookies
9	Egg Baked in Avocado	Tomato Bulgur	Pistachio Mint Pesto Pasta	Orange–Olive Oil Cupcakes
10	Peachy Oatmeal with Pecans	Domatorizo (Greek Tomato Rice)	Eggplant Parmesan	Pomegranate-Quinoa Dark Chocolate Bark
11	Mediterranean Frittata	Freekeh, Chickpea, and Herb Salad	Citrus Fennel Salad	Individual Apple Pockets
12	Spinach and Feta Egg Bake	Tangy Asparagus and Broccoli	Pear-Fennel Salad with Pomegranate	Chocolate-Dipped Fruit Bites
13	Garlicky Beans and Greens with Polenta	Parmesan Artichokes	Orange-Tarragon Chicken Salad Wrap	Creamy Spiced Almond Milk
14	Blender Cinnamon Pancakes with Cacao Cream Topping	Cauliflower Rice-Stuffed Peppers	Zucchini and Ricotta Salad	Chocolate Lava Cakes
15	Warm Fava Beans with Whole-Wheat Pita	Turkish Red Lentil and Bulgur Kofte	Chopped Greek Antipasto Salad	Lemon Berry Cream Pops
16	Portobello Eggs Benedict	Stuffed Portobellos	Yellow and White Hearts of Palm Salad	Lemon-Pepper Chicken Drumsticks
17	Spinach, Sun-Dried Tomato, and Feta Egg Wraps	Eggs Poached in Moroccan Tomato Sauce	Italian Summer Vegetable Barley Salad	Savory Mediterranean Popcorn
18	Egg in a "Pepper Hole" with Avocado	Mushroom Ragù with Parmesan Polenta	Panzanella (Tuscan Bread and Tomatoes Salad)	Bravas-Style Potatoes
19	Almond Butter Banana Chocolate Smoothie	Eggplants Stuffed with Walnuts and Feta	Raw Zucchini Salad	Ranch Oyster Snack Crackers
20	Veggie Frittata	Cauliflower Tabbouleh Salad	Citrus Avocado Salad	Stuffed Dates with Feta, Parmesan, and Pine Nuts

DAYS	BREAKFAST	LUNCH	DINNER	SNACK/DESSERT
21	Crostini with Smoked Trout	Tabbouleh	Amaranth Salad	Citrus-Kissed Melon
22	Greek Eggs and Potatoes	Beets with Goat Cheese and Chermoula	Wheat Berry Salad	Cheese-Stuffed Dates
23	Amaranth Breakfast Bowl with Chocolate and Almonds	Mediterranean Potato Salad	Crunchy Pea and Barley Salad	Mediterranean-Style Stuffed Mushrooms
24	Marinara Eggs with Parsley	Greek Village Salad	Revithosoupa (Chickpea Soup)	Pita Pizza with Olives, Feta, and Red Onion
25	Green Spinach & Salmon Crepes	Wild Greens Salad with Fresh Herbs	Giant Beans with Tomato and Parsley	Seared Halloumi with Pesto and Tomato
26	Veggie Hash with Eggs	Arugula Spinach Salad with Shaved Parmesan	Lentils in Tomato Sauce	Pea and Arugula Crostini with Pecorino Romano
27	Feta and Herb Frittata	Grain-Free Kale Tabbouleh	Brown Rice and Chickpea Salad	Flatbread with Ricotta and Orange-Raisin Relish
28	Whole-Wheat Toast with Apricots, Blue Cheese, and Honey	Sicilian Salad	South Indian Split Yellow Pigeon Peas with Mixed Vegetables	Sardine and Herb Bruschetta
29	Savory Zucchini Muffins	Pipirrana (Spanish Summer Salad)	Mediterranean Bulgur Medley	Zucchini Feta Roulades
30	Power Peach Smoothie Bowl	Traditional Greek Salad	Lentil and Zucchini Boats	Cream Cheese Wontons

Start Your Journey Now!

This cookbook is not just about the tantalizing tastes and aromas that make Mediterranean cuisine truly special. The Mediterranean diet has been praised for its health benefits, with numerous studies showcasing its positive impact on heart health, longevity, and overall well-being. It's a cuisine that celebrates fresh, whole foods, and encourages a balanced and wholesome approach to eating, with an abundance of colorful fruits and vegetables, hearty grains, lean proteins, and healthy fats.

Whether you're a seasoned cook looking to expand your culinary repertoire or a culinary novice eager to explore new flavors, this cookbook is your passport to the Mediterranean. Get ready to embark on a culinary journey that will awaken your taste buds, nourish your body, and transport you to the enchanting world of Mediterranean cuisine. So, grab your apron, sharpen your knives, and let's embark on this delicious adventure together!

Chapter 1

Breakfasts

Gluten-Free Granola Cereal

Prep time: 7 minutes | Cook time: 30 minutes | Makes 3½ cups

Oil, for spraying	1 tablespoon toasted sesame oil
1½ cups gluten-free rolled oats	or vegetable oil
½ cup chopped walnuts	1 teaspoon ground cinnamon
½ cup chopped almonds	½ teaspoon salt
½ cup pumpkin seeds	½ cup dried cranberries
¼ cup maple syrup or honey	

1. Preheat the air fryer to 250°F (121°C). Line the air fryer basket with parchment and spray lightly with oil. (Do not skip the step of lining the basket; the parchment will keep the granola from falling through the holes.) 2. In a large bowl, mix together the oats, walnuts, almonds, pumpkin seeds, maple syrup, sesame oil, cinnamon, and salt. 3. Spread the mixture in an even layer in the prepared basket. 4. Cook for 30 minutes, stirring every 10 minutes. 5. Transfer the granola to a bowl, add the dried cranberries, and toss to combine. 6. Let cool to room temperature before storing in an airtight container.

Per Serving:

calories: 322 | fat: 17g | protein: 11g | carbs: 35g | fiber: 6g | sodium: 170mg

Greek Yogurt and Berries

Prep time: 5 minutes | Cook time: 30 minutes | Serves 4

4 cups plain full-fat Greek yogurt	topping
1 cup granola	1 teaspoon chopped fresh mint leaves, for topping
½ cup blackberries	4 teaspoons honey, for topping
2 bananas, sliced and frozen	(optional)
1 teaspoon chia seeds, for	

1. Evenly divide the yogurt among four bowls. Top with the granola, blackberries, bananas, chia seeds, mint, and honey (if desired), dividing evenly among the bowls. Serve.

Per Serving:

calories: 283 | fat: 9g | protein: 12g | carbs: 42g | fiber: 5g | sodium: 115mg

Egg Baked in Avocado

Prep time: 5 minutes | Cook time: 15 minutes | Serves 2

1 ripe large avocado	serving
2 large eggs	2 tablespoons chopped tomato, for serving
Salt	
Freshly ground black pepper	2 tablespoons crumbled feta, for serving (optional)
4 tablespoons jarred pesto, for	

1. Preheat the oven to 425°F(220°C). 2. Slice the avocado in half and remove the pit. Scoop out about 1 to 2 tablespoons from each half to create a hole large enough to fit an egg. Place the avocado halves on a baking sheet, cut-side up. 3. Crack 1 egg in each avocado half and season with salt and pepper. 4. Bake until the eggs are set and cooked to desired level of doneness, 10 to 15 minutes. 5. Remove from oven and top each avocado with 2 tablespoons pesto, 1 tablespoon chopped tomato, and 1 tablespoon crumbled feta (if using).

Per Serving:

calories: 248 | fat: 23g | protein: 10g | carbs: 2g | fiber: 1g | sodium: 377mg

Heart-Healthy Hazelnut-Collagen Shake

Prep time: 5 minutes | Cook time: 0 minutes | Serves 1

1½ cups unsweetened almond milk	⅛ teaspoon LoSalt or pink Himalayan salt
2 tablespoons hazelnut butter	⅛ teaspoon sugar-free almond extract
2 tablespoons grass-fed collagen powder	1 tablespoon macadamia oil or hazelnut oil
½–1 teaspoon cinnamon	

1. Place all of the ingredients in a blender and pulse until smooth and frothy. Serve immediately.

Per Serving:

calories: 507 | fat: 41g | protein: 3g | carbs: 35g | fiber: 12g | sodium: 569mg

Baked Ricotta with Pears

Prep time: 5 minutes |Cook time: 25 minutes| Serves: 4

Nonstick cooking spray	1 tablespoon sugar
1 (16-ounce / 454-g) container whole-milk ricotta cheese	1 teaspoon vanilla extract
2 large eggs	¼ teaspoon ground nutmeg
¼ cup white whole-wheat flour or whole-wheat pastry flour	1 pear, cored and diced
	2 tablespoons water
	1 tablespoon honey

1. Preheat the oven to 400°F(205°C). Spray four 6-ounce ramekins with nonstick cooking spray. 2. In a large bowl, beat together the ricotta, eggs, flour, sugar, vanilla, and nutmeg. Spoon into the ramekins. Bake for 22 to 25 minutes, or until the ricotta is just about set. Remove from the oven and cool slightly on racks. 3. While the ricotta is baking, in a small saucepan over medium heat, simmer the pear in the water for 10 minutes, until slightly softened. Remove from the heat, and stir in the honey. 4. Serve the ricotta ramekins topped with the warmed pear.

Per Serving:

calories: 306 | fat: 17g | protein: 17g | carbs: 21g | fiber: 1g | sodium: 131mg

Veggie Frittata

Prep time: 7 minutes | Cook time: 21 to 23 minutes | Serves 2

Avocado oil spray	3 ounces (85 g) shredded sharp Cheddar cheese, divided
¼ cup diced red onion	½ teaspoon dried thyme
¼ cup diced red bell pepper	Sea salt and freshly ground black pepper, to taste
¼ cup finely chopped broccoli	
4 large eggs	

1. Spray a pan well with oil. Put the onion, pepper, and broccoli in the pan, place the pan in the air fryer, and set to 350°F (177°C). Bake for 5 minutes. 2. While the vegetables cook, beat the eggs in a medium bowl. Stir in half of the cheese, and season with the thyme, salt, and pepper. 3. Add the eggs to the pan and top with the remaining cheese. Set the air fryer to 350°F (177°C). Bake for 16 to 18 minutes, until cooked through.

Per Serving:

calories: 326 | fat: 23g | protein: 24g | carbs: 4g | fiber: 1g | sodium: 156mg

Berry Baked Oatmeal

Prep time: 10 minutes | Cook time: 45 to 50 minutes | Serves 8

2 cups gluten-free rolled oats	2 tablespoons extra-virgin olive oil
2 cups (10-ounce / 283-g bag) frozen mixed berries (blueberries and raspberries work best)	2 teaspoons ground cinnamon
	1 teaspoon baking powder
	1 teaspoon vanilla extract
2 cups plain, unsweetened almond milk	½ teaspoon kosher salt
1 cup plain Greek yogurt	¼ teaspoon ground nutmeg
¼ cup maple syrup	⅛ teaspoon ground cloves

1. Preheat the oven to 375ºF (190ºC). 2. Mix all the ingredients together in a large bowl. Pour into a 9-by-13-inch baking dish. Bake for 45 to 50 minutes, or until golden brown.

Per Serving:
calories: 180 | fat: 6g | protein: 6g | carbs: 28g | fiber: 4g | sodium: 180mg

Harissa Shakshuka with Bell Peppers and Tomatoes

Prep time: 10 minutes | Cook time: 20 minutes | Serves 4

1½ tablespoons extra-virgin olive oil	1 (28-ounce / 794-g) can no-salt-added diced tomatoes
2 tablespoons harissa	½ teaspoon kosher salt
1 tablespoon tomato paste	4 large eggs
½ onion, diced	2 to 3 tablespoons fresh basil, chopped or cut into ribbons
1 bell pepper, seeded and diced	
3 garlic cloves, minced	

1. Preheat the oven to 375ºF (190ºC). 2. Heat the olive oil in a 12-inch cast-iron pan or ovenproof skillet over medium heat. Add the harissa, tomato paste, onion, and bell pepper; sauté for 3 to 4 minutes. Add the garlic and cook until fragrant, about 30 seconds. Add the diced tomatoes and salt and simmer for about 10 minutes. 3. Make 4 wells in the sauce and gently break 1 egg into each. Transfer to the oven and bake until the whites are cooked and the yolks are set, 10 to 12 minutes. 4. Allow to cool for 3 to 5 minutes, garnish with the basil, and carefully spoon onto plates.

Per Serving:
calories: 190 | fat: 10g | protein: 9g | carbs: 15g | fiber: 4g | sodium: 255mg

Peachy Oatmeal with Pecans

Prep time: 10 minutes | Cook time: 4 minutes | Serves 4

4 cups water	and diced
2 cups rolled oats	¼ teaspoon salt
1 tablespoon light olive oil	½ cup toasted pecans
1 large peach, peeled, pitted,	2 tablespoons maple syrup

1. Place water, oats, oil, peach, and salt in the Instant Pot®. Stir well. Close lid, set steam release to Sealing, press the Manual button, and set time to 4 minutes. 2. When the timer beeps, quick-release the pressure until the float valve drops. Press the Cancel button, open lid, and stir well. Serve oatmeal topped with pecans and maple syrup.

Per Serving:

calories: 399 | fat: 27g | protein: 8g | carbs: 35g | fiber: 7g | sodium: 148mg

Egg and Pepper Pita

Prep time: 10 minutes | Cook time: 10 minutes | Serves 4

2 pita breads	Freshly ground black pepper
2 tablespoons olive oil	Pinch dried oregano
1 red or yellow bell pepper, diced	2 avocados, sliced
2 zucchini, quartered lengthwise and sliced	½ to ¾ cup crumbled feta cheese
4 large eggs, beaten	2 tablespoons chopped scallion, green part only, for garnish
Sea salt	Hot sauce, for serving

1. In a large skillet, heat the pitas over medium heat until warmed through and lightly toasted, about 2 minutes. Remove the pitas from the skillet and set aside. 2. In the same skillet, heat the olive oil over medium heat. Add the bell pepper and zucchini and sauté for 4 to 5 minutes. Add the eggs and season with salt, black pepper, and the oregano. Cook, stirring, for 2 to 3 minutes, until the eggs are cooked through. Remove from the heat. 3. Slice the pitas in half crosswise and fill each half with the egg mixture. Divide the avocado and feta among the pita halves. Garnish with the scallion and serve with hot sauce.

Per Serving:
calories: 476 | fat: 31g | protein: 17g | carbs: 36g | fiber: 11g | sodium: 455mg

Golden Egg Skillet

Prep time: 15 minutes | Cook time: 20 minutes | Serves 2

2 tablespoons extra-virgin avocado oil or ghee	2 tablespoons water
2 medium spring onions, white and green parts separated, sliced	1 teaspoon Dijon or yellow mustard
	½ teaspoon ground turmeric
1 clove garlic, minced	¼ teaspoon black pepper
3½ ounces (99 g) Swiss chard or collard greens, stalks and leaves separated, chopped	Salt, to taste
	4 large eggs
	¾ cup grated Manchego or Pecorino Romano cheese
1 medium zucchini, sliced into coins	2 tablespoons (30 ml) extra-virgin olive oil

1. Preheat the oven to 360°F (182ºC) fan assisted or 400°F (205ºC) conventional. 2. Grease a large, ovenproof skillet (with a lid) with the avocado oil. Cook the white parts of the spring onions and the garlic for about 1 minute, until just fragrant. Add the chard stalks, zucchini, and water. Stir, then cover with a lid. Cook over medium-low heat for about 10 minutes or until the zucchini is tender. Add the mustard, turmeric, pepper, and salt. Add the chard leaves and cook until just wilted. 3. Use a spatula to make 4 wells in the mixture. Crack an egg into each well and cook until the egg whites start to set while the yolks are still runny. Top with the cheese, transfer to the oven, and bake for 5 to 7 minutes. Remove from the oven and sprinkle with the reserved spring onions. Drizzle with the olive oil and serve warm.

Per Serving:
calories: 600 | fat: 49g | protein: 31g | carbs: 10g | fiber: 4g | sodium: 213mg

Mediterranean Frittata

Prep time: 10 minutes | Cook time: 15 minutes | Serves 2

4 large eggs	1 cup fresh spinach, arugula, kale, or other leafy greens
2 tablespoons fresh chopped herbs, such as rosemary, thyme, oregano, basil or 1 teaspoon dried herbs	4 ounces (113 g) quartered artichoke hearts, rinsed, drained, and thoroughly dried
¼ teaspoon salt	8 cherry tomatoes, halved
Freshly ground black pepper	½ cup crumbled soft goat cheese
4 tablespoons extra-virgin olive oil, divided	

1. Preheat the oven to broil on low. 2. In small bowl, combine the eggs, herbs, salt, and pepper and whisk well with a fork. Set aside. 3. In a 4- to 5-inch oven-safe skillet or omelet pan, heat 2 tablespoons olive oil over medium heat. Add the spinach, artichoke hearts, and cherry tomatoes and sauté until just wilted, 1 to 2 minutes. 4. Pour in the egg mixture and let it cook undisturbed over medium heat for 3 to 4 minutes, until the eggs begin to set on the bottom. 5. Sprinkle the goat cheese across the top of the egg mixture and transfer the skillet to the oven. 6. Broil for 4 to 5 minutes, or until the frittata is firm in the center and golden brown on top. 7. Remove from the oven and run a rubber spatula around the edge to loosen the sides. Invert onto a large plate or cutting board and slice in half. Serve warm and drizzled with the remaining 2 tablespoons olive oil.

Per Serving:
calories: 520 | fat: 44g | protein: 22g | carbs: 10g | fiber: 5g | sodium: 665mg

Blender Cinnamon Pancakes with Cacao Cream Topping

Prep time: 10 minutes | Cook time: 10 minutes | Serves 4

Cinnamon Pancakes:

2 cups pecans	or ghee
4 large eggs	Cacao Cream Topping:
1 tablespoon cinnamon	1 cup coconut cream
½ teaspoon baking soda	1½ tablespoons raw cacao powder
1 teaspoon fresh lemon juice or apple cider vinegar	Optional: low-carb sweetener, to taste
1 tablespoon virgin coconut oil	
To Serve:	
9 medium strawberries, sliced	shredded coconut
1 tablespoon unsweetened	

1. To make the pancakes: Place the pecans in a blender and process until powdered. Add all of the remaining ingredients apart from the ghee. Blend again until smooth. 2. Place a nonstick pan greased with 1 teaspoon of the coconut oil over low heat. Using a ¼-cup (60 ml) measure per pancake, cook in batches of 2 to 3 small pancakes over low heat until bubbles begin to form on the pancakes. Use a spatula to flip over, then cook for 30 to 40 seconds and place on a plate. Grease the pan with more coconut oil between batches. Transfer the pancakes to a plate. 3. To make the cacao cream topping: Place the coconut cream in a bowl. Add the cacao powder and sweetener, if using. Whisk until well combined and creamy. 4. Serve the pancakes with the cacao cream, sliced strawberries and a sprinkle of shredded coconut. You can enhance the flavor of the shredded coconut by toasting it in a dry pan for about 1 minute.

Per Serving:
calories: 665 | fat: 65g | protein: 14g | carbs: 17g | fiber: 9g | sodium: 232mg

Spinach and Feta Egg Bake

Prep time: 7 minutes | Cook time: 23 to 25 minutes | Serves 2

Avocado oil spray	Sea salt and freshly ground black pepper, to taste
⅓ cup diced red onion	¼ teaspoon cayenne pepper
1 cup frozen chopped spinach, thawed and drained	½ cup crumbled feta cheese
4 large eggs	¼ cup shredded Parmesan cheese
¼ cup heavy (whipping) cream	

1. Spray a deep pan with oil. Put the onion in the pan, and place the pan in the air fryer basket. Set the air fryer to 350ºF (177ºC) and bake for 7 minutes. 2. Sprinkle the spinach over the onion. 3. In a medium bowl, beat the eggs, heavy cream, salt, black pepper, and cayenne. Pour this mixture over the vegetables. 4. Top with the feta and Parmesan cheese. Bake for 16 to 18 minutes, until the eggs are set and lightly brown.

Per Serving:
calories: 366 | fat: 26g | protein: 25g | carbs: 8g | fiber: 3g | sodium: 520mg

Garlicky Beans and Greens with Polenta

Prep time: 5 minutes | Cook time: 20 minutes | Serves 4

2 tablespoons olive oil, divided	or chard
1 roll (18-ounce / 510-g) precooked polenta, cut into ½"-thick slices	2 tomatoes, seeded and diced
	1 can (15-ounce / 425-g) small white beans, drained and rinsed
4 cloves garlic, minced	Kosher salt and ground black pepper, to taste
4 cups chopped greens, such as kale, mustard greens, collards,	

1. In a large skillet over medium heat, warm 1 tablespoon of the oil. Cook the polenta slices, flipping once, until golden and crispy, about 5 minutes per side. Remove the polenta and keep warm. 2. Add the remaining 1 tablespoon oil to the skillet. Cook the garlic until softened, 1 minute. Add the greens, tomatoes, and beans and cook until the greens are wilted and bright green and the beans are heated through, 10 minutes. Season to taste with the salt and pepper. To serve, top the polenta with the beans and greens.

Per Serving:
calories: 329 | fat: 8g | protein: 12g | carbs: 54g | fiber: 9g | sodium: 324mg

Almond Butter Banana Chocolate Smoothie

Prep time: 5 minutes | Cook time: 0 minutes | Serves 1

¾ cup almond milk	1 tablespoon almond butter
½ medium banana, preferably frozen	1 tablespoon unsweetened cocoa powder
¼ cup frozen blueberries	1 tablespoon chia seeds

1. In a blender or Vitamix, add all the ingredients. Blend to combine.

Per Serving:
calories: 300 | fat: 16g | protein: 8g | carbs: 37g | fiber: 10g | sodium: 125mg

Spinach, Sun-Dried Tomato, and Feta Egg Wraps

Prep time: 10 minutes | Cook time: 7 minutes | Serves 2

1 tablespoon olive oil	1½ cups packed baby spinach
¼ cup minced onion	1 ounce (28 g) crumbled feta
3 to 4 tablespoons minced sun-dried tomatoes in olive oil and herbs	cheese
	Salt
3 large eggs, beaten	2 (8-inch) whole-wheat tortillas

1. In a large skillet, heat the olive oil over medium-high heat. Add the onion and tomatoes and sauté for about 3 minutes. 2. Turn the heat down to medium. Add the beaten eggs and stir to scramble them. 3. Add the spinach and stir to combine. Sprinkle the feta cheese over the eggs. Add salt to taste. 4. Warm the tortillas in the microwave for about 20 seconds each. 5. Fill each tortilla with half of the egg mixture. Fold in half or roll them up and serve.

Per Serving:
calories: 435 | fat: 28g | protein: 17g | carbs: 31g | fiber: 6g | sodium: 552mg

Egg in a "Pepper Hole" with Avocado

Prep time: 15 minutes | Cook time: 5 minutes | Serves 4

4 bell peppers, any color	black pepper, divided
1 tablespoon extra-virgin olive oil	1 avocado, peeled, pitted, and diced
8 large eggs	¼ cup red onion, diced
¾ teaspoon kosher salt, divided	¼ cup fresh basil, chopped
¼ teaspoon freshly ground	Juice of ½ lime

1. Stem and seed the bell peppers. Cut 2 (2-inch-thick) rings from each pepper. Chop the remaining bell pepper into small dice, and set aside. 2. Heat the olive oil in a large skillet over medium heat. Add 4 bell pepper rings, then crack 1 egg in the middle of each ring. Season with ¼ teaspoon of the salt and ⅛ teaspoon of the black pepper. Cook until the egg whites are mostly set but the yolks are still runny, 2 to 3 minutes. Gently flip and cook 1 additional minute for over easy. Move the egg-bell pepper rings to a platter or onto plates, and repeat with the remaining 4 bell pepper rings. 3. In a medium bowl, combine the avocado, onion, basil, lime juice, reserved diced bell pepper, the remaining ¼ teaspoon kosher salt, and the remaining ⅛ teaspoon black pepper. Divide among the 4 plates.

Per Serving:
2 egg-pepper rings: calories: 270 | fat: 19g | protein: 15g | carbs: 12g | fiber: 5g | sodium: 360mg

Crostini with Smoked Trout

Prep time: 10 minutes | Cook time: 5 minutes | Serves 4

½ French baguette, cut into 1-inch-thick slices	trout
	¼ cup crème fraîche
1 tablespoon olive oil	¼ teaspoon chopped fresh dill, for garnish
¼ teaspoon onion powder	
1 (4-ounce / 113-g) can smoked	

1. Drizzle the bread on both sides with the olive oil and sprinkle with the onion powder. 2. Place the bread in a single layer in a large skillet and toast over medium heat until lightly browned on both sides, 3 to 4 minutes total. 3. Transfer the toasted bread to a serving platter and place 1 or 2 pieces of the trout on each slice. Top with the crème fraîche, garnish with the dill, and serve immediately.

Per Serving:
calories: 206 | fat: 10g | protein: 13g | carbs: 15g | fiber: 1g | sodium: 350mg

Warm Fava Beans with Whole-Wheat Pita

Prep time: 5 minutes | Cook time: 10 minutes | Serves 4

1½ tablespoons olive oil	¼ cup chopped fresh parsley
1 large onion, diced	¼ cup lemon juice
1 large tomato, diced	Salt
1 clove garlic, crushed	Freshly ground black pepper
1 (15-ounce / 425-g) can fava beans, not drained	Crushed red pepper flakes
	4 whole-grain pita bread pockets
1 teaspoon ground cumin	

1. Heat the olive oil in a large skillet set over medium-high heat. Add the onion, tomato, and garlic and cook, stirring, for about 3 minutes, until the vegetables soften. 2. Add the fava beans, along with the liquid from the can, and bring to a boil. 3. Lower the heat to medium and stir in the cumin, parsley, and lemon juice. Season with salt, pepper, and crushed red pepper. Simmer over medium heat, stirring occasionally, for 5 minutes. 4. While the beans are simmering, heat the pitas in a toaster oven or in a cast-iron skillet over medium heat. To serve, cut the pitas into triangles for dipping into and scooping the bean mixture, or halve the pitas and fill the pockets up with beans.

Per Serving:
calories: 524 | fat: 8g | protein: 32g | carbs: 86g | fiber: 31g | sodium: 394mg

Green Spinach & Salmon Crepes

Prep time: 10 minutes | Cook time: 5 minutes | Serves 1

Green Spinach Crepe:	
1 cup fresh spinach or thawed and drained frozen spinach	1 tablespoon flax meal
	Salt and black pepper, to taste
1 small bunch fresh parsley	2 large eggs
½ teaspoon fresh thyme leaves or ¼ teaspoon dried thyme	2 teaspoons extra-virgin avocado oil or ghee for cooking
1 tablespoon nutritional yeast	

Salmon Filling:	
3 ounces (85 g) wild smoked salmon	1 teaspoon fresh lemon or lime juice
½ large avocado, sliced	Optional: fresh herbs or microgreens, to taste
2 tablespoons crumbled goat's cheese or feta	

Make the green spinach crepe: 1. Place the spinach, herbs, nutritional yeast, flax meal, salt, and pepper in a food processor or blender. Process well until the spinach is finely chopped. Add the eggs and process on low speed until the mixture is just combined. 2. Heat half of the oil in a large skillet and add half of the mixture. Swirl the pan so the mixture completely covers the bottom. Cook for about 3 minutes or until just set, then add the salmon and avocado. Sprinkle the crepe with the goat's cheese and drizzle with the lemon juice. Slide onto a plate and optionally garnish with fresh herbs or microgreens. Serve warm.

Per Serving:
calories: 673 | fat: 48g | protein: 44g | carbs: 23g | fiber: 15g | sodium: 762mg

Portobello Eggs Benedict

Prep time: 10 minutes | Cook time: 10 to 14 minutes | Serves 2

1 tablespoon olive oil	pepper, to taste
2 cloves garlic, minced	2 large eggs
¼ teaspoon dried thyme	2 tablespoons grated Pecorino
2 portobello mushrooms, stems removed and gills scraped out	Romano cheese
	1 tablespoon chopped fresh
2 Roma tomatoes, halved lengthwise	parsley, for garnish
	1 teaspoon truffle oil (optional)
Salt and freshly ground black	

1. Preheat the air fryer to **400°F** (204°C). 2. In a small bowl, combine the olive oil, garlic, and thyme. Brush the mixture over the mushrooms and tomatoes until thoroughly coated. Season to taste with salt and freshly ground black pepper. 3. Arrange the vegetables, cut side up, in the air fryer basket. Crack an egg into the center of each mushroom and sprinkle with cheese. Air fry for 10 to 14 minutes until the vegetables are tender and the whites are firm. When cool enough to handle, coarsely chop the tomatoes and place on top of the eggs. Scatter parsley on top and drizzle with truffle oil, if desired, just before serving.

Per Serving:

calories: 189 | fat: 13g | protein: 11g | carbs: 7g | fiber: 2g | sodium: 87mg

Feta and Herb Frittata

Prep time : 10 minutes | Cook time: 30 minutes | Serves 6

¼ cup olive oil, divided	¼ cup chopped flat-leaf parsley, plus additional for garnish
1 medium onion, halved and thinly sliced	1 teaspoon salt
1 clove garlic, minced	½ teaspoon freshly ground black pepper
8 sheets phyllo dough	
8 eggs	4 ounces (113 g) crumbled feta
¼ cup chopped fresh basil, plus additional for garnish	cheese

1. Preheat the oven to 400°F(205°C). 2. Heat 2 tablespoons of the olive oil in a medium skillet over medium-high heat. Add the onions and cook, stirring frequently, until softened, about 5 minutes. Add the garlic and cook, stirring, for 1 minute more. Remove from the heat and set aside to cool. 3. While the onion mixture is cooling, make the crust. Place a damp towel on the counter and cover with a sheet of parchment paper. Lay the phyllo sheets in a stack on top of the parchment and cover with a second sheet of parchment and then a second damp towel. 4. Brush some of the remaining olive oil in a 9-by-9-inch baking dish or a 9-inch pie dish. Layer the softened phyllo sheets in the prepared dish, brushing each with some of the olive oil before adding the next phyllo sheet. 5. Next, make the filling. In a large bowl, whisk the eggs with the onion mixture, basil, parsley, salt, and pepper. Add the feta cheese and mix well. Pour the egg mixture into the prepared crust, folding any excess phyllo inside the baking dish. 6. Bake in the preheated oven for about 25 to 30 minutes, until the crust is golden brown and the egg filling is completely set in the center. Cut into rectangles or wedges and serve garnished with basil and parsley.

Per Serving:

calories: 298 | fat: 20g | protein: 12g | carbs: 17g | fiber: 1g | sodium: 769mg

Greek Eggs and Potatoes

Prep time: 5 minutes | Cook time: 30 minutes | Serves 4

3 medium tomatoes, seeded and coarsely chopped	Sea salt and freshly ground pepper, to taste
2 tablespoons fresh chopped basil	3 large russet potatoes
1 garlic clove, minced	4 large eggs
2 tablespoons plus ½ cup olive oil, divided	1 teaspoon fresh oregano, chopped

1. Put tomatoes in a food processor and purée them, skins and all. 2. Add the basil, garlic, 2 tablespoons olive oil, sea salt, and freshly ground pepper, and pulse to combine. 3. Put the mixture in a large skillet over low heat and cook, covered, for 20–25 minutes, or until the sauce has thickened and is bubbly. 4. Meanwhile, dice the potatoes into small cubes. Put ½ cup olive oil in a nonstick skillet over medium-low heat. 5. Fry the potatoes for 5 minutes until crisp and browned on the outside, then cover and reduce heat to low. Steam potatoes until done. 6. Carefully crack the eggs into the tomato sauce. Cook over low heat until the eggs are set in the sauce, about 6 minutes. 7. Remove the potatoes from the pan and drain them on paper towels, then place them in a bowl. 8. Sprinkle with sea salt and freshly ground pepper to taste and top with the oregano. 9. Carefully remove the eggs with a slotted spoon and place them on a plate with the potatoes. Spoon sauce over the top and serve.

Per Serving:

calories: 548 | fat: 32g | protein: 13g | carbs: 54g | fiber: 5g | sodium: 90mg

Marinara Eggs with Parsley

Prep time: 5 minutes |Cook time: 15 minutes| Serves: 6

1 tablespoon extra-virgin olive oil	undrained, no salt added
	6 large eggs
1 cup chopped onion (about ½ medium onion)	½ cup chopped fresh flat-leaf (Italian) parsley
2 garlic cloves, minced (about 1 teaspoon)	Crusty Italian bread and grated Parmesan or Romano cheese, for serving (optional)
2 (14½-ounce / 411-g) cans Italian diced tomatoes,	

1. In a large skillet over medium-high heat, heat the oil. Add the onion and cook for 5 minutes, stirring occasionally. Add the garlic and cook for 1 minute. 2. Pour the tomatoes with their juices over the onion mixture and cook until bubbling, 2 to 3 minutes. While waiting for the tomato mixture to bubble, crack one egg into a small custard cup or coffee mug. 3. When the tomato mixture bubbles, lower the heat to medium. Then use a large spoon to make six indentations in the tomato mixture. Gently pour the first cracked egg into one indentation and repeat, cracking the remaining eggs, one at a time, into the custard cup and pouring one into each indentation. Cover the skillet and cook for 6 to 7 minutes, or until the eggs are done to your liking (about 6 minutes for soft-cooked, 7 minutes for harder cooked). 4. Top with the parsley, and serve with the bread and grated cheese, if desired.

Per Serving:

calories: 127 | fat: 7g | protein: 8g | carbs: 8g | fiber: 2g | sodium: 82mg

Veggie Hash with Eggs

Prep time: 20 minutes | Cook time: 6¼ hours | Serves 2

Nonstick cooking spray	chopped
1 onion, chopped	¼ cup vegetable broth
2 garlic cloves, minced	½ teaspoon salt
1 red bell pepper, chopped	⅛ teaspoon freshly ground
1 yellow summer squash, chopped	black pepper
2 carrots, chopped	½ teaspoon dried thyme leaves
2 Yukon Gold potatoes, peeled and chopped	3 or 4 eggs
2 large tomatoes, seeded and	½ teaspoon ground sweet paprika

1. Spray the slow cooker with the nonstick cooking spray. 2. In the slow cooker, combine all the ingredients except the eggs and paprika, and stir. 3. Cover and cook on low for 6 hours. 4. Uncover and make 1 indentation in the vegetable mixture for each egg. Break 1 egg into a small cup and slip the egg into an indentation. Repeat with the remaining eggs. Sprinkle with the paprika. 5. Cover and cook on low for 10 to 15 minutes, or until the eggs are just set, and serve.

Per Serving:
calories: 381 | fat: 8g | protein: 17g | carbs: 64g | fiber: 12g | sodium: 747mg

Whole-Wheat Toast with Apricots, Blue Cheese, and Honey

Prep time: 5 minutes | Cook time: 5 minutes | Serves 2

2 thick slices crusty whole-wheat bread	2 ounces (57 g) blue cheese
1 tablespoon olive oil	2 tablespoons honey
2 apricots, halved and cut into ¼-inch-thick slices	2 tablespoons toasted slivered almonds

1. Preheat the broiler to high. 2. Brush the bread on both sides with the olive oil. Arrange the slices on a baking sheet and broil until lightly browned, about 2 minutes per side. 3. Arrange the apricot slices on the toasted bread, dividing equally. Sprinkle the cheese over the top, dividing equally. Return the baking sheet to the broiler and broil for 1 to 2 minutes until the cheese melts and just begins to brown. Remove from the oven and serve drizzled with honey and garnished with the toasted almonds.

Per Serving:
calories: 379 | fat: 20g | protein: 13g | carbs: 40g | fiber: 4g | sodium: 595mg

Power Peach Smoothie Bowl

Prep time: 15 minutes | Cook time: 0 minutes | Serves 2

2 cups packed partially thawed frozen peaches	2 tablespoons flax meal
½ cup plain or vanilla Greek yogurt	1 teaspoon vanilla extract
	1 teaspoon orange extract
½ ripe avocado	1 tablespoon honey (optional)

1. Combine all of the ingredients in a blender and blend until smooth. 2. Pour the mixture into two bowls, and, if desired, sprinkle with additional toppings.

Per Serving:
calories: 213 | fat: 13g | protein: 6g | carbs: 23g | fiber: 7g | sodium: 41mg

Amaranth Breakfast Bowl with Chocolate and Almonds

Prep time: 10 minutes | Cook time: 6 minutes | Serves 6

2 cups amaranth, rinsed and drained	1 teaspoon vanilla extract
2 cups almond milk	¼ teaspoon salt
2 cups water	½ cup toasted sliced almonds
¼ cup maple syrup	⅓ cup miniature semisweet chocolate chips
3 tablespoons cocoa powder	

1. Place amaranth, almond milk, water, maple syrup, cocoa powder, vanilla, and salt in the Instant Pot®. Stir to combine. Close lid, set steam release to Sealing, press the Rice button, and set time to 6 minutes. When the timer beeps, quick-release the pressure until the float valve drops, press the Cancel button, open lid, and stir well. 2. Serve hot, topped with almonds and chocolate chips.

Per Serving:
calories: 263 | fat: 12g | protein: 5g | carbs: 35g | fiber: 5g | sodium: 212mg

Savory Zucchini Muffins

Prep time: 10 minutes | Cook time: 35 minutes | Serves 13

1 tablespoon extra virgin olive oil plus extra for brushing	1 tablespoon chopped fresh dill
2 medium zucchini, grated	1 tablespoon chopped fresh mint
⅛ teaspoon fine sea salt	¼ teaspoon freshly ground
1 large egg, lightly beaten	black pepper
1½ ounces (43 g) crumbled feta	3 tablespoons unseasoned
¼ medium onion (any variety), finely chopped	breadcrumbs
1 tablespoon chopped fresh parsley	1 tablespoon grated Parmesan cheese

1. Preheat the oven to 400°F (205°C), and line a medium muffin pan with 6 muffin liners. Lightly brush the bottoms of the liners with olive oil. 2. Place the grated zucchini in a colander and sprinkle with the sea salt. Set aside for 10 minutes to allow the salt to penetrate. 3. Remove the zucchini from the colander, and place it on a tea towel. Pull the edges of the towel in and then twist and squeeze the towel to remove as much of the water from the zucchini as possible. (This will prevent the muffins from becoming soggy.) 4. In a large bowl, combine the egg, feta, onions, parsley, dill, mint, pepper, and the remaining tablespoon of olive oil. Mix well, and add the zucchini to the bowl. Mix again, and add the breadcrumbs. Use a fork to mash the ingredients until well combined. 5. Divide the mixture among the prepared muffins liners and then sprinkle ½ teaspoon grated Parmesan over each muffin. Transfer to the oven, and bake for 35 minutes or until the muffins turn golden brown. 6. When the baking time is complete, remove the muffins from the oven and set aside to cool for 5 minutes before removing from the pan. Store in an airtight container in the refrigerator for 3 days, or tightly wrap individual muffins in plastic wrap and freeze for up to 3 months.

Per Serving:
calories: 39 | fat: 2g | protein: 2g | carbs: 3g | fiber: 1g | sodium: 80mg

Chapter 2

Poultry

Mediterranean Roasted Turkey Breast

Prep time: 15 minutes | Cook time: 6 to 8 hours | Serves 4

3 garlic cloves, minced	2 tablespoons freshly squeezed
1 teaspoon sea salt	lemon juice
1 teaspoon dried oregano	1 (4- to 6-pound / 1.8- to 2.7-
½ teaspoon freshly ground	kg) boneless or bone-in turkey
black pepper	breast
½ teaspoon dried basil	1 onion, chopped
½ teaspoon dried parsley	½ cup low-sodium chicken
½ teaspoon dried rosemary	broth
½ teaspoon dried thyme	4 ounces (113 g) whole
¼ teaspoon dried dill	Kalamata olives, pitted
¼ teaspoon ground nutmeg	1 cup sun-dried tomatoes
2 tablespoons extra-virgin olive	(packaged, not packed in oil),
oil	chopped

1. In a small bowl, stir together the garlic, salt, oregano, pepper, basil, parsley, rosemary, thyme, dill, and nutmeg. 2. Drizzle the olive oil and lemon juice all over the turkey breast and generously season it with the garlic-spice mix. 3. In a slow cooker, combine the onion and chicken broth. Place the seasoned turkey breast on top of the onion. Top the turkey with the olives and sun-dried tomatoes. 4. Cover the cooker and cook for 6 to 8 hours on Low heat. 5. Slice or shred the turkey for serving.

Per Serving:
calories: 676 | fat: 19g | protein: 111g | carbs: 14g | fiber: 3g | sodium: 626mg

Catalonian Chicken with Spiced Lemon Rice

Prep time: 10 minutes | Cook time: 4 hours 10 minutes | Serves 4

3 tablespoons all-purpose flour	2-inch pieces
2 tablespoons paprika	1 large yellow onion, sliced into
1 tablespoon garlic powder	thick pieces
Sea salt	2 tablespoons tomato paste
Black pepper	4 cups chicken stock
6 chicken thighs	1 cup uncooked brown rice
¼ cup olive oil	½ teaspoon red pepper flakes
1 (15-ounce / 425-g) can diced	Zest and juice from 1 lemon
tomatoes, with the juice	½ cup pitted green olives
2 green bell peppers, diced into	

1. In a large resealable bag, mix together the flour, paprika, and garlic powder and season with salt and pepper. Add the chicken, reseal the bag, and toss to coat. 2. In a large skillet over medium heat, heat the olive oil. Add the chicken and brown on both sides, 3 to 4 minutes per side. 3. While the chicken is cooking, add the tomatoes, bell peppers, and onion to the slow cooker. 4. Place the browned chicken thighs in the slow cooker. 5. In same skillet used to brown the chicken, add the tomato paste and cook for 1 minute, stirring constantly. 6. Add 2 cups of the chicken stock to the skillet and bring to a simmer, stirring with a wooden spoon to scrape up the flavorful browned bits off the bottom of the pan. Pour over the top of the chicken in the slow cooker. 7. Cook on low for 4 hours, or until the chicken is extremely tender. 8. In a heavy medium saucepan over medium-high heat, combine the remaining 2 cups stock, the rice, red pepper flakes, lemon zest, and juice of one-half of the lemon, and season with salt. Bring to a boil, reduce the heat to low, and simmer, covered, until the rice is tender and has absorbed all the liquid, about 25 minutes. 9. To serve, spoon the rice onto plates and ladle the Catalonian chicken and vegetables over the top. Garnish with the olives and squeeze the juice from the remaining one-half lemon over the dish.

Per Serving:
calories: 791 | fat: 31g | protein: 69g | carbs: 60g | fiber: 8g | sodium: 497mg

Chicken Avgolemono

Prep time: 10 minutes | Cook time: 50 minutes | Serves 4

1½ pounds (680 g) boneless,	3 large eggs
skinless chicken breasts	Juice of 2 lemons
6 cups chicken broth, as needed	Sea salt
¾ cup dried Greek orzo	Freshly ground black pepper

1. Place the chicken in a stockpot and add enough broth to cover the chicken by 1 inch. Bring to a boil over high heat, then reduce the heat to low, cover, and simmer for 30 to 45 minutes, until the chicken is cooked through. Remove the chicken from the stockpot and set aside in a medium bowl. 2. Increase the heat to medium-high and bring the broth back to a boil. Add the orzo and cook for 7 to 10 minutes, until tender. 3. While the orzo is cooking, shred the chicken with two forks and return it to the pot when orzo is done. 4. Crack the eggs into a small bowl and whisk until frothy, then whisk in the lemon juice. While whisking continuously, slowly pour in 1 cup of the hot broth to temper the eggs. Pour the egg mixture back into the pot and stir. Simmer for 1 minute more, season with salt and pepper, and serve.

Per Serving:
calories: 391 | fat: 9g | protein: 46g | carbs: 29g | fiber: 1g | sodium: 171mg

Chicken Shawarma

Prep time: 30 minutes | Cook time: 15 minutes | Serves 4

Shawarma Spice:	
2 teaspoons dried oregano	1 teaspoon kosher salt
1 teaspoon ground cinnamon	½ teaspoon ground allspice
1 teaspoon ground cumin	½ teaspoon cayenne pepper
1 teaspoon ground coriander	
Chicken:	
1 pound (454 g) boneless,	large bite-size chunks
skinless chicken thighs, cut into	2 tablespoons vegetable oil
For Serving:	
Tzatziki	Pita bread

1. For the shawarma spice: In a small bowl, combine the oregano, cayenne, cumin, coriander, salt, cinnamon, and allspice. 2. For the chicken: In a large bowl, toss together the chicken, vegetable oil, and shawarma spice to coat. Marinate at room temperature for 30 minutes or cover and refrigerate for up to 24 hours. 3. Place the chicken in the air fryer basket. Set the air fryer to 350ºF (177ºC) for 15 minutes, or until the chicken reaches an internal temperature of 165ºF (74ºC). 4. Transfer the chicken to a serving platter. Serve with tzatziki and pita bread.

Per Serving:
calories: 202 | fat: 12g | protein: 23g | carbs: 1g | fiber: 1g | sodium: 690mg

Moroccan-Spiced Chicken Thighs with Saffron Basmati Rice

Prep time: 15 minutes | Cook time: 15 minutes | Serves 2

For the chicken

½ teaspoon paprika	⅛ teaspoon cayenne pepper (a
½ teaspoon cumin	pinch—or more if you like it
½ teaspoon cinnamon	spicy)
¼ teaspoon salt	10 ounces (283 g) boneless,
¼ teaspoon garlic powder	skinless chicken thighs (about
¼ teaspoon ginger powder	4 pieces)
¼ teaspoon coriander	

For the rice

1 tablespoon olive oil	¼ teaspoon salt
½ small onion, minced	1 cup low-sodium chicken
½ cup basmati rice	stock
2 pinches saffron	

Make the chicken 1. Preheat the oven to 350°F (180°C) and set the rack to the middle position. 2. In a small bowl, combine the paprika, cumin, cinnamon, salt, garlic powder, ginger powder, coriander, and cayenne pepper. Add chicken thighs and toss, rubbing the spice mix into the chicken. 3. Place the chicken in a baking dish and roast it for 35 to 40 minutes, or until the chicken reaches an internal temperature of 165°F(74ºC). Let the chicken rest for 5 minutes before serving. Make the rice 1. While the chicken is roasting, heat the oil in a sauté pan over medium-high heat. Add the onion and sauté for 5 minutes. 2. Add the rice, saffron, salt, and chicken stock. Cover the pot with a tight-fitting lid and reduce the heat to low. Let the rice simmer for 15 minutes, or until it is light and fluffy and the liquid has been absorbed.

Per Serving:
calories: 401 | fat: 10g | protein: 37g | carbs: 41g | fiber: 2g | sodium: 715mg

Fiesta Chicken Plate

Prep time: 15 minutes | Cook time: 12 to 15 minutes | Serves 4

1 pound (454 g) boneless,	beans
skinless chicken breasts (2 large	½ cup salsa
breasts)	2 cups shredded lettuce
2 tablespoons lime juice	1 medium tomato, chopped
1 teaspoon cumin	2 avocados, peeled and sliced
½ teaspoon salt	1 small onion, sliced into thin
½ cup grated Pepper Jack	rings
cheese	Sour cream
1 (16-ounce / 454-g) can refried	Tortilla chips (optional)

1. Split each chicken breast in half lengthwise. 2. Mix lime juice, cumin, and salt together and brush on all surfaces of chicken breasts. 3. Place in air fryer basket and air fry at 390ºF (199ºC) for 12 to 15 minutes, until well done. 4. Divide the cheese evenly over chicken breasts and cook for an additional minute to melt cheese. 5. While chicken is cooking, heat refried beans on stovetop or in microwave. 6. When ready to serve, divide beans among 4 plates. Place chicken breasts on top of beans and spoon salsa over. Arrange the lettuce, tomatoes, and avocados artfully on each plate and scatter with the onion rings. 7. Pass sour cream at the table and serve with tortilla chips if desired.

Per Serving:
calories: 497 | fat: 27g | protein: 38g | carbs: 26g | fiber: 12g |

sodium: 722mg

Apricot-Glazed Turkey Tenderloin

Prep time: 20 minutes | Cook time: 30 minutes | Serves 4

Olive oil	1½ pounds (680 g) turkey
¼ cup sugar-free apricot	breast tenderloin
preserves	Salt and freshly ground black
½ tablespoon spicy brown	pepper, to taste
mustard	

1. Spray the air fryer basket lightly with olive oil. 2. In a small bowl, combine the apricot preserves and mustard to make a paste. 3. Season the turkey with salt and pepper. Spread the apricot paste all over the turkey. 4. Place the turkey in the air fryer basket and lightly spray with olive oil. 5. Air fry at 370ºF (188ºC) for 15 minutes. Flip the turkey over and lightly spray with olive oil. Air fry until the internal temperature reaches at least 170ºF (77ºC), an additional 10 to 15 minutes. 6. Let the turkey rest for 10 minutes before slicing and serving.

Per Serving:
calories: 204 | fat: 3g | protein: 40g | carbs: 3g | fiber: 0g | sodium: 214mg

Sautéed Chicken with Tomatoes over Haricots Verts

Prep time: 5 minutes | Cook time: 25 minutes | Serves 4

2 tablespoons olive oil	1 medium onion, diced, or 1
8 thin-cut boneless, skinless	cup frozen diced onions
chicken breasts	1 small handful of mixed fresh
3 cups haricots verts (very thin	parsley, oregano, and basil,
whole green beans)	minced, or 2 teaspoons Italian
2 cups cherry or grape	seasoning
tomatoes, halved	½ cup low-sodium chicken
1 or 2 garlic cloves, minced or	broth or white wine
pressed (½ teaspoon; optional)	

1. Preheat the oven (or a toaster oven) to 250ºF (121ºC). 2. In a large nonstick skillet, heat the olive oil over medium-high heat in a nonstick skillet. Working in batches as needed (you may only be able to do 2 to 4 breasts at a time, depending on the size of your skillet), add the chicken and cook for 1 minute, then reduce the heat to medium and cook for 2 to 3 minutes more. Turn the breast and cook for 2 minutes more, until browned on both sides but not cooked through (the chicken will finish cooking in the sauce). Remove and place on baking sheet in oven or transfer the chicken to a platter and cover to keep warm. Repeat until you have cooked all the chicken. 3. Immediately start cooking the green beans in a microwave or in a steamer basket over a pot of boiling water for about 5 minutes, or until crisp-tender. 4. In the same skillet, sauté the tomatoes, garlic (if using), and frozen diced onions (no need to thaw them first) over medium-low heat. Add the herbs and the broth and cook until the liquid has reduced and thickened slightly. Return all the chicken to the skillet and spoon the sauce over the chicken. 5. Divide the haricots verts among four plates. Place two chicken breasts on top of the beans on each plate, top with the sauce, and serve.

Per Serving:
1 cup: calories: 232 | fat: 10g | protein: 25g | carbs: 11g | fiber: 4g | sodium: 168mg

Chicken Pesto Parmigiana

Prep time: 10 minutes | Cook time: 23 minutes | Serves 4

2 large eggs	thighs, pounded to ¼ inch thick
1 tablespoon water	1 cup pesto
Fine sea salt and ground black pepper, to taste	1 cup shredded Mozzarella cheese (about 4 ounces / 113 g)
1 cup powdered Parmesan cheese (about 3 ounces / 85 g)	Finely chopped fresh basil, for garnish (optional)
2 teaspoons Italian seasoning	Grape tomatoes, halved, for serving (optional)
4 (5-ounce / 142-g) boneless, skinless chicken breasts or	

1. Spray the air fryer basket with avocado oil. Preheat the air fryer to 400ºF (204ºC). 2. Crack the eggs into a shallow baking dish, add the water and a pinch each of salt and pepper, and whisk to combine. In another shallow baking dish, stir together the Parmesan and Italian seasoning until well combined. 3. Season the chicken breasts well on both sides with salt and pepper. Dip one chicken breast in the eggs and let any excess drip off, then dredge both sides of the breast in the Parmesan mixture. Spray the breast with avocado oil and place it in the air fryer basket. Repeat with the remaining 3 chicken breasts. 4. Air fry the chicken in the air fryer for 20 minutes, or until the internal temperature reaches 165ºF (74ºC) and the breading is golden brown, flipping halfway through. 5. Dollop each chicken breast with ¼ cup of the pesto and top with the Mozzarella. Return the breasts to the air fryer and cook for 3 minutes, or until the cheese is melted. Garnish with basil and serve with halved grape tomatoes on the side, if desired. 6. Store leftovers in an airtight container in the refrigerator for up to 4 days. Reheat in a preheated 400ºF (204ºC) air fryer for 5 minutes, or until warmed through.

Per Serving:
calories: 631 | fat: 45g | protein: 52g | carbs: 4g | fiber: 0g | sodium: 607mg

Chicken Gyros with Grilled Vegetables and Tzatziki Sauce

Prep time: 15 minutes | Cook time: 15 minutes | Serves 2

For the chicken

2 tablespoons freshly squeezed lemon juice	1 small zucchini, cut into ½-inch strips lengthwise
2 tablespoons olive oil, divided, plus extra for oiling the grill	1 small eggplant, cut into 1-inch strips lengthwise
1 teaspoon minced fresh oregano, or ½ teaspoon dry oregano	½ red pepper, seeded and cut in half lengthwise
½ teaspoon garlic powder	¾ cup plain Greek yogurt
½ teaspoon salt, divided, plus more to season vegetables	½ English cucumber, peeled and minced
8 ounces (227 g) chicken tenders	1 tablespoon minced fresh dill
	2 (8-inch) pita breads

1. In a medium bowl, combine the lemon juice, 1 tablespoon of olive oil, the oregano, garlic powder, and ¼ teaspoon of salt. Add the chicken and marinate for 30 minutes. 2. Place the zucchini, eggplant, and red pepper in a large mixing bowl and sprinkle liberally with salt and the remaining 1 tablespoon of olive oil. Toss them well to coat. Let the vegetables rest while the chicken is marinating. 3. In a medium bowl, combine the yogurt, the cucumber, the remaining salt, and the dill. Stir well to combine and set aside in the refrigerator. 4. When ready to grill, heat the grill to medium-high and oil the grill grate. 5. Drain any liquid from the vegetables and place them on the grill. Remove the chicken tenders from the marinade and place them on the grill. 6. Cook chicken and vegetables for 3 minutes per side, or until the chicken is no longer pink inside and the vegetables have grill marks. 7. Remove the chicken and vegetables from the grill and set aside. On the grill, heat the pitas for about 30 seconds, flipping them frequently so they don't burn. 8. Divide the chicken tenders and vegetables between the pitas and top each with ¼ cup of the tzatziki sauce. Roll the pitas up like a cone to eat.

Per Serving:
calories: 584 | fat: 21g | protein: 38g | carbs: 64g | fiber: 12g | sodium: 762mg

Chicken in Cream Sauce

Prep time: 10 minutes | Cook time: 35 minutes | Serves 6

3 tablespoons olive oil	3 garlic cloves, minced
6 (4-ounce / 113-g) boneless, skinless chicken breasts	½ teaspoon dried thyme
½ zucchini, chopped into 2-inch pieces	½ teaspoon dried marjoram
1 celery stalk, chopped	½ teaspoon dried basil
1 red bell pepper, thinly sliced	½ cup baby spinach
2 tomatoes on the vine, chopped	1 cup heavy (whipping) cream
	¼ cup chopped fresh Italian parsley (optional)

1. In a large skillet, heat the olive oil over medium-high heat. Add the chicken and cook for 8 to 10 minutes on each side, until cooked through. Transfer the chicken to a plate and set aside. 2. Add the zucchini, celery, bell pepper, tomatoes, and garlic and sauté for 8 to 10 minutes, until the vegetables are softened. Add the thyme, marjoram, and basil and cook for 1 minute. Add the spinach and cook until wilted, about 3 minutes. 3. Add the cream and mix well. Return the chicken to the skillet and cook until warmed through, about 4 minutes. 4. Garnish with the parsley, if desired, and serve.

Per Serving:
calories: 341 | fat: 24g | protein: 27g | carbs: 4g | fiber: 1g | sodium: 83mg

Cajun-Breaded Chicken Bites

Prep time: 10 minutes | Cook time: 12 minutes | Serves 4

1 pound (454 g) boneless, skinless chicken breasts, cut into 1-inch cubes	pepper
½ cup heavy whipping cream	1 ounce (28 g) plain pork rinds, finely crushed
½ teaspoon salt	¼ cup unflavored whey protein powder
¼ teaspoon ground black	½ teaspoon Cajun seasoning

1. Place chicken in a medium bowl and pour in cream. Stir to coat. Sprinkle with salt and pepper. 2. In a separate large bowl, combine pork rinds, protein powder, and Cajun seasoning. Remove chicken from cream, shaking off any excess, and toss in dry mix until fully coated. 3. Place bites into ungreased air fryer basket. Adjust the temperature to 400ºF (204ºC) and air fry for 12 minutes, shaking the basket twice during cooking. Bites will be done when golden brown and have an internal temperature of at least 165ºF (74ºC). Serve warm.

Per Serving:
calories: 272 | fat: 13g | protein: 35g | carbs: 2g | fiber: 1g | sodium: 513mg

Chicken Legs with Leeks

Prep time: 30 minutes | Cook time: 18 minutes | Serves 6

2 leeks, sliced	skinless
2 large-sized tomatoes, chopped	½ teaspoon smoked cayenne pepper
3 cloves garlic, minced	2 tablespoons olive oil
½ teaspoon dried oregano	A freshly ground nutmeg
6 chicken legs, boneless and	

1. In a mixing dish, thoroughly combine all ingredients, minus the leeks. Place in the refrigerator and let it marinate overnight. 2. Lay the leeks onto the bottom of the air fryer basket. Top with the chicken legs. 3. Roast chicken legs at 375ºF (191ºC) for 18 minutes, turning halfway through. Serve with hoisin sauce.

Per Serving:

calories: 390 | fat: 16g | protein: 52g | carbs: 7g | fiber: 1g | sodium: 264mg

Old Delhi Butter Chicken

Prep time: 15 minutes | Cook time: 3 to 7 hours | Serves 6

Tomato Sauce:

3 medium red onions, roughly chopped	1 teaspoon salt
2 to 3 fresh green chiles	10 ripe red tomatoes, roughly chopped, or 1 (14-ounce / 397-g) can plum tomatoes
1 tablespoon freshly grated ginger	1 tablespoon tomato paste
6 garlic cloves, roughly chopped	½ teaspoon turmeric
2¾-inch piece cassia bark	1 tablespoon Kashmiri chili powder
5 green cardamom pods	2 teaspoons coriander seeds, ground
4 cloves	2 cups hot water
10 black peppercorns	

Chicken:

2 tablespoons ghee or butter	leaves
1 tablespoon cumin seeds	⅓ cup heavy cream (optional)
12 chicken thighs, skinned, trimmed, and cut into cubes	1 tablespoon butter (optional)
1 to 2 tablespoons honey	Coriander leaves to garnish (optional)
1 tablespoon dried fenugreek	

Make the Tomato Sauce: 1. Heat the slow cooker to high and add the onion, chiles, ginger, garlic, cassia bark, green cardamom pods, cloves, black peppercorns, salt, tomatoes, tomato paste, turmeric, chili powder, ground coriander seeds, and water. 2. Cover and cook on high for 1 to 2 hours, or on low for 3 hours. By the end, the tomatoes should have broken down. 3. Remove the cassia bark (this is important, because if you grind the cassia in the sauce it will turn out much darker) and blend the sauce with an immersion or regular blender until it's smooth. You can strain this to get a fine, glossy sauce, if you'd like, or leave it as it is. Return the sauce to the slow cooker. Make the Chicken: 4. In a frying pan, heat the ghee. Add cumin seeds and cook until fragrant, about 1 minute. Pour into the sauce in the slow cooker. 5. Add the diced chicken, cover the slow cooker, and cook on high for 2 hours, or on low for 4 hours. 6. When the chicken is cooked, stir in the honey, dried fenugreek leaves, and cream (if using). If you want to thicken the sauce you can turn the cooker to high and reduce for a while with the cover off. Add some butter, a little extra drizzle of cream, and garnish with coriander leaves (if using) just before serving.

Per Serving:

calories: 600 | fat: 21g | protein: 80g | carbs: 22g | fiber: 5g | sodium: 814mg

Chipotle Drumsticks

Prep time: 5 minutes | Cook time: 25 minutes | Serves 4

1 tablespoon tomato paste	8 chicken drumsticks
½ teaspoon chipotle powder	½ teaspoon salt
¼ teaspoon apple cider vinegar	⅛ teaspoon ground black pepper
¼ teaspoon garlic powder	

1. In a small bowl, combine tomato paste, chipotle powder, vinegar, and garlic powder. 2. Sprinkle drumsticks with salt and pepper, then place into a large bowl and pour in tomato paste mixture. Toss or stir to evenly coat all drumsticks in mixture. 3. Place drumsticks into ungreased air fryer basket. Adjust the temperature to 400ºF (204ºC) and air fry for 25 minutes, turning drumsticks halfway through cooking. Drumsticks will be dark red with an internal temperature of at least 165ºF (74ºC) when done. Serve warm.

Per Serving:

calories: 306 | fat: 10g | protein: 51g | carbs: 1g | fiber: 0g | sodium: 590mg

Blackened Chicken

Prep time: 10 minutes | Cook time: 20 minutes | Serves 4

1 large egg, beaten	chicken breasts (about 1 pound / 454 g each), halved
¾ cup Blackened seasoning	1 to 2 tablespoons oil
2 whole boneless, skinless	

1. Place the beaten egg in one shallow bowl and the Blackened seasoning in another shallow bowl. 2. One at a time, dip the chicken pieces in the beaten egg and the Blackened seasoning, coating thoroughly. 3. Preheat the air fryer to 360ºF (182ºC). Line the air fryer basket with parchment paper. 4. Place the chicken pieces on the parchment and spritz with oil. 5. Cook for 10 minutes. Flip the chicken, spritz it with oil, and cook for 10 minutes more until the internal temperature reaches 165ºF (74ºC) and the chicken is no longer pink inside. Let sit for 5 minutes before serving.

Per Serving:

calories: 225 | fat: 10g | protein: 28g | carbs: 8g | fiber: 6g | sodium: 512mg

Roasted Cornish Hen with Figs

Prep time: 10 minutes | Cook time: 45 minutes | Serves 2

2 Cornish game hens	Sea salt and freshly ground pepper, to taste
2 tablespoons olive oil	1 pound (454 g) fresh figs
1 tablespoon Herbes de Provence	1 cup dry white wine

1. Preheat the oven to 350ºF (180ºC). 2. Place the Cornish hens in a shallow roasting pan and brush them with olive oil. 3. Season liberally with Herbes de Provence, sea salt, and freshly ground pepper. Roast the hens for 15 minutes, or until golden brown. 4. Add the figs and white wine, and cover the hens with aluminum foil. Cook an additional 20–30 minutes, or until the hens are cooked through. Allow to rest for 10 minutes before serving.

Per Serving:

calories: 660 | fat: 22g | protein: 50g | carbs: 48g | fiber: 7g | sodium: 166mg

Tex-Mex Chicken Roll-Ups

Prep time: 10 minutes | Cook time: 14 to 17 minutes | Serves 8

2 pounds (907 g) boneless, skinless chicken breasts or thighs 1 teaspoon chili powder ½ teaspoon smoked paprika ½ teaspoon ground cumin Sea salt and freshly ground	black pepper, to taste 6 ounces (170 g) Monterey Jack cheese, shredded 4 ounces (113 g) canned diced green chiles Avocado oil spray

1. Place the chicken in a large zip-top bag or between two pieces of plastic wrap. Using a meat mallet or heavy skillet, pound the chicken until it is about ¼ inch thick. 2. In a small bowl, combine the chili powder, smoked paprika, cumin, and salt and pepper to taste. Sprinkle both sides of the chicken with the seasonings. 3. Sprinkle the chicken with the Monterey Jack cheese, then the diced green chiles. 4. Roll up each piece of chicken from the long side, tucking in the ends as you go. Secure the roll-up with a toothpick. 5. Set the air fryer to 350ºF (177ºC). Spray the outside of the chicken with avocado oil. Place the chicken in a single layer in the basket, working in batches if necessary, and roast for 7 minutes. Flip and cook for another 7 to 10 minutes, until an instant-read thermometer reads 160ºF (71ºC). 6. Remove the chicken from the air fryer and allow it to rest for about 5 minutes before serving.

Per Serving:

calories: 220 | fat: 10g | protein: 31g | carbs: 1g | fiber: 0g | sodium: 355mg

Fenugreek Chicken

Prep time: 15 minutes | Cook time: 6½ hours | Serves 6

1 tablespoon vegetable oil 2 teaspoons cumin seeds 2 onions, finely diced 2 tablespoons freshly grated ginger 3 garlic cloves, finely chopped 1 teaspoon turmeric 2 tomatoes, puréed 1 teaspoon chili powder 1 teaspoon coriander seeds, ground 1 teaspoon salt	1 or 2 fresh green chiles, chopped 8 boneless chicken thighs, skinned, trimmed, and cut into chunks 2 bunches fresh fenugreek leaves, washed and finely chopped (or 3 tablespoons dried fenugreek leaves) 2 tablespoons yogurt 2 teaspoons garam masala

1. Heat the oil in a frying pan (or in the slow cooker if you have a sear setting). Add the cumin seeds. Once fragrant, add the onions and cook until they begin to brown, about 10 minutes. Add the ginger, garlic, and turmeric, and cook for a few minutes. 2. Stir in the puréed tomatoes, chili powder, ground coriander seeds, salt, and green chiles. Put everything in the slow cooker and set the cooker to high. 3. Stir in the chicken pieces. Cover and cook on high for 4 hours, or on low for 6 hours. 4. Add the fenugreek leaves and stir into the sauce. Leave the cover off and cook for another half hour on high. This will also reduce the sauce and thicken it slightly. 5. Turn the cooker to low and stir in the yogurt, 1 tablespoon at a time, until it's fully incorporated into the sauce. 6. Turn off the heat, stir in the garam masala, and serve.

Per Serving:

calories: 405 | fat: 14g | protein: 54g | carbs: 15g | fiber: 3g | sodium: 664mg

Baked Chicken Caprese

Prep time: 5minutes |Cook time: 25 minutes| Serves: 4

Nonstick cooking spray 1 pound (454 g) boneless, skinless chicken breasts 2 tablespoons extra-virgin olive oil ¼ teaspoon freshly ground black pepper ¼ teaspoon kosher or sea salt 1 large tomato, sliced thinly	1 cup shredded mozzarella or 4 ounces (113 g) fresh mozzarella cheese, diced 1 (14½-ounce / 411-g) can low-sodium or no-salt-added crushed tomatoes 2 tablespoons fresh torn basil leaves 4 teaspoons balsamic vinegar

1. Set one oven rack about 4 inches below the broiler element. Preheat the oven to 450ºF(235ºC). Line a large, rimmed baking sheet with aluminum foil. Place a wire cooling rack on the aluminum foil, and spray the rack with nonstick cooking spray. Set aside. 2. Cut the chicken into 4 pieces (if they aren't already). Put the chicken breasts in a large zip-top plastic bag. With a rolling pin or meat mallet, pound the chicken so it is evenly flattened, about ¼-inch thick. Add the oil, pepper, and salt to the bag. Reseal the bag, and massage the ingredients into the chicken. Take the chicken out of the bag and place it on the prepared wire rack. 3. Cook the chicken for 15 to 18 minutes, or until the internal temperature of the chicken is 165ºF(74ºC) on a meat thermometer and the juices run clear. Turn the oven to the high broiler setting. Layer the tomato slices on each chicken breast, and top with the mozzarella. Broil the chicken for another 2 to 3 minutes, or until the cheese is melted (don't let the chicken burn on the edges). Remove the chicken from the oven. 4. While the chicken is cooking, pour the crushed tomatoes into a small, microwave-safe bowl. Cover the bowl with a paper towel, and microwave for about 1 minute on high, until hot. When you're ready to serve, divide the tomatoes among four dinner plates. Place each chicken breast on top of the tomatoes. Top with the basil and a drizzle of balsamic vinegar.

Per Serving:

calories: 304 | fat: 15g | protein: 34g | carbs: 7g | fiber: 3g | sodium: 215mg

Chicken Patties

Prep time: 15 minutes | Cook time: 12 minutes | Serves 4

1 pound (454 g) ground chicken thigh meat ½ cup shredded Mozzarella cheese 1 teaspoon dried parsley	½ teaspoon garlic powder ¼ teaspoon onion powder 1 large egg 2 ounces (57 g) pork rinds, finely ground

1. In a large bowl, mix ground chicken, Mozzarella, parsley, garlic powder, and onion powder. Form into four patties. 2. Place patties in the freezer for 15 to 20 minutes until they begin to firm up. 3. Whisk egg in a medium bowl. Place the ground pork rinds into a large bowl. 4. Dip each chicken patty into the egg and then press into pork rinds to fully coat. Place patties into the air fryer basket. 5. Adjust the temperature to 360ºF (182ºC) and air fry for 12 minutes. 6. Patties will be firm and cooked to an internal temperature of 165ºF (74ºC) when done. Serve immediately.

Per Serving:

calories: 265 | fat: 15g | protein: 29g | carbs: 1g | fiber: 0g | sodium: 285mg

Personal Cauliflower Pizzas

Prep time: 10 minutes | Cook time: 25 minutes | Serves 2

1 (12-ounce / 340-g) bag frozen riced cauliflower	4 tablespoons no-sugar-added marinara sauce, divided
⅓ cup shredded Mozzarella cheese	4 ounces (113 g) fresh Mozzarella, chopped, divided
¼ cup almond flour	1 cup cooked chicken breast, chopped, divided
¼ grated Parmesan cheese	½ cup chopped cherry tomatoes, divided
1 large egg	
½ teaspoon salt	¼ cup fresh baby arugula, divided
1 teaspoon garlic powder	
1 teaspoon dried oregano	

1. Preheat the air fryer to 400ºF (204ºC). Cut 4 sheets of parchment paper to fit the basket of the air fryer. Brush with olive oil and set aside. 2. In a large glass bowl, microwave the cauliflower according to package directions. Place the cauliflower on a clean towel, draw up the sides, and squeeze tightly over a sink to remove the excess moisture. Return the cauliflower to the bowl and add the shredded Mozzarella along with the almond flour, Parmesan, egg, salt, garlic powder, and oregano. Stir until thoroughly combined. 3. Divide the dough into two equal portions. Place one piece of dough on the prepared parchment paper and pat gently into a thin, flat disk 7 to 8 inches in diameter. Air fry for 15 minutes until the crust begins to brown. Let cool for 5 minutes. 4. Transfer the parchment paper with the crust on top to a baking sheet. Place a second sheet of parchment paper over the crust. While holding the edges of both sheets together, carefully lift the crust off the baking sheet, flip it, and place it back in the air fryer basket. The new sheet of parchment paper is now on the bottom. Remove the top piece of paper and air fry the crust for another 15 minutes until the top begins to brown. Remove the basket from the air fryer. 5. Spread 2 tablespoons of the marinara sauce on top of the crust, followed by half the fresh Mozzarella, chicken, cherry tomatoes, and arugula. Air fry for 5 to 10 minutes longer, until the cheese is melted and beginning to brown. Remove the pizza from the oven and let it sit for 10 minutes before serving. Repeat with the remaining ingredients to make a second pizza.

Per Serving:
calories: 655 | fat: 35g | protein: 67g | carbs: 20g | fiber: 7g | sodium: 741mg

Pesto-Glazed Chicken Breasts

Prep time: 5 minutes | Cook time: 20 minutes | Serves 4

¼ cup plus 1 tablespoon extra-virgin olive oil, divided	black pepper
4 boneless, skinless chicken breasts	1 packed cup fresh basil leaves
	1 garlic clove, minced
½ teaspoon salt	¼ cup grated Parmesan cheese
¼ teaspoon freshly ground	¼ cup pine nuts

1. In a large, heavy skillet, heat 1 tablespoon of the olive oil over medium-high heat. 2. Season the chicken breasts on both sides with salt and pepper and place in the skillet. Cook for 10 minutes on the first side, then turn and cook for 5 minutes. 3. Meanwhile, in a blender or food processor, combine the basil, garlic, Parmesan cheese, and pine nuts, and blend on high. Gradually pour in the remaining ¼ cup olive oil and blend until smooth. 4. Spread 1 tablespoon pesto on each chicken breast, cover the skillet, and cook

for 5 minutes. Serve the chicken pesto side up.
Per Serving:
calories: 531 | fat: 28g | protein: 64g | carbs: 2g | fiber: 0g | sodium: 572mg

Braised Chicken with Mushrooms and Tomatoes

Prep time: 20 minutes | Cook time: 25 minutes | Serves 4

1 tablespoon extra-virgin olive oil	2 teaspoons minced fresh sage
	½ cup dry red wine
1 pound (454 g) portobello mushroom caps, gills removed, caps halved and sliced ½ inch thick	1 (14½-ounce / 411-g) can diced tomatoes, drained
	4 (5- to 7-ounce / 142- to 198-g) bone-in chicken thighs, skin removed, trimmed
1 onion, chopped fine	
¾ teaspoon salt, divided	¼ teaspoon pepper
4 garlic cloves, minced	2 tablespoons chopped fresh parsley
1 tablespoon tomato paste	
1 tablespoon all-purpose flour	Shaved Parmesan cheese

1. Using highest sauté function, heat oil in Instant Pot until shimmering. Add mushrooms, onion, and ¼ teaspoon salt. Partially cover and cook until mushrooms are softened and have released their liquid, about 5 minutes. Stir in garlic, tomato paste, flour, and sage and cook until fragrant, about 1 minute. Stir in wine, scraping up any browned bits, then stir in tomatoes. 2. Sprinkle chicken with remaining ½ teaspoon salt and pepper. Nestle chicken skinned side up into pot and spoon some of sauce on top. Lock lid in place and close pressure release valve. Select high pressure cook function and cook for 15 minutes. 3. Turn off Instant Pot and quick-release pressure. Carefully remove lid, allowing steam to escape away from you. Transfer chicken to serving dish, tent with aluminum foil, and let rest while finishing sauce. 4. Using highest sauté function, bring sauce to simmer and cook until thickened slightly, about 5 minutes. Season sauce with salt and pepper to taste. Spoon sauce over chicken and sprinkle with parsley and Parmesan. Serve.

Per Serving:
calories: 230 | fat: 7g | protein: 21g | carbs: 15g | fiber:2g | sodium: 730mg

Honey-Glazed Chicken Thighs

Prep time: 5 minutes | Cook time: 14 minutes | Serves 4

Oil, for spraying	1 tablespoon balsamic vinegar
4 boneless, skinless chicken thighs, fat trimmed	2 teaspoons honey
	2 teaspoons minced garlic
3 tablespoons soy sauce	1 teaspoon ground ginger

1. Preheat the air fryer to 400ºF (204ºC). Line the air fryer basket with parchment and spray lightly with oil. 2. Place the chicken in the prepared basket. 3. Cook for 7 minutes, flip, and cook for another 7 minutes, or until the internal temperature reaches 165ºF (74ºC) and the juices run clear. 4. In a small saucepan, combine the soy sauce, balsamic vinegar, honey, garlic, and ginger and cook over low heat for 1 to 2 minutes, until warmed through. 5. Transfer the chicken to a serving plate and drizzle with the sauce just before serving.

Per Serving:
calories: 286 | fat: 10g | protein: 39g | carbs: 7g | fiber: 0g | sodium: 365mg

Chapter 3

Beans and Grains

Moroccan Vegetables and Chickpeas

Prep time: 25 minutes | Cook time: 6 hours | Serves 6

1 large carrot, cut into ¼-inch rounds	tomatoes, with the juice
2 large baking potatoes, peeled and cubed	3 cups canned chickpeas, rinsed and drained
1 large bell pepper, any color, chopped	1¾ cups vegetable stock
6 ounces (170 g) green beans, trimmed and cut into bite-size pieces	1 tablespoon ground coriander
	1 teaspoon ground cumin
	¼ teaspoon ground red pepper
	Sea salt
1 large yellow onion, chopped	Black pepper
2 garlic cloves, minced	8 ounces (227 g) fresh baby spinach
1 teaspoon peeled, grated fresh ginger	¼ cup diced dried apricots
	¼ cup diced dried figs
1 (15-ounce / 425-g) can diced	1 cup plain greek yogurt

1. Put the carrot, potatoes, bell pepper, green beans, onion, garlic, and ginger in the slow cooker. Stir in the diced tomatoes, chickpeas, and vegetable stock. Sprinkle with coriander, cumin, red pepper, salt, and black pepper. 2. Cover and cook on high for 6 hours or until the vegetables are tender. 3. Add the spinach, apricots, figs, and Greek yogurt, and cook and stir until the spinach wilts, about 4 minutes. Serve hot.

Per Serving:
calories: 307 | fat: 5g | protein: 13g | carbs: 57g | fiber: 12g | sodium: 513mg

Buckwheat Bake with Root Vegetables

Prep time: 15 minutes | Cook time: 30 minutes | Serves 6

Olive oil cooking spray	oil, divided
2 large potatoes, cubed	2 rosemary sprigs
2 carrots, sliced	1 cup buckwheat groats
1 small rutabaga, cubed	2 cups vegetable broth
2 celery stalks, chopped	2 garlic cloves, minced
½ teaspoon smoked paprika	½ yellow onion, chopped
¼ cup plus 1 tablespoon olive	1 teaspoon salt

1. Preheat the air fryer to 380°F(193°C). Lightly coat the inside of a 5-cup capacity casserole dish with olive oil cooking spray. (The shape of the casserole dish will depend upon the size of the air fryer, but it needs to be able to hold at least 5 cups.) 2. In a large bowl, toss the potatoes, carrots, rutabaga, and celery with the paprika and ¼ cup olive oil. 3. Pour the vegetable mixture into the prepared casserole dish and top with the rosemary sprigs. Place the casserole dish into the air fryer and bake for 15 minutes. 4. While the vegetables are cooking, rinse and drain the buckwheat groats. 5. In a medium saucepan over medium-high heat, combine the groats, vegetable broth, garlic, onion, and salt with the remaining 1 tablespoon olive oil. Bring the mixture to a boil, then reduce the heat to low, cover, and cook for 10 to 12 minutes. 6. Remove the casserole dish from the air fryer. Remove the rosemary sprigs and discard. Pour the cooked buckwheat into the dish with the vegetables and stir to combine. Cover with aluminum foil and bake for an additional 15 minutes. 7. Stir before serving.

Per Serving:
calories: 229 | fat: 10.2g | protein: 4g | carbs: 32.2g | fiber: 4.6g | sodium: 720mg

Sun-Dried Tomato Rice

Prep time: 10 minutes | Cook time: 30 minutes | Serves 8

2 tablespoons extra-virgin olive oil	1 tablespoon tomato paste
½ medium yellow onion, peeled and chopped	2 cups brown rice
	2¼ cups water
2 cloves garlic, peeled and minced	½ cup chopped fresh basil
	¼ teaspoon salt
1 cup chopped sun-dried tomatoes in oil, drained	½ teaspoon ground black pepper

1. Press the Sauté button on the Instant Pot® and heat oil. Add onion and cook until soft, about 6 minutes. Add garlic and sun-dried tomatoes and cook until fragrant, about 30 seconds. Add tomato paste, rice, and water, and stir well. Press the Cancel button. 2. Close lid, set steam release to Sealing, press the Manual button, and set time to 22 minutes. When the timer beeps, let pressure release naturally for 10 minutes, then quick-release the remaining pressure. Open lid and fold in basil. Season with salt and pepper. Serve warm.

Per Serving:
calories: 114 | fat: 4g | protein: 2g | carbs: 18g | fiber: 2g | sodium: 112mg

Creamy Thyme Polenta

Prep time: 5 minutes | Cook time: 10 minutes | Serves 6

3½ cups water	1 cup corn kernels
½ cup coarse polenta	1 teaspoon dried thyme
½ cup fine cornmeal	1 teaspoon salt

1. Add all ingredients to the Instant Pot® and stir. 2. Close lid, set steam release to Sealing, press the Manual button, and set time to 10 minutes. When the timer beeps, quick-release the pressure until the float valve drops and open lid. Serve immediately.

Per Serving:
calories: 74 | fat: 1g | protein: 2g | carbs: 14g | fiber: 2g | sodium: 401mg

Revithosoupa (Chickpea Soup)

Prep time: 10 minutes | Cook time: 30 minutes | Serves 8

1 pound (454 g) dried chickpeas	2 medium onions, peeled and diced
4 cups water	1 cup extra-virgin olive oil
¾ teaspoon salt	1 teaspoon dried oregano
½ teaspoon ground black pepper	3 tablespoons lemon juice
	2 tablespoons chopped fresh parsley
10 strands saffron	

1. Add chickpeas, water, salt, pepper, saffron, onions, oil, and oregano to the Instant Pot® and stir well. Close lid, set steam release to Sealing, press the Bean button, and cook for the default time of 30 minutes. 2. When the timer beeps, let pressure release naturally, about 25 minutes. Open lid. Serve hot or cold, sprinkled with lemon juice. Garnish with chopped parsley.

Per Serving:
calories: 464 | fat: 30g | protein: 12g | carbs: 38g | fiber: 10g | sodium: 236mg

Greek Baked Beans

Prep time: 5 minutes | Cook time: 30 minutes | Serves 4

Olive oil cooking spray	¼ cup olive oil
1 (15-ounce/ 425-g) can cannellini beans, drained and rinsed	2 garlic cloves, minced
	2 tablespoons chopped fresh dill
1 (15-ounce/ 425-g) can great northern beans, drained and rinsed	½ teaspoon salt
	½ teaspoon black pepper
½ yellow onion, diced	1 bay leaf
1 (8-ounce/ 227-g) can tomato sauce	1 tablespoon balsamic vinegar
	2 ounces (57 g) feta cheese, crumbled, for serving
1½ tablespoons raw honey	

1. Preheat the air fryer to 360°F(182ºC). Lightly coat the inside of a 5-cup capacity casserole dish with olive oil cooking spray. (The shape of the casserole dish will depend upon the size of the air fryer, but it needs to be able to hold at least 5 cups.) 2. In a large bowl, combine all ingredients except the feta cheese and stir until well combined. 3. Pour the bean mixture into the prepared casserole dish. 4. Bake in the air fryer for 30 minutes. 5. Remove from the air fryer and remove and discard the bay leaf. Sprinkle crumbled feta over the top before serving.

Per Serving:

calories: 336 | fat: 19g | protein: 11g | carbs: 34g | fiber: 9.4g | sodium: 497mg

South Indian Split Yellow Pigeon Peas with Mixed Vegetables

Prep time: 20 minutes | Cook time: 4½ to 6½ minutes | Serves 6

Sambar Masala:

1 teaspoon rapeseed oil	½ teaspoon fenugreek seeds
3 tablespoons coriander seeds	½ teaspoon mustard seeds
2 tablespoons split gram	¼ teaspoon cumin seeds
1 teaspoon black peppercorns	12 whole dried red chiles

Sambar:

1½ cups split yellow pigeon peas, washed	1 tomato, roughly chopped
	4 cups water
2 fresh green chiles, sliced lengthwise	2 to 3 moringa seed pods, or ⅓ pound (151 g) green beans or asparagus, chopped into 2¾-inch lengths
2 garlic cloves, chopped	
6 pearl onions	
4 to 5 tablespoons sambar masala	2 tablespoons tamarind paste
	½ teaspoon asafetida
2 teaspoons salt	2 teaspoons coconut oil
1 to 2 carrots, peeled and chopped	1 teaspoon mustard seeds
	20 curry leaves
1 red potato, peeled and diced	2 dried red chilies
1 white radish (mooli), peeled and chopped into 2¾-inch sticks	Handful fresh coriander leaves, chopped (optional)

Make the Sambar Masala: 1. Add the oil to a medium nonstick skillet. Add all of the remaining ingredients and roast for a few minutes until fragrant. The spices will brown a little, but don't let them burn. 2. Remove from the heat and pour onto a plate to cool. Once cooled, place into your spice grinder or mortar and pestle and grind to a powder. Set aside. Make the Sambar: 3. Heat the slow cooker to high and add the pigeon peas, green chiles, garlic, pearl onions, sambar masala, salt, carrots, potatoes, radish, tomato, and water. 4. Cover and cook for 4 hours on high, or for 6 hours on low. 5. Add the moringa (or green beans or asparagus), tamarind paste, and asafetida. Cover and cook for another 30 minutes. 6. When you're ready to serve, heat the coconut oil in a frying pan and pop the mustard seeds with the curry leaves and dried chiles. Pour over the sambar. Top with coriander leaves (if using) and serve.

Per Serving:

calories: 312 | fat: 7g | protein: 12g | carbs: 59g | fiber: 16g | sodium: 852mg

Fava Beans with Ground Meat

Prep time: 15 minutes | Cook time: 6 to 8 hours | Serves 6

8 ounces (227 g) raw ground meat	1 bell pepper, any color, seeded and diced
1 pound (454 g) dried fava beans, rinsed well under cold water and picked over to remove debris, or 1 (15-ounce/ 425-g) can fava beans, drained and rinsed	1 teaspoon sea salt
	1 teaspoon garlic powder
	1 teaspoon dried parsley
	1 teaspoon dried oregano
	1 teaspoon paprika
	1 teaspoon cayenne pepper
10 cups water or 5 cups water and 5 cups low-sodium vegetable broth	½ teaspoon freshly ground black pepper
	½ teaspoon dried thyme
1 small onion, diced	

1. In a large skillet over medium-high heat, cook the ground meat for 3 to 5 minutes, stirring and breaking it up with a spoon, until it has browned and is no longer pink. Drain any grease and put the meat in a slow cooker. 2. Add the fava beans, water, onion, bell pepper, salt, garlic powder, parsley, oregano, paprika, cayenne pepper, black pepper, and thyme to the meat. Stir to mix well. 3. Cover the cooker and cook for 6 to 8 hours on Low heat, or until the beans are tender.

Per Serving:

calories: 308 | fat: 4g | protein: 26g | carbs: 43g | fiber: 19g | sodium: 417mg

Falafel

Prep time: 10 minutes | Cook time: 6 to 8 hours | Serves 4

Nonstick cooking spray	¼ cup chopped fresh cilantro
2 cups canned reduced-sodium chickpeas, rinsed and drained	1 teaspoon sea salt
	1 teaspoon ground cumin
4 garlic cloves, peeled	½ teaspoon ground coriander
¼ cup chickpea flour or all-purpose flour	½ teaspoon freshly ground black pepper
¼ cup diced onion	⅛ teaspoon cayenne pepper
¼ cup chopped fresh parsley	

1. Generously coat a slow cooker insert with cooking spray. 2. In a blender or food processor, combine the chickpeas, garlic, flour, onion, parsley, cilantro, salt, cumin, coriander, black pepper, and cayenne pepper. Process until smooth. Form the mixture into 6 to 8 (2-inch) round patties and place them in a single layer in the prepared slow cooker. 3. Cover the cooker and cook for 6 to 8 hours on Low heat.

Per Serving:

calories: 174 | fat: 3g | protein: 9g | carbs: 30g | fiber: 8g | sodium: 594mg

Rice and Lentils

Prep time: 10 minutes | Cook time: 55 minutes | Serves 4

2 cups green or brown lentils	pepper
1 cup brown rice	½ teaspoon dried thyme
5 cups water or chicken stock	¼ cup olive oil
½ teaspoon sea salt	3 onions, peeled and sliced
½ teaspoon freshly ground	

1. Place the lentils and rice in a large saucepan with water or chicken stock. Bring to a boil, cover, and simmer for 20–25 minutes, or until almost tender. 2. Add the seasonings and cook an additional 20–30 minutes, or until the rice is tender and the water is absorbed. 3. In another saucepan, heat the olive oil over medium heat. Add the onions and cook very slowly, stirring frequently, until the onions become browned and caramelized, about 20 minutes. 4. To serve, ladle the lentils and rice into bowls and top with the caramelized onions.

Per Serving:
calories: 661 | fat: 16g | protein: 28g | carbs: 104g | fiber: 13g | sodium: 303mg

Domatorizo (Greek Tomato Rice)

Prep time: 10 minutes | Cook time: 12 minutes | Serves 6

2 tablespoons extra-virgin olive oil	½ teaspoon salt
1 large onion, peeled and diced	½ teaspoon ground black pepper
1 cup Arborio rice	½ cup crumbled or cubed feta cheese
1 cup tomato juice	⅛ teaspoon dried Greek oregano
3 tablespoons dry white wine	
2 cups water	1 scallion, thinly sliced
1 tablespoon tomato paste	

1. Press the Sauté button on the Instant Pot® and heat oil. Add onion and cook until just tender, about 3 minutes. Stir in rice and cook for 2 minutes. 2. Add tomato juice and wine to rice. Cook, stirring often, until the liquid is absorbed, about 1 minute. 3. In a small bowl, whisk together water and tomato paste. Add to pot along with salt and pepper and stir well. Press the Cancel button. 4. Close lid, set steam release to Sealing, press the Manual button, and set time to 5 minutes. When the timer beeps, let pressure release naturally for 10 minutes, then quick-release any remaining pressure until the float valve drops. 5. Open lid and stir well. Spoon rice into bowls and top with feta, oregano, and scallion. Serve immediately.

Per Serving:
calories: 184 | fat: 9g | protein: 6g | carbs: 20g | fiber: 1g | sodium: 537mg

Amaranth Salad

Prep time: 5 minutes | Cook time: 6 minutes | Serves 4

2 cups water	pepper
1 cup amaranth	1 tablespoon extra-virgin olive oil
1 teaspoon dried Greek oregano	
½ teaspoon salt	2 teaspoons red wine vinegar
½ teaspoon ground black	

1. Add water and amaranth to the Instant Pot®. Close lid, set steam release to Sealing, press the Manual button, and set time to 6 minutes. When the timer beeps, quick-release the pressure until the float valve drops. 2. Open lid and fluff amaranth with a fork. Add oregano, salt, and pepper. Mix well. Drizzle with olive oil and wine vinegar. Serve hot.

Per Serving:
calories: 93 | fat: 5g | protein: 3g | carbs: 12g | fiber: 3g | sodium: 299mg

Mediterranean "Fried" Rice

Prep time: 15 minutes | Cook time: 3 to 5 hours | Serves 4

Nonstick cooking spray	2 garlic cloves, minced
1 cup raw long-grain brown rice, rinsed	1 carrot, diced
2½ cups low-sodium chicken broth	1 bell pepper, any color, seeded and diced
2 tablespoons extra-virgin olive oil	¼ cup peas (raw, frozen, or canned)
2 tablespoons balsamic vinegar	1 teaspoon sea salt
2 zucchini, diced	1 pound (454 g) boneless, skinless chicken breast, cut into ½-inch pieces
4 ounces (113 g) mushrooms, diced	
1 small onion, diced	2 large eggs

1. Generously coat a slow-cooker insert with cooking spray. Put the rice, chicken broth, olive oil, vinegar, zucchini, mushrooms, onion, garlic, carrot, bell pepper, peas, and salt in a slow cooker. Stir to mix well. 2. Nestle the chicken into the rice mixture. 3. Cover the cooker and cook for 3 to 5 hours on Low heat. 4. In a small bowl, whisk the eggs. Pour the eggs over the chicken and rice. Replace the cover on the cooker and cook for 15 to 30 minutes on Low heat, or until the eggs are scrambled and cooked through. 5. Fluff the rice with a fork before serving.

Per Serving:
calories: 431 | fat: 14g | protein: 35g | carbs: 48g | fiber: 5g | sodium: 876mg

Lentils in Tomato Sauce

Prep time: 10 minutes | Cook time: 11 minutes | Serves 6

2 cups red, green, or brown dried lentils, rinsed and drained	1 tablespoon chopped fresh oregano
½ teaspoon salt	1 teaspoon ground fennel
4 cups water	¼ teaspoon ground black pepper
1 (24-ounce / 680-g) jar marinara sauce	½ cup grated Parmesan cheese
1 tablespoon extra-virgin olive oil	½ cup minced fresh flat-leaf parsley

1. Add lentils, salt, and water to the Instant Pot®. Close lid, set steam release to Sealing, press the Manual button, and set time to 6 minutes. When the timer beeps, quick-release the pressure until the float valve drops. Press the Cancel button. Open lid and drain off any excess liquid. 2. Add sauce, oil, oregano, fennel, and pepper to pot and stir well. Close lid, set steam release to Sealing, press the Manual button, and set time to 5 minutes. When the timer beeps, let pressure release naturally for 10 minutes, then quick-release any remaining pressure until the float valve drops. Open lid and top with cheese and parsley.

Per Serving:
calories: 342 | fat: 8g | protein: 21g | carbs: 48g | fiber: 9g | sodium: 640mg

Tomato Bulgur

Prep time: 10 minutes | Cook time: 25 minutes | Serves 4

3 tablespoons olive oil	juices
1 onion, diced	Juice of ½ lemon
1 garlic clove, minced	¼ teaspoon sea salt, plus more
1 tablespoon tomato paste	as needed
½ teaspoon paprika	1 cup dried bulgur
3 Roma (plum) tomatoes, finely	2 cups vegetable broth, chicken
chopped, or 1 cup canned	broth, or water
crushed tomatoes with their	

1. In a large saucepan, heat the olive oil over medium-high heat. Add the onion and garlic and sauté for 4 to 5 minutes, until the onion is soft. Add the tomato paste and paprika and stir for about 30 seconds. 2. Add the chopped tomatoes, lemon juice, and salt and cook for 1 to 2 minutes more. 3. Add the bulgur and stir for about 30 seconds. Add the broth, bring to a simmer, reduce the heat to low, cover, and simmer for 13 to 15 minutes, until the liquid has been absorbed. Uncover and stir, then remove from the heat, cover, and let stand for 5 minutes. 4. Taste and adjust the seasoning, then serve.
Per Serving:
calories: 243 | fat: 11g | protein: 6g | carbs: 34g | fiber: 6g | sodium: 92mg

Southwestern Rice Casserole

Prep time: 20 minutes | Cook time: 4 to 6 hours | Serves 2

1 teaspoon extra-virgin olive oil	1 teaspoon dried oregano
1 cup brown rice	⅛ teaspoon cayenne pepper
1 cup canned black beans,	⅛ teaspoon sea salt
drained and rinsed	1½ cups low-sodium vegetable
1 cup frozen corn, thawed	broth or water
1 cup canned fire-roasted diced	¼ cup fresh cilantro
tomatoes, undrained	¼ cup sharp cheddar cheese

1. Grease the inside of the slow cooker with the olive oil. 2. Add the brown rice, beans, corn, tomatoes, oregano, cayenne, and salt. Pour in the broth and stir to mix thoroughly. 3. Cover and cook on low for 4 to 6 hours. 4. Stir in the cilantro and cheddar cheese before serving.
Per Serving:
calories: 681 | fat: 12g | protein: 25g | carbs: 126g | fiber: 17g | sodium: 490mg

Crunchy Pea and Barley Salad

Prep time: 10 minutes | Cook time: 15 minutes | Serves 4

2 cups water	½ small red onion, diced
1 cup quick-cooking barley	2 tablespoons olive oil
2 cups sugar snap pea pods	Juice of 1 lemon
Small bunch flat-leaf parsley,	Sea salt and freshly ground
chopped	pepper, to taste

1. Bring water to boil in a saucepan. Stir in the barley and cover. 2. Simmer for 10 minutes until all water is absorbed, and then let stand about 5 minutes covered. 3. Rinse the barley under cold water and combine it with the peas, parsley, onion, olive oil, and lemon juice. 4. Season with sea salt and freshly ground pepper to taste.
Per Serving:

calories: 277 | fat: 8g | protein: 8g | carbs: 47g | fiber: 11g | sodium: 19mg

Giant Beans with Tomato and Parsley

Prep time: 10 minutes | Cook time: 54 minutes | Serves 8

2 tablespoons light olive oil	tomatoes, drained
1 medium white onion, peeled	1 (8-ounce / 227-g) can tomato
and chopped	sauce
2 cloves garlic, peeled and	¼ cup chopped fresh flat-leaf
minced	parsley
1 pound (454 g) dried giant	2 tablespoons chopped fresh
beans, soaked overnight and	oregano
drained	1 tablespoon chopped fresh dill
2 thyme sprigs	½ cup crumbled feta cheese
1 bay leaf	1 small lemon, cut into 8
5 cups water	wedges
1 (15-ounce / 425-g) can diced	

1. Press the Sauté button on the Instant Pot® and heat oil. Add onion and cook until tender, about 3 minutes. Add garlic and cook until fragrant, about 30 seconds. Press the Cancel button. 2. Add beans, thyme, bay leaf, and water to the Instant Pot®. Close lid, set steam release to Sealing, press the Manual button, and set time to 50 minutes. When the timer beeps, quick-release the pressure until the float valve drops. Open lid and check that beans are soft. If they are not tender, close lid and cook under pressure for 10 minutes more. 3. Add diced tomatoes and tomato sauce. Close lid and let stand on the Keep Warm setting for 10 minutes to heat through. Remove and discard bay leaf. Stir in herbs and ladle into soup bowls. Garnish with feta and lemon slices, and serve hot.
Per Serving:
calories: 241 | fat: 6g | protein: 14g | carbs: 33g | fiber: 10g | sodium: 458mg

Mediterranean Bulgur Medley

Prep time: 15 minutes | Cook time: 20 minutes | Serves 6

2 tablespoons extra-virgin olive oil	1 teaspoon ground cumin
	½ teaspoon salt
1 medium onion, peeled and	½ teaspoon ground black
diced	pepper
½ cup chopped button	1 cup medium bulgur wheat
mushrooms	1 tablespoon petimezi or honey
½ cup golden raisins (sultanas)	12 chestnuts, roasted, peeled,
¼ cup pine nuts	and halved
2 cups vegetable stock	1 teaspoon sesame seeds

1. Press the Sauté button on the Instant Pot® and heat oil. Add onion and sauté 3 minutes. Add mushrooms, raisins, and pine nuts and cook 2 minutes. 2. Add stock, cumin, salt, pepper, bulgur, and petimezi. Cook, stirring, for 3 minutes. Add chestnuts, then press the Cancel button. 3. Close lid, set steam release to Sealing, press the Rice button, and set time to 12 minutes. When the timer beeps, quick-release the pressure until the float valve drops and open lid. Stir well, then let stand, uncovered, on the Keep Warm setting for 10 minutes. Sprinkle with sesame seeds and serve.
Per Serving:
calories: 129 | fat: 1g | protein: 3g | carbs: 28g | fiber: 2g | sodium: 219mg

Wheat Berry Salad

Prep time: 20 minutes | Cook time: 50 minutes | Serves 12

1½ tablespoons vegetable oil
6¾ cups water
1½ cups wheat berries
1½ teaspoons Dijon mustard
1 teaspoon sugar
1 teaspoon salt
½ teaspoon ground black pepper
¼ cup white wine vinegar
½ cup extra-virgin olive oil
½ small red onion, peeled and diced

1⅓ cups frozen corn, thawed
1 medium zucchini, trimmed, grated, and drained
2 stalks celery, finely diced
1 medium red bell pepper, seeded and diced
4 scallions, diced
¼ cup diced sun-dried tomatoes
¼ cup chopped fresh parsley

1. Add vegetable oil, water, and wheat berries to the Instant Pot®. Close lid, set steam release to Sealing, press the Manual button, and set time to 50 minutes. When the timer beeps, quick-release the pressure until the float valve drops and open lid. Fluff wheat berries with a fork. Drain any excess liquid, transfer to a large bowl, and set aside to cool. 2. Purée mustard, sugar, salt, black pepper, vinegar, olive oil, and onion in a blender. Stir dressing into wheat berries. Stir in rest of ingredients. Serve.

Per Serving:
calories: 158 | fat: 10g | protein: 2g | carbs: 16g | fiber: 2g | sodium: 268mg

Creamy Lima Bean Soup

Prep time: 10 minutes | Cook time: 17 minutes | Serves 6

1 tablespoon olive oil
1 small onion, peeled and diced
1 clove garlic, peeled and minced
2 cups vegetable stock
½ cup water
2 cups dried lima beans, soaked

overnight and drained
½ teaspoon salt
½ teaspoon ground black pepper
2 tablespoons thinly sliced chives

1. Press the Sauté button on the Instant Pot® and heat oil. Add onion and cook until golden brown, about 10 minutes. Add garlic and cook until fragrant, about 30 seconds. Press the Cancel button. 2. Add stock, water, and lima beans. Close lid, set steam release to Sealing, press the Manual button, and set time to 6 minutes. When the timer beeps, let pressure release naturally, about 20 minutes. 3. Open lid and purée soup with an immersion blender or in batches in a blender. Season with salt and pepper, then sprinkle with chives before serving.

Per Serving:
calories: 67 | fat: 2g | protein: 2g | carbs: 9g | fiber: 2g | sodium: 394mg

Lemon and Garlic Rice Pilaf

Prep time: 10 minutes | Cook time: 34 minutes | Serves 8

2 tablespoons olive oil
1 medium yellow onion, peeled and chopped
4 cloves garlic, peeled and minced
1 tablespoon grated lemon zest
½ teaspoon ground black pepper

1 teaspoon dried thyme
1 teaspoon dried oregano
¼ teaspoon salt
2 tablespoons white wine
2 tablespoons lemon juice
2 cups brown rice
2 cups vegetable broth

1. Press the Sauté button on the Instant Pot® and heat oil. Add onion and cook until soft, about 6 minutes. Add garlic and cook until fragrant, about 30 seconds. Add lemon zest, pepper, thyme, oregano, and salt. Cook until fragrant, about 1 minute. 2. Add wine and lemon juice and cook, stirring well, until liquid has almost evaporated, about 1 minute. Add rice and cook, stirring constantly, until coated and starting to toast, about 3 minutes. Press the Cancel button. 3. Stir in broth. Close lid, set steam release to Sealing, press the Manual button, and set time to 22 minutes. 4. When the timer beeps, let pressure release naturally for 10 minutes, then quick-release the remaining pressure until the float valve drops. Open lid and fluff rice with a fork. Serve warm.

Per Serving:
calories: 202 | fat: 5g | protein: 4g | carbs: 37g | fiber: 1g | sodium: 274mg

Black-Eyed Peas with Olive Oil and Herbs

Prep time: 15 minutes | Cook time: 20 minutes | Serves 8

¼ cup extra-virgin olive oil
4 sprigs oregano, leaves minced and stems reserved
2 sprigs thyme, leaves stripped and stems reserved
4 sprigs dill, fronds chopped and stems reserved

1 pound (454 g) dried black-eyed peas, soaked overnight and drained
¼ teaspoon salt
1 teaspoon ground black pepper
4 cups water

1. In a small bowl, combine oil, oregano leaves, thyme leaves, and dill fronds, and mix to combine. Cover and set aside. 2. Tie herb stems together with butcher's twine. Add to the Instant Pot® along with black-eyed peas, salt, pepper, and water. Close lid, set steam release to Sealing, press the Manual button, and set time to 20 minutes. When the timer beeps, let pressure release naturally, about 20 minutes. 3. Open lid, remove and discard herb stem bundle, and drain off any excess liquid. Stir in olive oil mixture. Serve hot.

Per Serving:
calories: 119 | fat: 7g | protein: 6g | carbs: 9g | fiber: 3g | sodium: 76mg

Brown Rice and Chickpea Salad

Prep time: 5 minutes | Cook time: 22 minutes | Serves 8

2 cups brown rice
2¼ cups vegetable broth
2 tablespoons light olive oil
1 (15-ounce/ 425-g) can chickpeas, drained and rinsed
½ cup diced tomato
½ cup chopped red onion
½ cup diced cucumber

¼ cup chopped fresh basil
3 tablespoons extra-virgin olive oil
2 tablespoons balsamic vinegar
½ teaspoon ground black pepper
¼ teaspoon salt
¼ cup crumbled feta cheese

1. Place rice, broth, and light oil in the Instant Pot®. Close lid, set steam release to Sealing, press the Manual button, and set time to 22 minutes. 2. When the timer beeps, let pressure release naturally for 10 minutes, then quick-release the remaining pressure. Open lid, transfer rice to a large bowl, and set aside for 20 minutes. Fold in chickpeas, tomato, onion, cucumber, and basil. 3. In a small bowl, whisk together extra-virgin olive oil, balsamic vinegar, pepper, and salt. Pour over rice mixture and toss to coat. Top with feta. Serve at room temperature or refrigerate for at least 2 hours.

Per Serving:
calories: 417 | fat: 21g | protein: 13g | carbs: 45g | fiber: 7g | sodium: 366mg

Lentil and Zucchini Boats

Prep time: 15 minutes | Cook time: 50 minutes | Serves 4

1 cup dried green lentils, rinsed and drained
¼ teaspoon salt
2 cups water
1 tablespoon olive oil
½ medium red onion, peeled and diced
1 clove garlic, peeled and minced

1 cup marinara sauce
¼ teaspoon crushed red pepper flakes
4 medium zucchini, trimmed and cut lengthwise
½ cup shredded part-skim mozzarella cheese
¼ cup chopped fresh flat-leaf parsley

1. Add lentils, salt, and water to the Instant Pot®. Close lid, set steam release to Sealing, press the Manual button, and set time to 12 minutes. When the timer beeps, quick-release the pressure until the float valve drops. Press the Cancel button. Open lid and drain off any excess liquid. Transfer lentils to a medium bowl. Set aside. 2. Press the Sauté button and heat oil. Add onion and cook until tender, about 3 minutes. Add garlic and cook until fragrant, about 30 seconds. Add marinara sauce and crushed red pepper flakes and stir to combine. Press the Cancel button. Stir in lentils. 3. Preheat oven to 350°F (180°C) and spray a 9" × 13" baking dish with nonstick cooking spray. 4. Using a teaspoon, hollow out each zucchini half. Lay zucchini in prepared baking dish. Divide lentil mixture among prepared zucchini. Top with cheese. Bake for 30–35 minutes, or until zucchini are tender and cheese is melted and browned. Top with parsley and serve hot.

Per Serving:
calories: 326 | fat: 10g | protein: 22g | carbs: 39g | fiber: 16g | sodium: 568mg

Chapter 4

Beef, Pork, and Lamb

Pork and Cabbage Egg Roll in a Bowl

Prep time: 10 minutes | Cook time: 10 minutes | Serves 6

1 tablespoon light olive oil	ginger
1 pound (454 g) ground pork	¼ cup low-sodium chicken broth
1 medium yellow onion, peeled and chopped	2 tablespoons soy sauce
1 clove garlic, peeled and minced	2 (10-ounce/ 283-g) bags shredded coleslaw mix
2 teaspoons minced fresh	1 teaspoon sesame oil
	1 teaspoon garlic chili sauce

1. Press the Sauté button on the Instant Pot® and heat olive oil. Add pork and sauté until cooked through, about 8 minutes. Add onion, garlic, and ginger, and cook until fragrant, about 2 minutes. Stir in chicken broth and soy sauce. Press the Cancel button. 2. Spread coleslaw mix over pork, but do not mix. Close lid, set steam release to Sealing, press the Manual button, and set time to 0 minutes. 3. When the timer beeps, quick-release the pressure until the float valve drops and open lid. Stir in sesame oil and garlic chili sauce. Serve hot.

Per Serving:
calories: 283 | fat: 24g | protein: 12g | carbs: 5g | fiber: 2g | sodium: 507mg

Bone-in Pork Chops

Prep time: 5 minutes | Cook time: 10 to 12 minutes | Serves 2

1 pound (454 g) bone-in pork chops	½ teaspoon onion powder
1 tablespoon avocado oil	¼ teaspoon cayenne pepper
1 teaspoon smoked paprika	Sea salt and freshly ground black pepper, to taste

1. Brush the pork chops with the avocado oil. In a small dish, mix together the smoked paprika, onion powder, cayenne pepper, and salt and black pepper to taste. Sprinkle the seasonings over both sides of the pork chops. 2. Set the air fryer to 400ºF (204ºC). Place the chops in the air fryer basket in a single layer, working in batches if necessary. Air fry for 10 to 12 minutes, until an instant-read thermometer reads 145ºF (63ºC) at the chops' thickest point. 3. Remove the chops from the air fryer and allow them to rest for 5 minutes before serving.

Per Serving:
calories: 356 | fat: 16g | protein: 50g | carbs: 1g | fiber: 1g | sodium: 133mg

Giouvarlakia Soup

Prep time: 10 minutes | Cook time: 5 minutes | Serves 6

1 pound (454 g) lean ground beef	¾ teaspoon salt, divided
1 medium onion, peeled and grated	¾ teaspoon ground black pepper, divided
3 large eggs, divided	8 cups low-sodium chicken broth
⅓ cup plus ½ cup Arborio rice, divided	1 tablespoon all-purpose flour
1 teaspoon ground allspice	2 tablespoons water
⅛ teaspoon ground nutmeg	3 tablespoons lemon juice

1. In a large bowl, combine beef, onion, 1 egg, ⅓ cup rice, allspice, nutmeg, ¼ teaspoon salt, and ¼ teaspoon pepper. Roll the mixture into 1" balls. Set aside. 2. Add broth, meatballs, remaining ½ cup rice, and remaining ½ teaspoon each salt and pepper to the Instant Pot®. Close lid, set steam release to Sealing, press the Manual button, and set time to 5 minutes. When the timer beeps, let pressure release naturally for 10 minutes. Quick-release any remaining pressure until the float valve drops. Press the Cancel button and open lid. 3. In a large bowl, whisk together flour and water to form a slurry. Whisk in lemon juice and remaining 2 eggs. Continuing to whisk vigorously, slowly add a ladle of soup liquid into egg mixture. Continue whisking and slowly add another 3–4 ladles of soup (one at a time) into egg mixture. 4. Slowly stir egg mixture back into the soup. 5. Allow the soup to cool for 5 minutes and then serve it immediately.

Per Serving:
calories: 262 | fat: 5g | protein: 25g | carbs: 18g | fiber: 0g | sodium: 670mg

Grilled Kefta

Prep time: 10 minutes | Cook time: 5 minutes | Serves 4

1 medium onion	¼ teaspoon cinnamon
⅓ cup fresh Italian parsley	1 teaspoon salt
1 pound (454 g) ground beef	½ teaspoon freshly ground black pepper
¼ teaspoon ground cumin	

1. Preheat a grill or grill pan to high. 2. Mince the onion and parsley in a food processor until finely chopped. 3. In a large bowl, using your hands, combine the beef with the onion mix, ground cumin, cinnamon, salt, and pepper. 4. Divide the meat into 6 portions. Form each portion into a flat oval. 5. Place the patties on the grill or grill pan and cook for 3 minutes on each side.

Per Serving:
calories: 203 | fat: 10g | protein: 24g | carbs: 3g | fiber: 1g | sodium: 655mg

Stuffed Flank Steak

Prep time: 20 minutes | Cook time: 6 hours | Serves 6

2 pounds (907 g) flank steak	½ cup dried tomatoes, chopped
Sea salt and freshly ground pepper, to taste	½ cup roasted red peppers, diced
1 tablespoon olive oil	½ cup almonds, toasted and chopped
¼ cup onion, diced	
1 clove garlic, minced	Kitchen twine
2 cups baby spinach, chopped	½ cup chicken stock

1. Lay the flank steak out on a cutting board, and generously season with sea salt and freshly ground pepper 2. Heat the olive oil in a medium saucepan. Add the onion and garlic. 3. Cook 5 minutes on medium heat, or until onion is tender and translucent, stirring frequently. 4. Add the spinach, tomatoes, peppers, and chopped almonds, and cook an additional 3 minutes, or until the spinach wilts slightly. 5. Let the tomato and spinach mixture cool to room temperature. Spread the tomato and spinach mixture evenly over the flank steak. 6. Roll the flank steak up slowly, and tie it securely with kitchen twine on both ends and in the middle. 7. Brown the flank steak in the same pan for 5 minutes, turning it carefully to brown all sides. 8. Place steak in a slow cooker with the chicken stock. Cover and cook on low for 4–6 hours. 9. Cut into rounds, discarding the twine, and serve.

Per Serving:
calories: 287 | fat: 14g | protein: 35g | carbs: 4g | fiber: 2g | sodium: 95mg

Flank Steak with Artichokes

Prep time: 15 minutes | Cook time: 60 minutes | Serves 4 to 6

4 tablespoons grapeseed oil, divided	diced tomatoes, drained
2 pounds (907 g) flank steak	1 cup tomato sauce
1 (14-ounce/ 397-g) can artichoke hearts, drained and roughly chopped	2 tablespoons tomato paste
	1 teaspoon dried oregano
	1 teaspoon dried parsley
1 onion, diced	1 teaspoon dried basil
8 garlic cloves, chopped	½ teaspoon ground cumin
1 (32-ounce/ 907-g) container low-sodium beef broth	3 bay leaves
	2 to 3 cups cooked couscous (optional)
1 (14½-ounce / 411-g) can	

1. Preheat the oven to 450ºF(235ºC). 2. In an oven-safe sauté pan or skillet, heat 3 tablespoons of oil on medium heat. Sear the steak for 2 minutes per side on both sides. Transfer the steak to the oven for 30 minutes, or until desired tenderness. 3. Meanwhile, in a large pot, combine the remaining 1 tablespoon of oil, artichoke hearts, onion, and garlic. Pour in the beef broth, tomatoes, tomato sauce, and tomato paste. Stir in oregano, parsley, basil, cumin, and bay leaves. 4. Cook the vegetables, covered, for 30 minutes. Remove bay leaf and serve with flank steak and ½ cup of couscous per plate, if using.

Per Serving:

calories: 577 | fat: 21g | protein: 45g | carbs: 54g | fiber: 5g | sodium: 150mg

Beef Sliders with Pepper Slaw

Prep time: 10 minutes |Cook time: 10 minutes| Serves: 4

Nonstick cooking spray	divided
1 (8-ounce / 227-g) package white button mushrooms	¼ teaspoon freshly ground black pepper
2 tablespoons extra-virgin olive oil, divided	1 tablespoon balsamic vinegar
	2 bell peppers of different colors, sliced into strips
1 pound (454 g) ground beef (93% lean)	2 tablespoons torn fresh basil or flat-leaf (Italian) parsley
2 garlic cloves, minced (about 1 teaspoon)	Mini or slider whole-grain rolls, for serving (optional)
½ teaspoon kosher or sea salt,	

1. Set one oven rack about 4 inches below the broiler element. Preheat the oven broiler to high. 2. Line a large, rimmed baking sheet with aluminum foil. Place a wire cooling rack on the aluminum foil, and spray the rack with nonstick cooking spray. Set aside. 3. Put half the mushrooms in the bowl of a food processor and pulse about 15 times, until the mushrooms are finely chopped but not puréed, similar to the texture of ground meat. Repeat with the remaining mushrooms. 4. In a large skillet over medium-high heat, heat 1 tablespoon of oil. Add the mushrooms and cook for 2 to 3 minutes, stirring occasionally, until the mushrooms have cooked down and some of their liquid has evaporated. Remove from the heat. 5. In a large bowl, combine the ground beef with the cooked mushrooms, garlic, ¼ teaspoon of salt, and pepper. Mix gently using your hands. Form the meat into 8 small (½-inch-thick) patties, and place on the prepared rack, making two lines of 4 patties down the center of the pan. 6. Place the pan in the oven so the broiler heating element is directly over as many burgers as possible. Broil for 4 minutes. Flip the burgers and rearrange them so any burgers

not getting brown are nearer to the heat source. Broil for 3 to 4 more minutes, or until the internal temperature of the meat is 160°F (71ºC) on a meat thermometer. Watch carefully to prevent burning. 7. While the burgers are cooking, in a large bowl, whisk together the remaining 1 tablespoon of oil, vinegar, and remaining ¼ teaspoon of salt. Add the peppers and basil, and stir gently to coat with the dressing. Serve the sliders with the pepper slaw as a topping or on the side. If desired, serve with the rolls, burger style.

Per Serving:

calories: 252 | fat: 13g | protein: 27g | carbs: 9g | fiber: 2g | sodium: 373mg

Poblano Pepper Cheeseburgers

Prep time: 5 minutes | Cook time: 30 minutes | Serves 4

2 poblano chile peppers	½ teaspoon freshly ground black pepper
1½ pounds (680 g) 85% lean ground beef	4 slices Cheddar cheese (about 3 ounces / 85 g)
1 clove garlic, minced	
1 teaspoon salt	4 large lettuce leaves

1. Preheat the air fryer to 400ºF (204ºC). 2. Arrange the poblano peppers in the basket of the air fryer. Pausing halfway through the cooking time to turn the peppers, air fry for 20 minutes, or until they are softened and beginning to char. Transfer the peppers to a large bowl and cover with a plate. When cool enough to handle, peel off the skin, remove the seeds and stems, and slice into strips. Set aside. 3. Meanwhile, in a large bowl, combine the ground beef with the garlic, salt, and pepper. Shape the beef into 4 patties. 4. Lower the heat on the air fryer to 360ºF (182ºC). Arrange the burgers in a single layer in the basket of the air fryer. Pausing halfway through the cooking time to turn the burgers, air fry for 10 minutes, or until a thermometer inserted into the thickest part registers 160ºF (71ºC). 5. Top the burgers with the cheese slices and continue baking for a minute or two, just until the cheese has melted. Serve the burgers on a lettuce leaf topped with the roasted poblano peppers.

Per Serving:

calories: 489 | fat: 35g | protein: 39g | carbs: 3g | fiber: 1g | sodium: 703mg

Pork and Cannellini Bean Stew

Prep time: 15 minutes | Cook time: 1 hour | Serves 6

1 cup dried cannellini beans	1 (8-ounce/ 227-g) can tomato paste
¼ cup olive oil	
1 medium onion, diced	¼ cup flat-leaf parsley, chopped
2 pounds (907 g) pork roast, cut into 1-inch chunks	½ teaspoon dried thyme
	Sea salt and freshly ground pepper, to taste
3 cups water	

1. Rinse and sort the beans. 2. Cover beans with water, and allow to soak overnight. Heat the olive oil in a large stew pot. 3. Add the onion, stirring occasionally, until golden brown. 4. Add the pork chunks and cook 5–8 minutes, stirring frequently, until the pork is browned. Drain and rinse the beans, and add to the pot. 5. Add the water, and bring to a boil. Reduce heat and simmer for 45 minutes, until beans are tender. 6. Add the tomato paste, parsley, and thyme, and simmer an additional 15 minutes, or until the sauce thickens slightly. Season to taste.

Per Serving:

calories: 373 | fat: 16g | protein: 39g | carbs: 19g | fiber: 4g | sodium: 107mg

Quinoa Pilaf–Stuffed Pork

Prep time: 15 minutes | Cook time: 45 minutes | Serves 6

1 (1½-pound / 680-g) pork tenderloin	parsley
2 tablespoons olive oil, divided	1 tablespoon lemon juice
1 clove garlic, peeled and minced	½ cup quinoa, rinsed and drained
½ medium tomato, diced	2 cups water, divided
¼ cup chopped fresh flat-leaf	¼ cup crumbled goat cheese
	¼ teaspoon salt

1. Butterfly pork tenderloin. Open tenderloin and top with a sheet of plastic wrap. Pound pork out to ½" thick. Wrap and refrigerate until ready to use. 2. Press the Sauté button on the Instant Pot® and heat 1 tablespoon oil. Add garlic and cook 30 seconds, then add tomato, parsley, and lemon juice. Cook an additional minute. Transfer mixture to a small bowl. Press the Cancel button. 3. Add quinoa and 1 cup water to the pot. Close lid, set steam release to Sealing, press the Multigrain button, and set time to 20 minutes. When the timer beeps, let pressure release naturally, about 20 minutes, then open lid. Press the Cancel button. Fluff quinoa with a fork. Transfer quinoa to bowl with tomato mixture and mix well. 4. Spread quinoa mixture over pork. Top with goat cheese. Season with salt. Roll pork over filling. Tie pork every 2" with butcher's twine to secure. 5. Press Sauté on the Instant Pot® and heat remaining 1 tablespoon oil. Brown pork on all sides, about 2 minutes per side. Press the Cancel button. Remove pork and clean out pot. Return to machine, add remaining 1 cup water, place rack in pot, and place pork on rack. 6. Close lid, set steam release to Sealing, Press the Manual button, and set time to 20 minutes. When the timer beeps, quick-release the pressure until the float valve drops. Open lid and transfer pork to cutting board. Let rest for 10 minutes, then remove twine and cut into 1" slices. Serve hot.

Per Serving:
calories: 207 | fat: 9g | protein: 25g | carbs: 11g | fiber: 1g | sodium: 525mg

Rosemary Roast Beef

Prep time: 30 minutes | Cook time: 30 to 35 minutes | Serves 8

1 (2-pound / 907-g) top round beef roast, tied with kitchen string	2 teaspoons minced garlic
	2 tablespoons finely chopped fresh rosemary
Sea salt and freshly ground black pepper, to taste	¼ cup avocado oil

1. Season the roast generously with salt and pepper. 2. In a small bowl, whisk together the garlic, rosemary, and avocado oil. Rub this all over the roast. Cover loosely with aluminum foil or plastic wrap and refrigerate for at least 12 hours or up to 2 days. 3. Remove the roast from the refrigerator and allow to sit at room temperature for about 1 hour. 4. Set the air fryer to 325ºF (163ºC). Place the roast in the air fryer basket and roast for 15 minutes. Flip the roast and cook for 15 to 20 minutes more, until the meat is browned and an instant-read thermometer reads 120ºF (49ºC) at the thickest part (for medium-rare). 5. Transfer the meat to a cutting board, and let it rest for 15 minutes before thinly slicing and serving.

Per Serving:
calories: 208 | fat: 12g | protein: 25g | carbs: 0g | fiber: 0g | sodium: 68mg

Lamb Tagine

Prep time: 15 minutes | Cook time: 7 hours | Serves 6

1 navel orange	¼ teaspoon saffron threads, crushed in your palm
2 tablespoons all-purpose flour	¼ teaspoon ground red pepper
2 pounds (907 g) boneless leg of lamb, trimmed and cut into 1½-inch cubes	1 cup pitted dates
	2 tablespoons honey
½ cup chicken stock	3 cups hot cooked couscous, for serving
2 large white onions, chopped	2 tablespoons toasted slivered almonds, for serving
1 teaspoon pumpkin pie spice	
1 teaspoon ground cumin	
½ teaspoon sea salt	

1. Grate 2 teaspoons of zest from the orange into a small bowl. Squeeze ¼ cup juice from the orange into another small bowl. 2. Add the flour to the orange juice, stirring with a whisk until smooth. Stir in the orange zest. 3. Heat a large nonstick skillet over medium-high heat. Add the lamb and sauté 7 minutes or until browned. Stir in the stock, scraping the bottom of the pan with a wooden spoon to loosen the flavorful brown bits. Stir in the orange juice mixture. 4. Stir the onions into the lamb mixture. Add the pumpkin pie spice, cumin, salt, saffron, and ground red pepper. 5. Pour the lamb mixture into the slow cooker. Cover and cook on low for 6 hours or until the lamb is tender. 6. Stir the dates and honey into the lamb mixture. Cover and cook on low for 1 hour or until thoroughly heated. 7. Serve the lamb tagine over the couscous and sprinkle with the almonds.

Per Serving:
calories: 451 | fat: 11g | protein: 37g | carbs: 53g | fiber: 5g | sodium: 329mg

Zesty London Broil

Prep time: 30 minutes | Cook time: 20 to 28 minutes | Serves 4 to 6

⅔ cup ketchup	½ teaspoon paprika
¼ cup honey	1 teaspoon salt
¼ cup olive oil	1 teaspoon freshly ground black pepper
2 tablespoons apple cider vinegar	2 pounds (907 g) London broil, top round or flank steak (about 1-inch thick)
2 tablespoons Worcestershire sauce	
2 tablespoons minced onion	

1. Combine the ketchup, honey, olive oil, apple cider vinegar, Worcestershire sauce, minced onion, paprika, salt and pepper in a small bowl and whisk together. 2. Generously pierce both sides of the meat with a fork or meat tenderizer and place it in a shallow dish. Pour the marinade mixture over the steak, making sure all sides of the meat get coated with the marinade. Cover and refrigerate overnight. 3. Preheat the air fryer to 400ºF (204ºC). 4. Transfer the London broil to the air fryer basket and air fry for 20 to 28 minutes, depending on how rare or well done you like your steak. Flip the steak over halfway through the cooking time. 5. Remove the London broil from the air fryer and let it rest for five minutes on a cutting board. To serve, thinly slice the meat against the grain and transfer to a serving platter.

Per Serving:
calories: 411 | fat: 21g | protein: 34g | carbs: 21g | fiber: 0g | sodium: 536mg

Steak with Bell Pepper

Prep time: 30 minutes | Cook time: 20 to 23 minutes | Serves 6

¼ cup avocado oil	steak or flank steak, thinly
¼ cup freshly squeezed lime	sliced against the grain
juice	1 red bell pepper, cored,
2 teaspoons minced garlic	seeded, and cut into ½-inch
1 tablespoon chili powder	slices
½ teaspoon ground cumin	1 green bell pepper, cored,
Sea salt and freshly ground	seeded, and cut into ½-inch
black pepper, to taste	slices
1 pound (454 g) top sirloin	1 large onion, sliced

1. In a small bowl or blender, combine the avocado oil, lime juice, garlic, chili powder, cumin, and salt and pepper to taste. 2. Place the sliced steak in a zip-top bag or shallow dish. Place the bell peppers and onion in a separate zip-top bag or dish. Pour half the marinade over the steak and the other half over the vegetables. Seal both bags and let the steak and vegetables marinate in the refrigerator for at least 1 hour or up to 4 hours. 3. Line the air fryer basket with an air fryer liner or aluminum foil. Remove the vegetables from their bag or dish and shake off any excess marinade. Set the air fryer to 400°F (204°C). Place the vegetables in the air fryer basket and cook for 13 minutes. 4. Remove the steak from its bag or dish and shake off any excess marinade. Place the steak on top of the vegetables in the air fryer, and cook for 7 to 10 minutes or until an instant-read thermometer reads 120°F (49°C) for medium-rare (or cook to your desired doneness). 5. Serve with desired fixings, such as keto tortillas, lettuce, sour cream, avocado slices, shredded Cheddar cheese, and cilantro.

Per Serving:

calories: 252 | fat: 18g | protein: 17g | carbs: 6g | fiber: 2g | sodium: 81mg

Short Ribs with Chimichurri

Prep time: 30 minutes | Cook time: 13 minutes | Serves 4

1 pound (454 g) boneless short	1 tablespoon freshly squeezed
ribs	lemon juice
1½ teaspoons sea salt, divided	½ teaspoon ground cumin
½ teaspoon freshly ground	¼ teaspoon red pepper flakes
black pepper, divided	2 tablespoons extra-virgin olive
½ cup fresh parsley leaves	oil
½ cup fresh cilantro leaves	Avocado oil spray
1 teaspoon minced garlic	

1. Pat the short ribs dry with paper towels. Sprinkle the ribs all over with 1 teaspoon salt and ¼ teaspoon black pepper. Let sit at room temperature for 45 minutes. 2. Meanwhile, place the parsley, cilantro, garlic, lemon juice, cumin, red pepper flakes, the remaining ½ teaspoon salt, and the remaining ¼ teaspoon black pepper in a blender or food processor. With the blender running, slowly drizzle in the olive oil. Blend for about 1 minute, until the mixture is smooth and well combined. 3. Set the air fryer to 400°F (204°C). Spray both sides of the ribs with oil. Place in the basket and air fry for 8 minutes. Flip and cook for another 5 minutes, until an instant-read thermometer reads 125°F (52°C) for medium-rare (or to your desired doneness). 4. Allow the meat to rest for 5 to 10 minutes, then slice. Serve warm with the chimichurri sauce.

Per Serving:

calories: 251 | fat: 17g | protein: 25g | carbs: 1g | fiber: 1g | sodium:

651mg

Herbs and Lamb Stew

Prep time: 25 minutes | Cook time: 55 minutes | Serves 8

1 pound (454 g) boneless lamb	3 cloves garlic, peeled and
shoulder, trimmed and cut into	minced
1" pieces	4 thyme sprigs
2 tablespoons all-purpose flour	1 sprig rosemary
¼ teaspoon salt	2 tablespoons chopped fresh
¼ teaspoon ground black	oregano
pepper	1 bay leaf
2 tablespoons olive oil, divided	2 cups low-sodium chicken
2 medium carrots, peeled and	broth
sliced	1 cup tomato sauce
2 stalks celery, sliced	1 medium russet potato, cut
1 medium onion, peeled and	into 1" pieces
chopped	¼ cup chopped fresh parsley

1. In a medium bowl, add lamb, flour, salt, and pepper. Toss until lamb is thoroughly coated. Set aside. 2. Press the Sauté button on the Instant Pot® and heat 1 tablespoon oil. Add half of the lamb pieces in a single layer, leaving space between each piece to prevent steaming, and brown well on all sides, about 3 minutes per side. Transfer lamb to a large bowl and repeat with remaining 1 tablespoon oil and lamb. 3. Add carrots, celery, and onion to the pot. Cook until tender, about 8 minutes. Add garlic and cook until fragrant, about 30 seconds. Add thyme, rosemary, oregano, and bay leaf. Stir well. 4. Slowly add chicken broth, scraping the bottom of the pot well to release any brown bits. Add tomato sauce, potato, and browned lamb along with any juices. Press the Cancel button. 5. Close lid, set steam release to Sealing, press the Stew button, and set time to 40 minutes. When the timer beeps, quick-release the pressure until the float valve drops, open lid, and stir well. Remove and discard thyme, rosemary, and bay leaf. Sprinkle with parsley and serve hot.

Per Serving:

calories: 222 | fat: 11g | protein: 18g | carbs: 11g | fiber: 2g | sodium: 285mg

Balsamic Pork Tenderloin

Prep time: 10 minutes | Cook time: 6 to 8 hours | Serves 6

1 small onion, sliced	2 tablespoons capers, undrained
1 (3-pound/ 1.4-kg) pork	1½ teaspoons olive oil
tenderloin	1 teaspoon dried rosemary
1 cup balsamic vinegar	1 teaspoon sea salt
½ cup low-sodium beef broth	½ teaspoon freshly ground
3 garlic cloves, crushed	black pepper

1. Put the onion in a slow cooker and arrange the pork tenderloin on top. 2. In a small bowl, whisk together the vinegar, beef broth, garlic, capers, olive oil, rosemary, salt, and pepper until combined. Pour the sauce over the pork. 3. Cover the cooker and cook for 6 to 8 hours on Low heat.

Per Serving:

calories: 281 | fat: 10g | protein: 45g | carbs: 7g | fiber: 0g | sodium: 523mg

Seasoned Beef Kebabs

Prep time: 15 minutes | Cook time: 10 minutes | Serves 6

2 pounds beef fillet	⅓ cup extra-virgin olive oil
1½ teaspoons salt	1 large onion, cut into 8
1 teaspoon freshly ground black	quarters
pepper	1 large red bell pepper, cut into
½ teaspoon ground allspice	1-inch cubes
½ teaspoon ground nutmeg	

1. Preheat a grill, grill pan, or lightly oiled skillet to high heat. 2. Cut the beef into 1-inch cubes and put them in a large bowl. 3. In a small bowl, mix together the salt, black pepper, allspice, and nutmeg. 4. Pour the olive oil over the beef and toss to coat the beef. Then evenly sprinkle the seasoning over the beef and toss to coat all pieces. 5. Skewer the beef, alternating every 1 or 2 pieces with a piece of onion or bell pepper. 6. To cook, place the skewers on the grill or skillet, and turn every 2 to 3 minutes until all sides have cooked to desired doneness, 6 minutes for medium-rare, 8 minutes for well done. Serve warm.

Per Serving:

calories: 326 | fat: 21g | protein: 32g | carbs: 4g | fiber: 1g | sodium: 714mg

Lebanese Malfouf (Stuffed Cabbage Rolls)

Prep time: 15 minutes | Cook time: 33 minutes | Serves 4

1 head green cabbage	1 teaspoon ground cinnamon
1 pound (454 g) lean ground	2 tablespoons chopped fresh
beef	mint
½ cup long-grain brown rice	Juice of 1 lemon
4 garlic cloves, minced	Olive oil cooking spray
1 teaspoon salt	½ cup beef broth
½ teaspoon black pepper	1 tablespoon olive oil

1. Cut the cabbage in half and remove the core. Remove 12 of the larger leaves to use for the cabbage rolls. 2. Bring a large pot of salted water to a boil, then drop the cabbage leaves into the water, boiling them for 3 minutes. Remove from the water and set aside. 3. In a large bowl, combine the ground beef, rice, garlic, salt, pepper, cinnamon, mint, and lemon juice, and mix together until combined. Divide this mixture into 12 equal portions. 4. Preheat the air fryer to 360°F(182°C). Lightly coat a small casserole dish with olive oil cooking spray. 5. Place a cabbage leaf on a clean work surface. Place a spoonful of the beef mixture on one side of the leaf, leaving space on all other sides. Fold the two perpendicular sides inward and then roll forward, tucking tightly as rolled (similar to a burrito roll). Place the finished rolls into the baking dish, stacking them on top of each other if needed. 6. Pour the beef broth over the top of the cabbage rolls so that it soaks down between them, and then brush the tops with the olive oil. 7. Place the casserole dish into the air fryer basket and bake for 30 minutes.

Per Serving:

calories: 329 | fat: 10g | protein: 29g | carbs: 33g | fiber: 7g | sodium: 700mg

Tenderloin with Crispy Shallots

Prep time: 30 minutes | Cook time: 18 to 20 minutes | Serves 6

1½ pounds (680 g) beef	4 medium shallots
tenderloin steaks	1 teaspoon olive oil or avocado
Sea salt and freshly ground	oil
black pepper, to taste	

1. Season both sides of the steaks with salt and pepper, and let them sit at room temperature for 45 minutes. 2. Set the air fryer to 400°F (204°C) and let it preheat for 5 minutes. 3. Working in batches if necessary, place the steaks in the air fryer basket in a single layer and air fry for 5 minutes. Flip and cook for 5 minutes longer, until an instant-read thermometer inserted in the center of the steaks registers 120°F (49°C) for medium-rare (or as desired). Remove the steaks and tent with aluminum foil to rest. 4. Set the air fryer to 300°F (149°C). In a medium bowl, toss the shallots with the oil. Place the shallots in the basket and air fry for 5 minutes, then give them a toss and cook for 3 to 5 minutes more, until crispy and golden brown. 5. Place the steaks on serving plates and arrange the shallots on top.

Per Serving:

calories: 166 | fat: 8g | protein: 24g | carbs: 1g | fiber: 0g | sodium: 72mg

Italian Steak Rolls

Prep time: 30 minutes | Cook time: 9 minutes | Serves 4

1 tablespoon vegetable oil	1 (10-ounce / 283-g) package
2 cloves garlic, minced	frozen spinach, thawed and
2 teaspoons dried Italian	squeezed dry
seasoning	½ cup diced jarred roasted red
1 teaspoon kosher salt	pepper
1 teaspoon black pepper	1 cup shredded Mozzarella
1 pound (454 g) flank or skirt	cheese
steak, ¼ to ½ inch thick	

1. In a large bowl, combine the oil, garlic, Italian seasoning, salt, and pepper. Whisk to combine. Add the steak to the bowl, turning to ensure the entire steak is covered with the seasonings. Cover and marinate at room temperature for 30 minutes or in the refrigerator for up to 24 hours. 2. Lay the steak on a flat surface. Spread the spinach evenly over the steak, leaving a ¼-inch border at the edge. Evenly top each steak with the red pepper and cheese. 3. Starting at a long end, roll up the steak as tightly as possible, ending seam side down. Use 2 or 3 wooden toothpicks to hold the roll together. Using a sharp knife, cut the roll in half so that it better fits in the air fryer basket. 4. Place the steak roll, seam side down, in the air fryer basket. Set the air fryer to 400°F (204°C) for 9 minutes. Use a meat thermometer to ensure the steak has reached an internal temperature of 145°F (63°C). (It is critical to not overcook flank steak, so as to not toughen the meat.) 5. Let the steak rest for 10 minutes before cutting into slices to serve.

Per Serving:

calories: 311 | fat: 15g | protein: 36g | carbs: 7g | fiber: 3g | sodium: 803mg

Hamburger Steak with Mushroom Gravy

Prep time: 20 minutes | Cook time: 29 to 34 minutes | Serves 4

Mushroom Gravy:

1 (1-ounce / 28-g) envelope dry onion soup mix	½ cup Italian-style bread crumbs
⅓ cup cornstarch	2 teaspoons Worcestershire sauce
1 cup diced mushrooms	
Hamburger Steak:	1 teaspoon salt
1 pound (454 g) ground beef (85% lean)	1 teaspoon freshly ground black pepper
¾ cup minced onion	1 to 2 tablespoons oil

Make the Mushroom Gravy 1. In a metal bowl, whisk the soup mix, cornstarch, mushrooms, and 2 cups water until blended. 2. Preheat the air fryer to 350ºF (177ºC). 3. Place the bowl in the air fryer basket. 4. Cook for 10 minutes. Stir and cook for 5 to 10 minutes more to your desired thickness. Make the Hamburger Steak 5. In a large bowl, mix the ground beef, onion, bread crumbs, Worcestershire sauce, salt, and pepper until blended. Shape the beef mixture into 4 patties. 6. Decrease the air fryer's temperature to 320ºF (160ºC). 7. Place the patties in the air fryer basket. 8. Cook for 7 minutes. Flip the patties, spritz them with oil, and cook for 7 minutes more, until the internal temperature reaches 145ºF (63ºC).

Per Serving:

calories: 383 | fat: 21g | protein: 24g | carbs: 23g | fiber: 1g | sodium: 810mg

Pork and Beef Egg Rolls

Prep time: 30 minutes | Cook time: 7 to 8 minutes per batch | Makes 8 egg rolls

¼ pound (113 g) very lean ground beef	¼ cup chopped water chestnuts
¼ pound (113 g) lean ground pork	¼ teaspoon salt
	¼ teaspoon garlic powder
1 tablespoon soy sauce	¼ teaspoon black pepper
1 teaspoon olive oil	1 egg
½ cup grated carrots	1 tablespoon water
2 green onions, chopped	8 egg roll wraps
2 cups grated Napa cabbage	Oil for misting or cooking spray

1. In a large skillet, brown beef and pork with soy sauce. Remove cooked meat from skillet, drain, and set aside. 2. Pour off any excess grease from skillet. Add olive oil, carrots, and onions. Sauté until barely tender, about 1 minute. 3. Stir in cabbage, cover, and cook for 1 minute or just until cabbage slightly wilts. Remove from heat. 4. In a large bowl, combine the cooked meats and vegetables, water chestnuts, salt, garlic powder, and pepper. Stir well. If needed, add more salt to taste. 5. Beat together egg and water in a small bowl. 6. Fill egg roll wrappers, using about ¼ cup of filling for each wrap. Roll up and brush all over with egg wash to seal. Spray very lightly with olive oil or cooking spray. 7. Place 4 egg rolls in air fryer basket and air fry at 390ºF (199ºC) for 4 minutes. Turn over and cook 3 to 4 more minutes, until golden brown and crispy. 8. Repeat to cook remaining egg rolls.

Per Serving:

calories: 176 | fat: 5g | protein: 11g | carbs: 22g | fiber: 2g | sodium: 339mg

Pork Milanese

Prep time: 10 minutes | Cook time: 12 minutes | Serves 4

4 (1-inch) boneless pork chops	cheese
Fine sea salt and ground black pepper, to taste	Chopped fresh parsley, for garnish
2 large eggs	Lemon slices, for serving
¾ cup powdered Parmesan	

1. Spray the air fryer basket with avocado oil. Preheat the air fryer to 400ºF (204ºC). 2. Place the pork chops between 2 sheets of plastic wrap and pound them with the flat side of a meat tenderizer until they're ¼ inch thick. Lightly season both sides of the chops with salt and pepper. 3. Lightly beat the eggs in a shallow bowl. Divide the Parmesan cheese evenly between 2 bowls and set the bowls in this order: Parmesan, eggs, Parmesan. Dredge a chop in the first bowl of Parmesan, then dip it in the eggs, and then dredge it again in the second bowl of Parmesan, making sure both sides and all edges are well coated. Repeat with the remaining chops. 4. Place the chops in the air fryer basket and air fry for 12 minutes, or until the internal temperature reaches 145ºF (63ºC), flipping halfway through. 5. Garnish with fresh parsley and serve immediately with lemon slices. Store leftovers in an airtight container in the refrigerator for up to 3 days. Reheat in a preheated 390ºF (199ºC) air fryer for 5 minutes, or until warmed through.

Per Serving:

calories: 349 | fat: 14g | protein: 50g | carbs: 3g | fiber: 0g | sodium: 464mg

Moroccan Lamb Roast

Prep time: 15 minutes | Cook time: 6 to 8 hours | Serves 6

¼ cup low-sodium beef broth or low-sodium chicken broth	½ teaspoon ground nutmeg
1 teaspoon dried ginger	½ teaspoon ground cloves
1 teaspoon dried cumin	½ teaspoon sea salt
1 teaspoon ground turmeric	½ teaspoon freshly ground black pepper
1 teaspoon paprika	1 (3-pound/ 1.4-kg) lamb roast
1 teaspoon garlic powder	4 ounces (113 g) carrots, chopped
1 teaspoon red pepper flakes	
½ teaspoon ground cinnamon	¼ cup sliced onion
½ teaspoon ground coriander	¼ cup chopped fresh mint

1. Pour the broth into a slow cooker. 2. In a small bowl, stir together the ginger, cumin, turmeric, paprika, garlic powder, red pepper flakes, cinnamon, coriander, nutmeg, cloves, salt, and black pepper. Rub the spice mix firmly all over the lamb roast. Put the lamb in the slow cooker and add the carrots and onion. 3. Top everything with the mint. 4. Cover the cooker and cook for 6 to 8 hours on Low heat.

Per Serving:

calories: 601 | fat: 39g | protein: 56g | carbs: 4g | fiber: 1g | sodium: 398mg

Chapter 5

Fish and Seafood

Sesame-Crusted Tuna Steak

Prep time: 5 minutes | Cook time: 8 minutes | Serves 2

2 (6-ounce / 170-g) tuna steaks	½ teaspoon garlic powder
1 tablespoon coconut oil, melted	2 teaspoons white sesame seeds
	2 teaspoons black sesame seeds

1. Brush each tuna steak with coconut oil and sprinkle with garlic powder. 2. In a large bowl, mix sesame seeds and then press each tuna steak into them, covering the steak as completely as possible. Place tuna steaks into the air fryer basket. 3. Adjust the temperature to 400°F (204°C) and air fry for 8 minutes. 4. Flip the steaks halfway through the cooking time. Steaks will be well-done at 145°F (63°C) internal temperature. Serve warm.

Per Serving:
calories: 281 | fat: 11g | protein: 43g | carbs: 1g | fiber: 1g | sodium: 80mg

Tuna Steaks with Olive Tapenade

Prep time: 10 minutes | Cook time: 10 minutes | Serves 4

4 (6-ounce / 170-g) ahi tuna steaks	½ cup pitted kalamata olives
1 tablespoon olive oil	1 tablespoon olive oil
Salt and freshly ground black pepper, to taste	1 tablespoon chopped fresh parsley
½ lemon, sliced into 4 wedges	1 clove garlic
Olive Tapenade:	2 teaspoons red wine vinegar
	1 teaspoon capers, drained

1. Preheat the air fryer to 400°F (204°C). 2. Drizzle the tuna steaks with the olive oil and sprinkle with salt and black pepper. Arrange the tuna steaks in a single layer in the air fryer basket. Pausing to turn the steaks halfway through the cooking time, air fry for 10 minutes until the fish is firm. 3. To make the tapenade: In a food processor fitted with a metal blade, combine the olives, olive oil, parsley, garlic, vinegar, and capers. Pulse until the mixture is finely chopped, pausing to scrape down the sides of the bowl if necessary. Spoon the tapenade over the top of the tuna steaks and serve with lemon wedges.

Per Serving:
calories: 269 | fat: 9g | protein: 42g | carbs: 2g | fiber: 1g | sodium: 252mg

Salmon with Lemon-Garlic Mashed Cauliflower

Prep time: 15 minutes | Cook time: 10 minutes | Serves 4

2 tablespoons extra-virgin olive oil	into 2-inch florets
4 garlic cloves, peeled and smashed	4 (6-ounce / 170-g) skinless salmon fillets, 1½ inches thick
½ cup chicken or vegetable broth	½ teaspoon ras el hanout
¾ teaspoon table salt, divided	½ teaspoon grated lemon zest
1 large head cauliflower (3 pounds / 1.4 kg), cored and cut	3 scallions, sliced thin
	1 tablespoon sesame seeds, toasted

1. Using highest sauté function, cook oil and garlic in Instant Pot until garlic is fragrant and light golden brown, about 3 minutes. Turn off Instant Pot, then stir in broth and ¼ teaspoon salt. Arrange cauliflower in pot in even layer. 2. Fold sheet of aluminum foil into 16 by 6-inch sling. Sprinkle flesh side of salmon with ras el hanout and remaining ½ teaspoon salt, then arrange skinned side down in center of sling. Using sling, lower salmon into Instant Pot on top of cauliflower; allow narrow edges of sling to rest along sides of insert. Lock lid in place and close pressure release valve. Select high pressure cook function and cook for 2 minutes. 3. Turn off Instant Pot and quick-release pressure. Carefully remove lid, allowing steam to escape away from you. Using sling, transfer salmon to large plate. Tent with foil and let rest while finishing cauliflower. 4. Using potato masher, mash cauliflower mixture until no large chunks remain. Using highest sauté function, cook cauliflower, stirring often, until slightly thickened, about 3 minutes. Stir in lemon zest and season with salt and pepper to taste. Serve salmon with cauliflower, sprinkling individual portions with scallions and sesame seeds.

Per Serving:
calories: 480 | fat: 31g | protein: 38g | carbs: 9g | fiber: 3g | sodium: 650mg

Snapper with Fruit

Prep time: 15 minutes | Cook time: 9 to 13 minutes | Serves 4

4 (4-ounce / 113-g) red snapper fillets	1 cup red grapes
2 teaspoons olive oil	1 tablespoon freshly squeezed lemon juice
3 nectarines, halved and pitted	1 tablespoon honey
3 plums, halved and pitted	½ teaspoon dried thyme

1. Put the red snapper in the air fryer basket and drizzle with the olive oil. Air fry at 390°F (199°C) for 4 minutes. 2. Remove the basket and add the nectarines and plums. Scatter the grapes over all. 3. Drizzle with the lemon juice and honey and sprinkle with the thyme. 4. Return the basket to the air fryer and air fry for 5 to 9 minutes more, or until the fish flakes when tested with a fork and the fruit is tender. Serve immediately.

Per Serving:
calories: 246 | fat: 4g | protein: 25g | carbs: 28g | fiber: 3g | sodium: 74mg

Shrimp with Marinara Sauce

Prep time: 15 minutes | Cook time: 6 to 7 hours | Serves 4

1 (15-ounce / 425-g) can diced tomatoes, with the juice	1 teaspoon garlic powder
1 (6-ounce / 170-g) can tomato paste	1½ teaspoons sea salt
1 clove garlic, minced	¼ teaspoon black pepper
2 tablespoons minced fresh flat-leaf parsley	1 pound (454 g) cooked shrimp, peeled and deveined
½ teaspoon dried basil	2 cups hot cooked spaghetti or linguine, for serving
1 teaspoon dried oregano	½ cup grated parmesan cheese, for serving

1. Combine the tomatoes, tomato paste, and minced garlic in the slow cooker. Sprinkle with the parsley, basil, oregano, garlic powder, salt, and pepper. 2. Cover and cook on low for 6 to 7 hours. 3. Turn up the heat to high, stir in the cooked shrimp, and cover and cook on high for about 15 minutes longer. 4. Serve hot over the cooked pasta. Top with Parmesan cheese.

Per Serving:
calories: 313 | fat: 5g | protein: 39g | carbs: 32g | fiber: 7g | sodium: 876mg

Spicy Trout over Sautéed Mediterranean Salad

Prep time: 10 minutes | Cook time: 30 minutes | Serves 4

2 pounds (907 g) rainbow trout fillets (about 6 fillets)	1 garlic clove, finely minced
Salt	1 large carrot, thinly sliced
Ground white pepper	2 Roma tomatoes, chopped
1 tablespoon extra-virgin olive oil	8 pitted kalamata olives, chopped
1 pound (454 g) asparagus	¼ cup ground cumin
4 medium golden potatoes, thinly sliced	2 tablespoons dried parsley
1 scallion, thinly sliced, green and white parts separated	2 tablespoons paprika
	1 tablespoon vegetable bouillon seasoning
	½ cup dry white wine

1. Lightly season the fish with salt and white pepper and set aside. 2. In a large sauté pan or skillet, heat the oil over medium heat. Add and stir in the asparagus, potatoes, the white part of the scallions, and garlic to the hot oil. Cook and stir for 5 minutes, until fragrant. Add the carrot, tomatoes, and olives; continue to cook for 5 to 7 minutes, until the carrots are slightly tender. 3. Sprinkle the cumin, parsley, paprika, and vegetable bouillon seasoning over the pan. Season with salt. Stir to incorporate. Put the trout on top of the vegetables and add the wine to cover the vegetables. 4. Reduce the heat to low, cover, and cook for 5 to 7 minutes, until the fish flakes easily with a fork and juices run clear. Top with scallion greens and serve.

Per Serving:
calories: 493 | fat: 19g | protein: 40g | carbs: 41g | fiber: 7g | sodium: 736mg

River Trout with Herb Sauce

Prep time: 10 minutes | Cook time: 3 minutes | Serves 4

4 (½-pound / 227-g) fresh river trout, rinsed and patted dry	2 tablespoons chopped fresh oregano
1 teaspoon salt, divided	1 teaspoon fresh thyme leaves
1 teaspoon white wine vinegar	1 small shallot, peeled and minced
½ cup water	2 tablespoons olive oil
½ cup minced fresh flat-leaf parsley	½ teaspoon lemon juice

1. Sprinkle trout with ¾ teaspoon salt inside and out. Combine vinegar and water, pour into the Instant Pot®, and place rack inside. Place trout on rack. 2. Close lid, set steam release to Sealing, press the Manual button, and set time to 3 minutes. When the timer beeps, let pressure release naturally for 3 minutes. Quick-release any remaining pressure until the float valve drops and then open lid. 3. Transfer fish to a serving plate. Peel and discard skin from fish. Remove and discard the heads if desired. 4. In a small bowl, mix together parsley, oregano, thyme, shallot, olive oil, lemon juice, and remaining ¼ teaspoon salt. Pour evenly over fish. Serve immediately.

Per Serving:
calories: 344 | fat: 18g | protein: 45g | carbs: 1g | fiber: 0g | sodium: 581mg

Cod Gratin

Prep time: 10 minutes | Cook time: 22 minutes | Serves 4

½ cup olive oil, divided	1 cup whole-wheat breadcrumbs
1 pound (454 g) fresh cod	¾ cup low-salt chicken stock
1 cup black olives, pitted and chopped	Sea salt and freshly ground pepper, to taste
4 leeks, trimmed and sliced	

1. Preheat the oven to 350ºF (180ºC). 2. Brush 4 gratin dishes with the olive oil. 3. Place the cod on a baking dish, and bake for 5–7 minutes. Cool and cut into 1-inch pieces. 4. Heat the remaining olive oil in a large skillet. 5. Add the olives and leeks, and cook over medium-low heat until the leeks are tender. 6. Add the breadcrumbs and chicken stock, stirring to mix. 7. Gently fold in the pieces of cod. Divide the mixture between the 4 gratin dishes, and drizzle with olive oil. 8. Season with sea salt and freshly ground pepper. Bake for 15 minutes or until warmed through.

Per Serving:
calories: 538 | fat: 33g | protein: 26g | carbs: 35g | fiber: 4g | sodium: 538mg

Monkfish with Sautéed Leeks, Fennel, and Tomatoes

Prep time: 20 minutes | Cook time: 35 minutes | Serves 4

1 to 1½ pounds (454 to 680 g) monkfish	½ onion, julienned
3 tablespoons lemon juice, divided	3 garlic cloves, minced
1 teaspoon kosher salt, divided	2 bulbs fennel, cored and thinly sliced, plus ¼ cup fronds for garnish
⅛ teaspoon freshly ground black pepper	1 (14½-ounce / 411-g) can no-salt-added diced tomatoes
2 tablespoons extra-virgin olive oil	2 tablespoons fresh parsley, chopped
1 leek, white and light green parts only, sliced in half lengthwise and thinly sliced	2 tablespoons fresh oregano, chopped
	¼ teaspoon red pepper flakes

1. Place the fish in a medium baking dish and add 2 tablespoons of the lemon juice, ¼ teaspoon of the salt, and the black pepper. Place in the refrigerator. 2. Heat the olive oil in a large skillet or sauté pan over medium heat. Add the leek and onion and sauté until translucent, about 3 minutes. Add the garlic and sauté for 30 seconds. Add the fennel and sauté 4 to 5 minutes. Add the tomatoes and simmer for 2 to 3 minutes. 3. Stir in the parsley, oregano, red pepper flakes, the remaining ¾ teaspoon salt, and the remaining 1 tablespoon lemon juice. Place the fish on top of the leek mixture, cover, and simmer for 20 to 25 minutes, turning over halfway through, until the fish is opaque and pulls apart easily. Garnish with the fennel fronds.

Per Serving:
calories: 220 | fat: 9g | protein: 22g | carbs: 11g | fiber: 3g | sodium: 345mg

Apple Cider Mussels

Prep time: 10 minutes | Cook time: 2 minutes | Serves 5

2 pounds (907 g) mussels, cleaned, peeled
1 teaspoon onion powder

1 teaspoon ground cumin
1 tablespoon avocado oil
¼ cup apple cider vinegar

1. Mix mussels with onion powder, ground cumin, avocado oil, and apple cider vinegar. 2. Put the mussels in the air fryer and cook at 395ºF (202ºC) for 2 minutes.
Per Serving:
calories: 187 | fat: 7g | protein: 22g | carbs: 7g | fiber: 0g | sodium: 521mg

Blackened Salmon

Prep time: 10 minutes | Cook time: 8 minutes | Serves 2

10 ounces (283 g) salmon fillet
½ teaspoon ground coriander
1 teaspoon ground cumin

1 teaspoon dried basil
1 tablespoon avocado oil

1. In the shallow bowl, mix ground coriander, ground cumin, and dried basil. 2. Then coat the salmon fillet in the spices and sprinkle with avocado oil. 3. Put the fish in the air fryer basket and cook at 395ºF (202ºC) for 4 minutes per side.
Per Serving:
calories: 249 | fat: 13g | protein: 29g | carbs: 1g | fiber: 1g | sodium: 109mg

Cod Stew with Olives

Prep time: 20 minutes | Cook time: 15 minutes | Serves 4

3 tablespoons olive oil
1 medium onion, peeled and diced
1 stalk celery, diced
1 medium carrot, peeled and chopped
2 cloves garlic, peeled and minced
1 tablespoon chopped fresh oregano
½ teaspoon ground fennel

1 sprig fresh thyme
1 (14½-ounce / 411-g) can diced tomatoes
1½ cups vegetable broth
1 pound (454 g) cod fillets, cut into 1" pieces
⅓ cup sliced green olives
¼ teaspoon ground black pepper
2 tablespoons chopped fresh dill

1. Press the Sauté button on the Instant Pot® and heat oil. Add onion, celery, and carrot. Cook until vegetables are soft, about 6 minutes. Add garlic, oregano, fennel, and thyme. Cook for 30 seconds, then add tomatoes and vegetable broth. Stir well. Press the Cancel button. 2. Close lid, set steam release to Sealing, press the Manual button, and set time to 3 minutes. 3. When the timer beeps, quick-release the pressure until the float valve drops and open lid. Press the Cancel button, then press the Sauté button and add fish, olives, and pepper. Cook until fish is opaque, 3–5 minutes. Sprinkle with dill and serve hot.
Per Serving:
calories: 200 | fat: 16g | protein: 7g | carbs: 14g | fiber: 3g | sodium: 379mg

Mediterranean Garlic and Herb-Roasted Cod

Prep time: 10 minutes | Cook time: 15 minutes | Serves 3

4½ tablespoons extra virgin olive oil plus 1 teaspoon for brushing
1½ tablespoons dried oregano
1 teaspoon paprika
1½ teaspoons dried onion flakes
½ teaspoon salt
¼ teaspoon freshly ground black pepper
1½ tablespoons fresh lemon juice plus extra for serving

1 garlic clove, minced
3 teaspoons Dijon mustard
1 pound (454 g) cod fillets, patted dry
2 tablespoons chopped fresh parsley
Topping:
1½ tablespoons extra virgin olive oil
4 tablespoons unseasoned breadcrumbs

1. Preheat the oven to 425ºF (220ºC). Brush a baking dish large enough to hold the fish in a single layer with 1 teaspoon of the olive oil. 2. In a small bowl, combine the oregano, paprika, onion flakes, salt, and black pepper. Mix well and set aside. 3. In a medium bowl, combine 4½ tablespoons of the olive oil, lemon juice, garlic, and Dijon mustard. Add the dry ingredients to the wet ingredients and mix well. 4. Dip each fillet in the coating and toss to coat, then place the fillets in the dish and drizzle the leftover coating over the top of the fillets. 5. Make the breadcrumb topping by combining the breadcrumbs and olive oil in a small bowl and mixing with a fork. Sprinkle the breadcrumb mixture over the fillets. 6. Place in the oven and roast for 15 minutes or until the breadcrumb topping becomes golden brown. 7. Transfer to a plate and top with the chopped parsley and a squeeze of lemon. (This recipe is best eaten fresh.)
Per Serving:
calories: 410 | fat: 29g | protein: 29g | carbs: 9g | fiber: 1g | sodium: 593mg

Shrimp and Fish Chowder

Prep time: 20 minutes | Cook time: 4 to 6 hours | Serves 4

3 cups low-sodium vegetable broth
1 (28-ounce / 794-g) can no-salt-added crushed tomatoes
1 large bell pepper, any color, seeded and diced
1 large onion, diced
2 zucchini, chopped
3 garlic cloves, minced
1 teaspoon dried thyme

1 teaspoon dried basil
½ teaspoon sea salt
¼ teaspoon freshly ground black pepper
¼ teaspoon red pepper flakes
8 ounces (227 g) whole raw medium shrimp, peeled and deveined
8 ounces (227 g) fresh cod fillets, cut into 1-inch pieces

1. In a slow cooker, combine the vegetable broth, tomatoes, bell pepper, onion, zucchini, garlic, thyme, basil, salt, black pepper, and red pepper flakes. Stir to mix well. 2. Cover the cooker and cook for 4 to 6 hours on Low heat. 3. Stir in the shrimp and cod. Replace the cover on the cooker and cook for 15 to 30 minutes on Low heat, or until the shrimp have turned pink and the cod is firm and flaky.
Per Serving:
calories: 201 | fat: 1g | protein: 26g | carbs: 24g | fiber: 7g | sodium: 598mg

Red Snapper with Peppers and Potatoes

Prep time: 15 minutes | Cook time: 4 to 6 hours | Serves 4

1 pound (454 g) red potatoes, chopped	5 garlic cloves, minced
1 green bell pepper, seeded and sliced	1 teaspoon dried thyme
1 red bell pepper, seeded and sliced	1 teaspoon dried rosemary
½ onion, sliced	Juice of 1 lemon
1 (15-ounce / 425-g) can no-salt-added diced tomatoes	Sea salt
	Freshly ground black pepper
⅓ cup whole Kalamata olives, pitted	1½ to 2 pounds (680 to 907 g) fresh red snapper fillets
	2 lemons, thinly sliced
	¼ cup chopped fresh parsley

1. In a slow cooker, combine the potatoes, green and red bell peppers, onion, tomatoes, olives, garlic, thyme, rosemary, and lemon juice. Season with salt and black pepper. Stir to mix well. 2. Nestle the snapper into the vegetable mixture in a single layer, cutting it into pieces to fit if needed. Top it with lemon slices. 3. Cover the cooker and cook for 4 to 6 hours on Low heat, or until the potatoes are tender. 4. Garnish with fresh parsley for serving.

Per Serving:
calories: 350 | fat: 5g | protein: 45g | carbs: 41g | fiber: 8g | sodium: 241mg

Ouzo Mussels

Prep time: 10 minutes | Cook time: 15 minutes | Serves 4

1 tablespoon olive oil	broth or water
2 shallots, chopped	½ cup ouzo
4 cloves garlic, sliced	Grated peel of 1 lemon
1 pound (454 g) mussels, scrubbed and debearded	2 tablespoons chopped fresh flat-leaf parsley
1 cup low-sodium chicken	

1. In a large pot over medium heat, warm the oil. Cook the shallots and garlic until softened, 5 minutes. Increase the heat and add the mussels, broth or water, and ouzo. Cover, bring to a boil, and cook until the mussels have opened, about 8 minutes. 2. Discard any unopened mussels. Sprinkle the lemon peel and parsley over the top. Serve the mussels with their broth.

Per Serving:
calories: 238 | fat: 6g | protein: 16g | carbs: 22g | fiber: 0g | sodium: 344mg

Shrimp in Creamy Pesto over Zoodles

Prep time: 10 minutes | Cook time: 10 minutes | Serves 4

1 pound (454 g) peeled and deveined fresh shrimp	jarred pesto
Salt	¾ cup crumbled goat or feta cheese, plus more for serving
Freshly ground black pepper	
2 tablespoons extra-virgin olive oil	6 cups zucchini noodles (from about 2 large zucchini), for serving
½ small onion, slivered	¼ cup chopped flat-leaf Italian parsley, for garnish
8 ounces (227 g) store-bought	

1. In a bowl, season the shrimp with salt and pepper and set aside. 2. In a large skillet, heat the olive oil over medium-high heat. Sauté the onion until just golden, 5 to 6 minutes. 3. Reduce the heat to low and add the pesto and cheese, whisking to combine and melt the cheese. Bring to a low simmer and add the shrimp. Reduce the heat back to low and cover. Cook until the shrimp is cooked through and pink, another 3 to 4 minutes. 4. Serve warm over zucchini noodles, garnishing with chopped parsley and additional crumbled cheese, if desired.

Per Serving:
calories: 608 | fat: 49g | protein: 37g | carbs: 9g | fiber: 3g | sodium: 564mg

Whitefish with Lemon and Capers

Prep time: 5 minutes | Cook time: 20 minutes | Serves 4

4 (4- to 5-ounce / 113- to 142-g) cod fillets (or any whitefish)	butter
	2 tablespoons capers, drained
1 tablespoon extra-virgin olive oil	3 tablespoons lemon juice
	½ teaspoon freshly ground black pepper
1 teaspoon salt, divided	
4 tablespoons (½ stick) unsalted	

1. Preheat the oven to 450°F(235ºC). Put the cod in a large baking dish and drizzle with the olive oil and ½ teaspoon of salt. Bake for 15 minutes. 2. Right before the fish is done cooking, melt the butter in a small saucepan over medium heat. Add the capers, lemon juice, remaining ½ teaspoon of salt, and pepper; simmer for 30 seconds. 3. Place the fish in a serving dish once it is done baking; spoon the caper sauce over the fish and serve.

Per Serving:
calories: 255 | fat: 16g | protein: 26g | carbs: 1g | fiber: 0g | sodium: 801mg

Halibut in Parchment with Zucchini, Shallots, and Herbs

Prep time: 15 minutes | Cook time: 15 minutes | Serves 4

½ cup zucchini, diced small	¼ teaspoon kosher salt
1 shallot, minced	⅛ teaspoon freshly ground black pepper
4 (5-ounce / 142-g) halibut fillets (about 1 inch thick)	
	1 lemon, sliced into ⅛-inch-thick rounds
4 teaspoons extra-virgin olive oil	8 sprigs of thyme

1. Preheat the oven to 450ºF (235ºC). Combine the zucchini and shallots in a medium bowl. 2. Cut 4 (15-by-24-inch) pieces of parchment paper. Fold each sheet in half horizontally. Draw a large half heart on one side of each folded sheet, with the fold along the center of the heart. Cut out the heart, open the parchment, and lay it flat. 3. Place a fillet near the center of each parchment heart. Drizzle 1 teaspoon olive oil on each fillet. Sprinkle with salt and pepper. Top each fillet with lemon slices and 2 sprigs of thyme. Sprinkle each fillet with one-quarter of the zucchini and shallot mixture. Fold the parchment over. 4. Starting at the top, fold the edges of the parchment over, and continue all the way around to make a packet. Twist the end tightly to secure. 5. Arrange the 4 packets on a baking sheet. Bake for about 15 minutes. Place on plates; cut open. Serve immediately.

Per Serving:
calories: 190 | fat: 7g | protein: 27g | carbs: 5g | fiber: 1g | sodium: 170mg

Sage-Stuffed Whole Trout with Roasted Vegetables

Prep time: 10 minutes | Cook time: 35 minutes | Serves 4

2 red bell peppers, seeded and cut into 1-inch-wide strips
1 (15-ounce / 425-g) can artichoke hearts, drained and cut into quarters
1 large red onion, halved through the stem and cut into 1-inch-wide wedges
4 cloves garlic, halved
3 tablespoons olive oil, divided

1½ teaspoons salt, divided
¾ teaspoon freshly ground black pepper, divided
2 whole rainbow trout, cleaned with head on
3 cups sage leaves
Juice of ½ lemon

1. Preheat the oven to 475ºF (245ºC). 2. In a large baking dish, toss the bell peppers, artichoke hearts, onion, and garlic with 2 tablespoons of the olive oil. Sprinkle with 1 teaspoon of salt and ½ teaspoon of pepper. Roast the vegetables in the preheated oven for 20 minutes. Reduce the heat to 375°F(190ºC). 3. While the vegetables are roasting, prepare the fish. Brush the fish inside and out with the remaining 1 tablespoon of olive oil and season with the remaining ½ teaspoon of salt and ¼ teaspoon of pepper. Stuff each fish with half of the sage leaves. 4. Remove the vegetables from the oven and place the fish on top. Put back in the oven and bake at 375°F (190ºC) for about 15 minutes more, until the fish is cooked through. Remove from the oven, squeeze the lemon juice over the fish, and let rest for 5 minutes. 5. To serve, halve the fish. Spoon roasted vegetables onto 4 serving plates and serve half a fish alongside each, topped with some of the sage leaves.

Per Serving:
calories: 349 | fat: 16g | protein: 24g | carbs: 34g | fiber: 17g | sodium: 879mg

Baked Red Snapper with Potatoes and Tomatoes

Prep time: 10 minutes | Cook time: 45 minutes | Serves 4

5 sprigs fresh thyme, divided
2 sprigs fresh oregano, divided
1½ pounds (680 g) new potatoes, halved (or quartered if large)
4 Roma tomatoes, quartered lengthwise
1 tablespoon plus 1 teaspoon olive oil
4 cloves garlic, halved, divided

1¼ teaspoons kosher salt, divided
¾ teaspoon ground black pepper, divided
1 cleaned whole red snapper (about 2 pounds / 907 g), scaled and fins removed
½–1 lemon, sliced
4 cups (4 ounces) baby spinach

1. Preheat the oven to 350°F(180ºC). 2. Strip the leaves off 2 sprigs thyme and 1 sprig oregano and chop. In a 9' × 13' baking dish, toss the potatoes and tomatoes with 1 tablespoon of the oil, the chopped thyme and oregano leaves, 2 cloves of the garlic, 1 teaspoon of the salt, and ½ teaspoon of the pepper. 3. Cut 3 or 4 diagonal slashes in the skin on both sides of the snapper. Rub the skin with the remaining 1 teaspoon oil. Sprinkle the cavity of the snapper with the remaining ¼ teaspoon salt and pepper. Fill it with the lemon slices, the remaining thyme and oregano sprigs, and the remaining 2 cloves garlic. Sprinkle the outside of the snapper with a pinch of salt and pepper. Set the fish on the vegetables. 4. Cover the baking dish with foil and bake for 20 minutes. Remove the foil and continue baking until the potatoes are tender and the fish flakes easily with a fork, 20 to 25 minutes. 5. Transfer the fish to a serving platter. Toss the spinach with the tomatoes and potatoes in the baking dish, until wilted. 6. Using forks, peel the skin off the fish fillets. Scatter the vegetables around the fish and serve.

Per Serving:
calories: 345 | fat: 6g | protein: 39g | carbs: 33g | fiber: 5g | sodium: 782mg

Breaded Shrimp Tacos

Prep time: 10 minutes | Cook time: 9 minutes | Makes 8 tacos

2 large eggs
1 teaspoon prepared yellow mustard
1 pound (454 g) small shrimp, peeled, deveined, and tails

removed
½ cup finely shredded Gouda or Parmesan cheese
½ cup pork dust

For Serving:
8 large Boston lettuce leaves
¼ cup pico de gallo
¼ cup shredded purple cabbage

1 lemon, sliced
Guacamole (optional)

1. Preheat the air fryer to 400ºF (204ºC). 2. Crack the eggs into a large bowl, add the mustard, and whisk until well combined. Add the shrimp and stir well to coat. 3. In a medium-sized bowl, mix together the cheese and pork dust until well combined. 4. One at a time, roll the coated shrimp in the pork dust mixture and use your hands to press it onto each shrimp. Spray the coated shrimp with avocado oil and place them in the air fryer basket, leaving space between them. 5. Air fry the shrimp for 9 minutes, or until cooked through and no longer translucent, flipping after 4 minutes. 6. To serve, place a lettuce leaf on a serving plate, place several shrimp on top, and top with 1½ teaspoons each of pico de gallo and purple cabbage. Squeeze some lemon juice on top and serve with guacamole, if desired. 7. Store leftover shrimp in an airtight container in the refrigerator for up to 3 days. Reheat in a preheated 400ºF (204ºC) air fryer for 5 minutes, or until warmed through.

Per Serving:
calories: 115 | fat: 4g | protein: 18g | carbs: 2g | fiber: 1g | sodium: 253mg

Shrimp Risotto

Prep time: 10 minutes | Cook time: 4 to 6 hours | Serves 4

1½ cups raw arborio rice
4½ cups low-sodium chicken broth
½ cup diced onion
2 garlic cloves, minced
½ teaspoon sea salt
½ teaspoon dried parsley

¼ teaspoon freshly ground black pepper
1 pound (454 g) whole raw medium shrimp, peeled and deveined
¼ cup grated Parmesan cheese

1. In a slow cooker, combine the rice, chicken broth, onion, garlic, salt, parsley, and pepper. Stir to mix well. 2. Cover the cooker and cook for 4 to 6 hours on Low heat. 3. Stir in the shrimp and Parmesan cheese. Replace the cover on the cooker and cook for 15 to 30 minutes on Low heat, or until the shrimp have turned pink and the cheese is melted.

Per Serving:
calories: 376 | fat: 3g | protein: 28g | carbs: 59g | fiber: 1g | sodium: 602mg

Tomato-Poached Fish

Prep time: 10 minutes | Cook time: 8 minutes | Serves 4

2 tablespoons olive oil	pepper
1 medium onion, peeled and chopped	¼ teaspoon crushed red pepper flakes
2 cloves garlic, peeled and minced	1 (14½-ounce / 411-g) can diced tomatoes
1 tablespoon chopped fresh oregano	1 cup vegetable broth
1 teaspoon fresh thyme leaves	1 pound (454 g) halibut fillets
½ teaspoon ground fennel	2 tablespoons chopped fresh parsley
¼ teaspoon ground black	

1. Press the Sauté button on the Instant Pot® and heat oil. Add onion and cook until soft, about 4 minutes. Add garlic, oregano, thyme, and fennel. Cook until fragrant, about 30 seconds, then add black pepper, red pepper flakes, tomatoes, and vegetable broth. Press the Cancel button. 2. Top vegetables with fish, close lid, set steam release to Sealing, press the Manual button, and set time to 3 minutes. 3. When the timer beeps, quick-release the pressure until the float valve drops and open lid. Carefully transfer fillets to a serving platter and spoon sauce over fillets. Sprinkle with parsley and serve hot.

Per Serving:

calories: 212 | fat: 8g | protein: 24g | carbs: 10g | fiber: 2g | sodium: 449mg

Shrimp and Feta Saganaki

Prep time: 10 minutes | Cook time: 35 minutes | Serves 2

1¼ pounds (567 g) raw medium shrimp (about 20), peeled and deveined	1 small hot chili, sliced
¼ teaspoon fine sea salt	1 teaspoon red pepper flakes
¼ teaspoon freshly ground black pepper	14 ounces (397 g) canned crushed tomatoes or whole tomatoes chopped in a food processor
4 tablespoons extra virgin olive oil, divided	1 teaspoon dried oregano, divided
5 garlic cloves, minced	3 ounces (85 g) crumbled feta, divided
¼ cup ouzo (anise-flavored liquor)	1 tablespoon chopped fresh basil
½ large onion (any variety), chopped	

1. Preheat the oven to 400°F (205°C). Pat the shrimp dry with paper towels, then season with the sea salt and black pepper. 2. Add 2 tablespoons of the olive oil to a large skillet over medium-high heat. When the oil begins to shimmer, add the shrimp and sauté for about 2 minutes and then add the garlic and sauté for 1 more minute or until the shrimp turn pink. 3. Add the ouzo and sauté for 2 minutes or until the alcohol has evaporated. Remove the pan from the heat and set aside. 4. Add the remaining 2 tablespoons of olive oil to a medium pot or saucepan placed over medium heat. When the olive oil begins to shimmer, add the onions and sauté for 5 minutes or until translucent. Add the sliced chili and red pepper flakes and sauté for 2 more minutes. Add the tomatoes, cover, and simmer for 7 minutes or until the sauce thickens. 5. Pour the tomato sauce into an oven-proof casserole dish or cast-iron skillet large enough to hold the shrimp in a single layer. Sprinkle ½ teaspoon of the oregano and half of the feta over the sauce, then place the shrimp on top of the sauce, lightly pressing each shrimp into the sauce. Sprinkle the remaining feta and oregano over the shrimp. 6. Transfer to the oven and bake for 15 minutes, then top with the chopped basil. Store covered in the refrigerator for up to 2 days.

Per Serving:

calories: 652 | fat: 38g | protein: 66g | carbs: 15g | fiber: 5g | sodium: 704mg

Pistachio-Crusted Halibut

Prep time: 5 minutes | Cook time: 7 minutes | Serves 2

1 tablespoon Dijon mustard	pistachios
1 teaspoon lemon juice	¼ teaspoon salt
2 tablespoons panko bread crumbs	2 (5-ounce / 142-g) halibut fillets
¼ cup chopped unsalted	1 cup water

1. Preheat broiler. Line a baking sheet with parchment paper. 2. In a small bowl, combine mustard, lemon juice, bread crumbs, pistachios, and salt to form a thick paste. 3. Pat fillets dry with a paper towel. Rub paste on the top of each fillet and place in the steamer basket. 4. Pour water in the Instant Pot® and insert rack. Place steamer basket on rack. Close lid, set steam release to Sealing, press the Manual button, and set time to 5 minutes. When the timer beeps, quick-release the pressure until the float valve drops and then open lid. Transfer fillets to prepared baking sheet. 5. Broil for approximately 1–2 minutes until tops are browned. Remove from oven and serve hot.

Per Serving:

calories: 235 | fat: 9g | protein: 35g | carbs: 4g | fiber: 2g | sodium: 411mg

Salmon with Cauliflower

Prep time: 10 minutes | Cook time: 25 minutes | Serves 4

1 pound (454 g) salmon fillet, diced	1 tablespoon coconut oil, melted
1 cup cauliflower, shredded	1 teaspoon ground turmeric
1 tablespoon dried cilantro	¼ cup coconut cream

1. Mix salmon with cauliflower, dried cilantro, ground turmeric, coconut cream, and coconut oil. 2. Transfer the salmon mixture into the air fryer and cook the meal at 350°F (177°C) for 25 minutes. Stir the meal every 5 minutes to avoid the burning.

Per Serving:

calories: 232 | fat: 14g | protein: 24g | carbs: 3g | fiber: 1g | sodium: 94mg

Coconut Cream Mackerel

Prep time: 10 minutes | Cook time: 6 minutes | Serves 4

2 pounds (907 g) mackerel fillet	1 teaspoon cumin seeds
1 cup coconut cream	1 garlic clove, peeled, chopped
1 teaspoon ground coriander	

1. Chop the mackerel roughly and sprinkle it with coconut cream, ground coriander, cumin seeds, and garlic. 2. Then put the fish in the air fryer and cook at 400°F (204°C) for 6 minutes.

Per Serving:

calories: 439 | fat: 25g | protein: 48g | carbs: 4g | fiber: 1g | sodium: 362mg

Chapter 6

Snacks and Appetizers

Lemon-Pepper Chicken Drumsticks

Prep time: 30 minutes | Cook time: 30 minutes | Serves 2

2 teaspoons freshly ground coarse black pepper	4 chicken drumsticks (4 ounces / 113 g each)
1 teaspoon baking powder	Kosher salt, to taste
½ teaspoon garlic powder	1 lemon

1. In a small bowl, stir together the pepper, baking powder, and garlic powder. Place the drumsticks on a plate and sprinkle evenly with the baking powder mixture, turning the drumsticks so they're well coated. Let the drumsticks stand in the refrigerator for at least 1 hour or up to overnight. 2. Sprinkle the drumsticks with salt, then transfer them to the air fryer, standing them bone-end up and leaning against the wall of the air fryer basket. Air fry at 375°F (191°C) until cooked through and crisp on the outside, about 30 minutes. 3. Transfer the drumsticks to a serving platter and finely grate the zest of the lemon over them while they're hot. Cut the lemon into wedges and serve with the warm drumsticks.

Per Serving:

calories: 438 | fat: 24g | protein: 48g | carbs: 6g | fiber: 2g | sodium: 279mg

Savory Mediterranean Popcorn

Prep time: 5 minutes | Cook time: 2 minutes | Serves 4 to 6

3 tablespoons extra-virgin olive oil	¼ teaspoon sea salt
¼ teaspoon garlic powder	⅛ teaspoon dried thyme
¼ teaspoon freshly ground black pepper	⅛ teaspoon dried oregano
	12 cups plain popped popcorn

1. In a large sauté pan or skillet, heat the oil over medium heat, until shimmering, and then add the garlic powder, pepper, salt, thyme, and oregano until fragrant. 2. In a large bowl, drizzle the oil over the popcorn, toss, and serve.

Per Serving:

calories: 183 | fat: 12g | protein: 3g | carbs: 19g | fiber: 4g | sodium: 146mg

Bravas-Style Potatoes

Prep time: 15 minutes | Cook time: 50 minutes | Serves 8

4 large russet potatoes (about 2½ pounds / 1.1 kg), scrubbed and cut into 1' cubes	½ small yellow onion, chopped
1 teaspoon kosher salt, divided	1 large tomato, chopped
½ teaspoon ground black pepper	1 tablespoon sherry vinegar
¼ teaspoon red-pepper flakes	1 teaspoon hot paprika
	1 tablespoon chopped fresh flat-leaf parsley Hot sauce (optional)

1. Preheat the oven to 450°F(235°C). Bring a large pot of well-salted water to a boil. 2. Boil the potatoes until just barely tender, 5 to 8 minutes. Drain and transfer the potatoes to a large rimmed baking sheet. Add 1 tablespoon of the oil, ½ teaspoon of the salt, the black pepper, and pepper flakes. With 2 large spoons, toss very well to coat the potatoes in the oil. Spread the potatoes out on the baking sheet. Roast until the bottoms are starting to brown and crisp, 20 minutes. Carefully flip the potatoes and roast until the other side is golden and crisp, 15 to 20 minutes. 3. Meanwhile, in a small skillet over medium heat, warm the remaining 1 teaspoon oil. Cook the onion until softened, 3 to 4 minutes. Add the tomato and cook until it's broken down and saucy, 5 minutes. Stir in the vinegar, paprika, and the remaining ½ teaspoon salt. Cook for 30 seconds, remove from the heat, and cover to keep warm. 4. Transfer the potatoes to a large serving bowl. Drizzle the tomato mixture over the potatoes. Sprinkle with the parsley. Serve with hot sauce, if using.

Per Serving:

calories: 173 | fat: 2g | protein: 4g | carbs: 35g | fiber: 3g | sodium: 251mg

Ranch Oyster Snack Crackers

Prep time: 3 minutes | Cook time: 12 minutes | Serves 6

Oil, for spraying	½ teaspoon dried dill
¼ cup olive oil	½ teaspoon granulated garlic
2 teaspoons dry ranch seasoning	½ teaspoon salt
1 teaspoon chili powder	1 (9-ounce / 255-g) bag oyster crackers

1. Preheat the air fryer to 325°F (163°C). Line the air fryer basket with parchment and spray lightly with oil. 2. In a large bowl, mix together the olive oil, ranch seasoning, chili powder, dill, garlic, and salt. Add the crackers and toss until evenly coated. 3. Place the mixture in the prepared basket. 4. Cook for 10 to 12 minutes, shaking or stirring every 3 to 4 minutes, or until crisp and golden brown.

Per Serving:

calories: 261 | fat: 13g | protein: 4g | carbs: 32g | fiber: 1g | sodium: 621mg

Baked Spanakopita Dip

Prep time: 10 minutes | Cook time: 15 minutes | Serves 2

Olive oil cooking spray	divided
3 tablespoons olive oil, divided	Zest of 1 lemon
2 tablespoons minced white onion	¼ teaspoon ground nutmeg
2 garlic cloves, minced	1 teaspoon dried dill
4 cups fresh spinach	½ teaspoon salt
4 ounces (113 g) cream cheese, softened	Pita chips, carrot sticks, or sliced bread for serving (optional)
4 ounces (113 g) feta cheese,	

1. Preheat the air fryer to 360°F(182°C). Coat the inside of a 6-inch ramekin or baking dish with olive oil cooking spray. 2. In a large skillet over medium heat, heat 1 tablespoon of the olive oil. Add the onion, then cook for 1 minute. 3. Add in the garlic and cook, stirring for 1 minute more. 4. Reduce the heat to low and mix in the spinach and water. Let this cook for 2 to 3 minutes, or until the spinach has wilted. Remove the skillet from the heat. 5. In a medium bowl, combine the cream cheese, 2 ounces (57 g) of the feta, and the remaining 2 tablespoons of olive oil, along with the lemon zest, nutmeg, dill, and salt. Mix until just combined. 6. Add the vegetables to the cheese base and stir until combined. 7. Pour the dip mixture into the prepared ramekin and top with the remaining 2 ounces (57 g) of feta cheese. 8. Place the dip into the air fryer basket and cook for 10 minutes, or until heated through and bubbling. 9. Serve with pita chips, carrot sticks, or sliced bread.

Per Serving:

calories: 376 | fat: 32g | protein: 14g | carbs: 11g | fiber: 2g | sodium: 737mg

Stuffed Dates with Feta, Parmesan, and Pine Nuts

Prep time: 5 minutes | Cook time: 10 minutes | Serves 4

1 ounce (28 g) feta	½ tablespoon raw pine nuts
1 ounce (28 g) Parmesan cheese	1 teaspoon extra virgin olive oil
12 dried dates, pitted	

1. Preheat the oven to 425°F (220°C). Line a small baking pan with parchment paper. 2. Cut the feta and Parmesan into 12 small thin sticks, each about ¾ inch long and ¼ inch thick. 3. Use a sharp knife to cut a small slit lengthwise into each date. Insert a piece of the Parmesan followed by a piece of the feta, and then press 2–3 pine nuts slightly into the feta. 4. Transfer the dates to the prepared baking pan and place in the oven to roast for 10 minutes. (The edges of the dates should begin to brown.) 5. Remove the dates from the oven and drizzle a few drops of the olive oil over each date. Serve promptly. (These do not store well and are best enjoyed fresh.)

Per Serving:
calories: 126 | fat: 5g | protein: 4g | carbs: 17g | fiber: 2g | sodium: 194mg

Citrus-Kissed Melon

Prep time: 5 minutes | Cook time: 0 minutes | Serves 4

2 cups cubed melon, such as Crenshaw, Sharlyn, or honeydew	juice
	¼ cup freshly squeezed lime juice
2 cups cubed cantaloupe	1 tablespoon orange zest
½ cup freshly squeezed orange	

1. In a large bowl, combine the melon cubes. In a small bowl, whisk together the orange juice, lime juice, and orange zest and pour over the fruit. 2. Cover and refrigerate for at least 4 hours, stirring occasionally. Serve chilled.

Per Serving:
calories: 80 | fat: 0g | protein: 2g | carbs: 20g | fiber: 2g | sodium: 30mg

Grilled Halloumi with Watermelon, Cherry Tomatoes, Olives, and Herb Oil

Prep time: 5 minutes | Cook time: 5 minutes | Serves 4

½ cup coarsely chopped fresh basil	black pepper, plus a pinch
3 tablespoons coarsely chopped fresh mint leaves, plus thinly sliced mint for garnish	¾ pound (340 g) cherry tomatoes
1 clove garlic, coarsely chopped	8 ounces (227 g) Halloumi cheese, cut crosswise into 8 slices
½ cup olive oil, plus more for brushing	2 cups thinly sliced watermelon, rind removed
½ teaspoon salt, plus a pinch	¼ cup sliced, pitted Kalamata olives
½ teaspoon freshly ground	

1. Heat a grill or grill pan to high. 2. In a food processor or blender, combine the basil, chopped mint, and garlic and pulse to chop. While the machine is running, add the olive oil in a thin stream. Strain the oil through a fine-meshed sieve and discard the solids. Stir in ½ teaspoon of salt and ½ teaspoon of pepper. 3. Brush the grill rack with olive oil. Drizzle 2 tablespoons of the herb oil over the tomatoes and cheese and season them with pinches of salt and pepper. Place the tomatoes on the grill and cook, turning occasionally, until their skins become blistered and begin to burst, about 4 minutes. Place the cheese on the grill and cook until grill marks appear and the cheese begins to get melty, about 1 minute per side. 4. Arrange the watermelon on a serving platter. Arrange the grilled cheese and tomatoes on top of the melon. Drizzle the herb oil over the top and garnish with the olives and sliced mint. Serve immediately.

Per Serving:
calories: 535 | fat: 50g | protein: 14g | carbs: 12g | fiber: 2g | sodium: 663mg

Cheese-Stuffed Dates

Prep time: 10 minutes | Cook time: 10 minutes | Serves 4

2 ounces (57 g) low-fat cream cheese, at room temperature	¼ teaspoon kosher salt
	⅛ teaspoon ground black pepper
2 tablespoons sweet pickle relish	Dash of hot sauce
1 tablespoon low-fat plain Greek yogurt	2 tablespoons pistachios, chopped
1 teaspoon finely chopped fresh chives	8 Medjool dates, pitted and halved

1. In a small bowl, stir together the cream cheese, relish, yogurt, chives, salt, pepper, and hot sauce. 2. Put the pistachios on a clean plate. Put the cream cheese mixture into a resealable plastic bag, and snip off 1 corner of the bag. Pipe the cream cheese mixture into the date halves and press the tops into the pistachios to coat.

Per Serving:
calories: 196 | fat: 4g | protein: 3g | carbs: 41g | fiber: 4g | sodium: 294mg

Mediterranean-Style Stuffed Mushrooms

Prep time: 10 minutes | Cook time: 20 minutes | Serves 4

2 ounces (57 g) feta	¼ teaspoon freshly ground black pepper
1 tablespoon cream cheese	
2 teaspoons dried oregano	3 tablespoons unseasoned breadcrumbs, divided
1 tablespoon finely chopped fresh parsley	2 tablespoons extra virgin olive oil, divided
2 tablespoons finely chopped fresh basil	20 medium button mushrooms, washed, dried, and stems removed
2 tablespoons finely chopped fresh mint	

1. Preheat the oven to 400°F (205°C). Line a large baking pan with foil. 2. In a medium bowl, combine the feta, cream cheese, oregano, parsley, basil, mint, black pepper, 2 tablespoons of the breadcrumbs, and 1 tablespoon of the olive oil. Use a fork to mash the ingredients until they're combined and somewhat creamy. 3. Stuff the mushrooms with the filling and then place them in the prepared pan. 4. Sprinkle the remaining 1 tablespoon of breadcrumbs over the mushrooms and then drizzle the remaining olive oil over the top. 5. Bake for 15–20 minutes or until the tops are golden brown. Serve promptly.

Per Serving:
calories: 151 | fat: 12g | protein: 6g | carbs: 8g | fiber: 1g | sodium: 186mg

Pita Pizza with Olives, Feta, and Red Onion

Prep time: 15 minutes | Cook time: 10 minutes | Serves 4

4 (6-inch) whole-wheat pitas	chopped
1 tablespoon extra-virgin olive oil	¼ cup crumbled feta cheese
½ cup hummus	¼ teaspoon red pepper flakes
½ bell pepper, julienned	¼ cup fresh herbs, chopped
½ red onion, julienned	(mint, parsley, oregano, or a
¼ cup olives, pitted and	mix)

1. Preheat the broiler to low. Line a baking sheet with parchment paper or foil. 2. Place the pitas on the prepared baking sheet and brush both sides with the olive oil. Broil 1 to 2 minutes per side until starting to turn golden brown. 3. Spread 2 tablespoons hummus on each pita. Top the pitas with bell pepper, onion, olives, feta cheese, and red pepper flakes. Broil again until the cheese softens and starts to get golden brown, 4 to 6 minutes, being careful not to burn the pitas. 4. Remove from broiler and top with the herbs.

Per Serving:
calories: 185 | fat: 11g | protein: 5g | carbs: 17g | fiber: 3g | sodium: 285mg

Seared Halloumi with Pesto and Tomato

Prep time: 2 minutes | Cook time: 5 minutes | Serves 2

3 ounces (85 g) Halloumi cheese, cut crosswise into 2 thinner, rectangular pieces	sauce, plus additional for drizzling if desired
2 teaspoons prepared pesto	1 medium tomato, sliced

1. Heat a nonstick skillet over medium-high heat and place the slices of Halloumi in the hot pan. After about 2 minutes, check to see if the cheese is golden on the bottom. If it is, flip the slices, top each with 1 teaspoon of pesto, and cook for another 2 minutes, or until the second side is golden. 2. Serve with slices of tomato and a drizzle of pesto, if desired, on the side.

Per Serving:
calories: 177 | fat: 14g | protein: 10g | carbs: 4g | fiber: 1g | sodium: 233mg

Pea and Arugula Crostini with Pecorino Romano

Prep time: 10 minutes | Cook time: 15 minutes | Serves 6 to 8

1½ cups fresh or frozen peas	½ teaspoon salt
1 loaf crusty whole-wheat bread, cut into thin slices	¼ teaspoon freshly ground black pepper
3 tablespoons olive oil, divided	1 cup (packed) baby arugula
1 small garlic clove, finely mined or pressed	¼ cup thinly shaved Pecorino Romano
Juice of ½ lemon	

1. Preheat the oven to 350°F(180°C). 2. Fill a small saucepan with about ½ inch of water. Bring to a boil over medium-high heat. Add the peas and cook for 3 to 5 minutes, until tender. Drain and rinse with cold water. 3. Arrange the bread slices on a large baking sheet and brush the tops with 2 tablespoons olive oil. Bake in the preheated oven for about 8 minutes, until golden brown. 4. Meanwhile, in a medium bowl, mash the peas gently with the back of a fork. They should be smashed but not mashed into a paste. Add the remaining 1 tablespoon olive oil, lemon juice, garlic, salt, and pepper and stir to mix. 5. Spoon the pea mixture onto the toasted bread slices and top with the arugula and cheese. Serve immediately.

Per Serving:
calories: 301 | fat: 13g | protein: 14g | carbs: 32g | fiber: 6g | sodium: 833mg

Flatbread with Ricotta and Orange-Raisin Relish

Prep time: 5 minutes | Cook time: 8 minutes | Serves 4 to 6

¾ cup golden raisins, roughly chopped	strips
1 shallot, finely diced	Pinch of salt
1 tablespoon olive oil	1 oval prebaked whole-wheat flatbread, such as naan or pocketless pita
1 tablespoon red wine vinegar	
1 tablespoon honey	8 ounces (227 g) whole-milk ricotta cheese
1 tablespoon chopped flat-leaf parsley	
1 tablespoon fresh orange zest	½ cup baby arugula

1. Preheat the oven to 450°F(235°C). 2. In a small bowl, stir together the raisins, shallot, olive oil, vinegar, honey, parsley, orange zest, and salt. 3. Place the flatbread on a large baking sheet and toast in the preheated oven until the edges are lightly browned, about 8 minutes. 4. Spoon the ricotta cheese onto the flatbread, spreading with the back of the spoon. Scatter the arugula over the cheese. Cut the flatbread into triangles and top each piece with a dollop of the relish. Serve immediately.

Per Serving:
calories: 195 | fat: 9g | protein: 6g | carbs: 25g | fiber: 1g | sodium: 135mg

Sardine and Herb Bruschetta

Prep time: 5 minutes | Cook time: 10 minutes | Serves 4

8 (1-inch) thick whole-grain baguette slices	2 tablespoons capers, drained
1½ tablespoons extra virgin olive oil	3 tablespoons finely chopped onion (any variety)
4 ounces (113 g) olive oil–packed sardines	½ teaspoon dried oregano
2 tablespoons fresh lemon juice	1 tablespoon finely chopped fresh mint
1 teaspoon red wine vinegar	1 garlic clove, halved

1. Preheat the oven to 400°F (205°C). 2. Place the baguette slices on a large baking sheet and brush them with the olive oil. Transfer to the oven and toast until the slices are golden, about 10 minutes. 3. While the baguette slices are toasting, make the sardine topping by combining the sardines, lemon juice, and vinegar in a medium bowl. Mash with a fork. Add the capers, onions, oregano, and mint, and stir to combine. 4. When the baguette slices are done toasting, remove them from the oven and rub them with the garlic. 5. Transfer the slices to a serving platter. Place 1 heaping tablespoon of the topping onto each baguette slice. Store the sardine topping in the refrigerator for up to 3 days.

Per Serving:
calories: 249 | fat: 11g | protein: 14g | carbs: 24g | fiber: 4g | sodium: 387mg

Zucchini Feta Roulades

Prep time: 10 minutes | Cook time: 10 minutes | Serves 6

½ cup feta	⅛ teaspoon salt
1 garlic clove, minced	⅛ teaspoon red pepper flakes
2 tablespoons fresh basil, minced	1 tablespoon lemon juice
	2 medium zucchini
1 tablespoon capers, minced	12 toothpicks

1. Preheat the air fryer to 360ºF (182ºC).(If using a grill attachment, make sure it is inside the air fryer during preheating.) 2. In a small bowl, combine the feta, garlic, basil, capers, salt, red pepper flakes, and lemon juice. 3. Slice the zucchini into ⅛-inch strips lengthwise. (Each zucchini should yield around 6 strips.) 4. Spread 1 tablespoon of the cheese filling onto each slice of zucchini, then roll it up and secure it with a toothpick through the middle. 5. Place the zucchini roulades into the air fryer basket in a single layer, making sure that they don't touch each other. 6. Bake or grill in the air fryer for 10 minutes. 7. Remove the zucchini roulades from the air fryer and gently remove the toothpicks before serving.

Per Serving:
calories: 36 | fat: 3g | protein: 2g | carbs: 1g | fiber: 0g | sodium: 200mg

Cream Cheese Wontons

Prep time: 15 minutes | Cook time: 6 minutes | Makes 20 wontons

Oil, for spraying	4 ounces (113 g) cream cheese
20 wonton wrappers	

1. Line the air fryer basket with parchment and spray lightly with oil. 2. Pour some water in a small bowl. 3. Lay out a wonton wrapper and place 1 teaspoon of cream cheese in the center. 4. Dip your finger in the water and moisten the edge of the wonton wrapper. Fold over the opposite corners to make a triangle and press the edges together. 5. Pinch the corners of the triangle together to form a classic wonton shape. Place the wonton in the prepared basket. Repeat with the remaining wrappers and cream cheese. You may need to work in batches, depending on the size of your air fryer. 6. Air fry at 400ºF (204ºC) for 6 minutes, or until golden brown around the edges.

Per Serving:
1 wonton: calories: 43 | fat: 2g | protein: 1g | carbs: 5g | fiber: 0g | sodium: 66mg

Bite-Size Stuffed Peppers

Prep time: 15 minutes | Cook time: 10 minutes | Serves 8 to 10

20 to 25 mini sweet bell peppers, assortment of colors	4 ounces (113 g) mascarpone cheese, at room temperature
1 tablespoon extra-virgin olive oil	1 tablespoon fresh chives, chopped
4 ounces (113 g) goat cheese, at room temperature	1 tablespoon lemon zest

1. Preheat the oven to 400ºF(205ºC). 2. Remove the stem, cap, and any seeds from the peppers. Put them into a bowl and toss to coat with the olive oil. 3. Put the peppers onto a baking sheet; bake for 8 minutes. 4. Remove the peppers from the oven and let cool completely. 5. In a medium bowl, add the goat cheese, mascarpone cheese, chives, and lemon zest. Stir to combine, then spoon mixture into a piping bag. 6. Fill each pepper to the top with the cheese mixture, using the piping bag. 7. Chill the peppers in the fridge for at least 30 minutes before serving.

Per Serving:
calories: 141 | fat: 11g | protein: 4g | carbs: 6g | fiber: 2g | sodium: 73mg

Heart-Healthful Trail Mix

Prep time: 15 minutes | Cook time: 30 minutes | Serves 10

1 cup raw almonds	chopped
1 cup walnut halves	1 cup golden raisins
1 cup pumpkin seeds	2 tablespoons extra-virgin olive oil
1 cup dried apricots, cut into thin strips	1 teaspoon salt
1 cup dried cherries, roughly	

1. Preheat the oven to 300°F(150ºC). Line a baking sheet with aluminum foil. 2. In a large bowl, combine the almonds, walnuts, pumpkin seeds, apricots, cherries, and raisins. Pour the olive oil over all and toss well with clean hands. Add salt and toss again to distribute. 3. Pour the nut mixture onto the baking sheet in a single layer and bake until the fruits begin to brown, about 30 minutes. Cool on the baking sheet to room temperature. 4. Store in a large airtight container or zipper-top plastic bag.

Per Serving:
calories: 346 | fat: 20g | protein: 8g | carbs: 39g | fiber: 5g | sodium: 240mg

Goat'S Cheese & Hazelnut Dip

Prep time: 10 minutes | Cook time: 0 minutes | Serves 8

2 heads yellow chicory or endive	leaves
	Pinch of salt
Enough ice water to cover the	
Dip:	
12 ounces (340 g) soft goat's cheese	lemon)
	1 clove garlic, minced
3 tablespoons extra-virgin olive oil	Freshly ground black pepper, to taste
1 tablespoon fresh lemon juice	Salt, if needed, to taste
1 teaspoon lemon zest (about ½	
Topping:	
2 tablespoons chopped fresh chives	1 tablespoon extra-virgin olive oil
¼ cup crushed hazelnuts, pecans, or walnuts	Chile flakes or black pepper, to taste

1. Cut off the bottom of the chicory and trim the leaves to get rid of any that are limp or brown. Place the leaves in salted ice water for 10 minutes. This will help the chicory leaves to become crisp. Drain and leave in the strainer. 2. To make the dip: Place the dip ingredients in a bowl and use a fork or spatula to mix until smooth and creamy. 3. Stir in the chives. Transfer to a serving bowl and top with the crushed hazelnuts, olive oil, and chile flakes. Serve with the crisp chicory leaves. Store in a sealed jar in the fridge for up to 5 days.

Per Serving:
calories: 219 | fat: 18g | protein: 10g | carbs: 5g | fiber: 4g | sodium: 224mg

Red Pepper Tapenade

Prep time: 5 minutes | Cook time: 5 minutes | Serves 4

1 large red bell pepper	and roughly chopped
2 tablespoons plus 1 teaspoon olive oil, divided	1 garlic clove, minced
½ cup Kalamata olives, pitted	½ teaspoon dried oregano
	1 tablespoon lemon juice

1. Preheat the air fryer to 380°F(193ºC). 2. Brush the outside of a whole red pepper with 1 teaspoon olive oil and place it inside the air fryer basket. Roast for 5 minutes. 3. Meanwhile, in a medium bowl combine the remaining 2 tablespoons of olive oil with the olives, garlic, oregano, and lemon juice. 4. Remove the red pepper from the air fryer, then gently slice off the stem and remove the seeds. Roughly chop the roasted pepper into small pieces. 5. Add the red pepper to the olive mixture and stir all together until combined. 6. Serve with pita chips, crackers, or crusty bread.

Per Serving:

calories: 94 | fat: 9g | protein: 1g | carbs: 4g | fiber: 2g | sodium: 125mg

Stuffed Figs with Goat Cheese and Honey

Prep time: 5 minutes | Cook time: 10 minutes | Serves 4

8 fresh figs	1 tablespoon honey, plus more for serving
2 ounces (57 g) goat cheese	
¼ teaspoon ground cinnamon	1 tablespoon olive oil

1. Preheat the air fryer to 360°F(182ºC). 2. Cut the stem off of each fig. 3. Cut an X into the top of each fig, cutting halfway down the fig. Leave the base intact. 4. In a small bowl, mix together the goat cheese, cinnamon, and honey. 5. Spoon the goat cheese mixture into the cavity of each fig. 6. Place the figs in a single layer in the air fryer basket. Drizzle the olive oil over top of the figs and roast for 10 minutes. 7. Serve with an additional drizzle of honey.

Per Serving:

calories: 152 | fat: 9g | protein: 5g | carbs: 16g | fiber: 2g | sodium: 62mg

Roasted Pearl Onion Dip

Prep time: 5 minutes | Cook time: 12 minutes | Serves 4

2 cups peeled pearl onions	¼ teaspoon black pepper
3 garlic cloves	⅛ teaspoon red pepper flakes
3 tablespoons olive oil, divided	Pita chips, vegetables, or toasted bread for serving (optional)
½ teaspoon salt	
1 cup nonfat plain Greek yogurt	
1 tablespoon lemon juice	

1. Preheat the air fryer to 360°F(182ºC). 2. In a large bowl, combine the pearl onions and garlic with 2 tablespoons of the olive oil until the onions are well coated. 3. Pour the garlic-and-onion mixture into the air fryer basket and roast for 12 minutes. 4. Transfer the garlic and onions to a food processor. Pulse the vegetables several times, until the onions are minced but still have some chunks. 5. In a large bowl, combine the garlic and onions and the remaining 1 tablespoon of olive oil, along with the salt, yogurt, lemon juice, black pepper, and red pepper flakes. 6. Cover and chill for 1 hour before serving with pita chips, vegetables, or toasted bread.

Per Serving:

calories: 152 | fat: 10g | protein: 4g | carbs: 11g | fiber: 1g | sodium: 341mg

Greens Chips with Curried Yogurt Sauce

Prep time: 10 minutes | Cook time: 5 to 6 minutes | Serves 4

1 cup low-fat Greek yogurt	leaves cut into 2- to 3-inch pieces
1 tablespoon freshly squeezed lemon juice	½ bunch chard, stemmed, ribs removed and discarded, leaves cut into 2- to 3-inch pieces
1 tablespoon curry powder	
½ bunch curly kale, stemmed, ribs removed and discarded,	1½ teaspoons olive oil

1. In a small bowl, stir together the yogurt, lemon juice, and curry powder. Set aside. 2. In a large bowl, toss the kale and chard with the olive oil, working the oil into the leaves with your hands. This helps break up the fibers in the leaves so the chips are tender. 3. Air fry the greens in batches at 390ºF (199ºC) for 5 to 6 minutes, until crisp, shaking the basket once during cooking. Serve with the yogurt sauce.

Per Serving:

calories: 98 | fat: 4g | protein: 7g | carbs: 13g | fiber: 4g | sodium: 186mg

Lemony Olives and Feta Medley

Prep time: 10 minutes | Cook time: 0 minutes | Serves 8

1 (1-pound / 454-g) block of Greek feta cheese	¼ cup extra-virgin olive oil
	3 tablespoons lemon juice
3 cups mixed olives (Kalamata and green), drained from brine; pitted preferred	1 teaspoon grated lemon zest
	1 teaspoon dried oregano
	Pita bread, for serving

1. Cut the feta cheese into ½-inch squares and put them into a large bowl. 2. Add the olives to the feta and set aside. 3. In a small bowl, whisk together the olive oil, lemon juice, lemon zest, and oregano. 4. Pour the dressing over the feta cheese and olives and gently toss together to evenly coat everything. 5. Serve with pita bread.

Per Serving:

calories: 269 | fat: 24g | protein: 9g | carbs: 6g | fiber: 2g | sodium: 891mg

Crunchy Tex-Mex Tortilla Chips

Prep time: 5 minutes | Cook time: 5 minutes | Serves 4

Olive oil	½ teaspoon paprika
½ teaspoon salt	Pinch cayenne pepper
½ teaspoon ground cumin	8 (6-inch) corn tortillas, each cut into 6 wedges
½ teaspoon chili powder	

1. Spray fryer basket lightly with olive oil. 2. In a small bowl, combine the salt, cumin, chili powder, paprika, and cayenne pepper. 3. Place the tortilla wedges in the air fryer basket in a single layer. Spray the tortillas lightly with oil and sprinkle with some of the seasoning mixture. You will need to cook the tortillas in batches. 4. Air fry at 375ºF (191ºC) for 2 to 3 minutes. Shake the basket and cook until the chips are light brown and crispy, an additional 2 to 3 minutes. Watch the chips closely so they do not burn.

Per Serving:

calories: 118 | fat: 1g | protein: 3g | carbs: 25g | fiber: 3g | sodium: 307mg

Black-Eyed Pea "Caviar"

Prep time: 10 minutes | Cook time: 30 minutes | Makes 5 cups

1 cup dried black-eyed peas	1 medium tomato, diced
4 cups water	2 tablespoons chopped fresh
1 pound (454 g) cooked corn	cilantro
kernels	¼ cup red wine vinegar
½ medium red onion, peeled	2 tablespoons extra-virgin olive
and diced	oil
½ medium green bell pepper,	1 teaspoon salt
seeded and diced	½ teaspoon ground black
2 tablespoons minced pickled	pepper
jalapeño pepper	½ teaspoon ground cumin

1. Add black-eyed peas and water to the Instant Pot®. Close lid, set steam release to Sealing, press the Manual button, and set time to 30 minutes. 2. When the timer beeps, let pressure release naturally, about 25 minutes, and open lid. Drain peas and transfer to a large mixing bowl. Add all remaining ingredients and stir until thoroughly combined. Cover and refrigerate for 2 hours before serving.

Per Serving:
½ cup: calories: 28 | fat: 1g | protein: 1g | carbs: 4 | fiber: 1g | sodium: 51mg

Roasted Chickpeas with Herbs and Spices

Prep time: 5 minutes | Cook time: 22 minutes | Serves 4

1 (15-ounce / 425-g) can	1 teaspoon Aleppo pepper
chickpeas, drained and rinsed	1 teaspoon brown sugar
1 tablespoon olive oil	½ teaspoon kosher salt
1 teaspoon za'atar	2 tablespoons chopped fresh
½ teaspoon ground sumac	parsley

1. Preheat the oven to 350°F (180°C). 2. Spread the chickpeas in an even layer on an ungreased rimmed baking sheet and bake for 10 minutes, or until they are dried. Remove from the oven; keep the oven on. 3. Meanwhile, in a medium bowl, whisk together the olive oil, za'atar, sumac, Aleppo pepper, brown sugar, and salt until well combined. 4. Add the warm chickpeas to the oil-spice mixture and stir until they are completely coated. Return the chickpeas to the baking sheet and spread them into an even layer. Bake for 10 to 12 minutes more, until fragrant. 5. Transfer the chickpeas to a serving bowl, toss with the parsley, and serve.

Per Serving:
1 cup: calories: 122 | fat: 5g | protein: 5g | carbs: 16g | fiber: 4g | sodium: 427mg

Vegetable Pot Stickers

Prep time: 12 minutes | Cook time: 11 to 18 minutes | Makes 12 pot stickers

1 cup shredded red cabbage	2 garlic cloves, minced
¼ cup chopped button	2 teaspoons grated fresh ginger
mushrooms	12 gyoza/pot sticker wrappers
¼ cup grated carrot	2½ teaspoons olive oil, divided
2 tablespoons minced onion	

1. In a baking pan, combine the red cabbage, mushrooms, carrot, onion, garlic, and ginger. Add 1 tablespoon of water. Place in the air fryer and air fry at 370°F (188°C) for 3 to 6 minutes, until the vegetables are crisp-tender. Drain and set aside. 2. Working one at a time, place the pot sticker wrappers on a work surface. Top each wrapper with a scant 1 tablespoon of the filling. Fold half of the wrapper over the other half to form a half circle. Dab one edge with water and press both edges together. 3. To another pan, add 1¼ teaspoons of olive oil. Put half of the pot stickers, seam-side up, in the pan. Air fry for 5 minutes, or until the bottoms are light golden brown. Add 1 tablespoon of water and return the pan to the air fryer. 4. Air fry for 4 to 6 minutes more, or until hot. Repeat with the remaining pot stickers, remaining 1¼ teaspoons of oil, and another tablespoon of water. Serve immediately.

Per Serving:
1 pot stickers: calories: 36 | fat: 1g | protein: 1g | carbs: 6g | fiber: 0g | sodium: 49mg

Garlic-Lemon Hummus

Prep time: 15 minutes | Cook time: 0 minutes | Serves 6

1 (15-ounce / 425-g) can	oil, divided
chickpeas, drained and rinsed	2 lemons, juice
4 to 5 tablespoons tahini	1 lemon, zested, divided
(sesame seed paste)	1 tablespoon minced garlic
4 tablespoons extra-virgin olive	Pinch salt

1. In a food processor, combine the chickpeas, tahini, 2 tablespoons of olive oil, lemon juice, half of the lemon zest, and garlic and blend for up to 1 minute. After 30 seconds of blending, stop and scrape the sides down with a spatula, before blending for another 30 seconds. At this point, you've made hummus! Taste and add salt as desired. Feel free to add 1 teaspoon of water at a time to help thin the hummus to a better consistency. 2. Scoop the hummus into a bowl, then drizzle with the remaining 2 tablespoons of olive oil and remaining lemon zest.

Per Serving:
calories: 216 | fat: 15g | protein: 5g | carbs: 17g | fiber: 5g | sodium: 12mg

Chapter 7

Vegetables and Sides

Lightened-Up Eggplant Parmigiana

Prep time: 10 minutes | Cook time: 1 hour 20 minutes | Serves 3

2 medium globe eggplants, sliced into ¼-inch rounds	purée
2 tablespoons extra virgin olive oil, divided	3 tablespoons chopped fresh basil, divided
1 teaspoon fine sea salt, divided	¼ teaspoon freshly ground black pepper
1 medium onion (any variety), diced	7 ounces (198 g) low-moisture mozzarella, thinly sliced or grated
1 garlic clove, finely chopped	
20 ounces (567g) canned crushed tomatoes or tomato	2 ounces (57 g) grated Parmesan cheese

1. Line an oven rack with aluminum foil and preheat the oven to 350ºF (180ºC). 2. Place the eggplant slices in a large bowl and toss with 1 tablespoon of the olive oil and ½ teaspoon of the sea salt. Arrange the slices on the prepared oven rack. Place the oven rack in the middle position and roast the eggplant for 15–20 minutes or until soft. 3. While the eggplant slices are roasting, heat the remaining tablespoon of olive oil in a medium pan over medium heat. When the oil begins to shimmer, add the onions and sauté for 5 minutes, then add the garlic and sauté for 1 more minute. Add the crushed tomatoes, 1½ tablespoons of the basil, the remaining ½ teaspoon of sea salt, and black pepper. Reduce the heat to low and simmer for 15 minutes, then remove from the heat. 4. When the eggplant slices are done roasting, remove them from the oven. Begin assembling the dish by spreading ½ cup of the tomato sauce over the bottom of a 11 × 7-inch (30 × 20cm) casserole dish. Place a third of the eggplant rounds in a single layer in the dish, overlapping them slightly, if needed. Layer half of the mozzarella on top of the eggplant, then spread ¾ cup tomato sauce over the cheese slices and then sprinkle 2½ tablespoons of the grated Parmesan cheese over the top. Repeat the process with a second layer of eggplant, sauce, and cheese, then add the remaining eggplant in a single layer on top of the cheese. Top with the remaining sauce and then sprinkle the remaining 1½ tablespoons of basil over the top. 5. Bake for 40–45 minutes or until browned, then remove from oven and set aside to cool for 10 minutes before cutting into 6 equal-size pieces and serving. Store covered in the refrigerator for up to 3 days.

Per Serving:

calories: 453 | fat: 28g | protein: 28g | carbs: 26g | fiber: 4g | sodium: 842mg

Parmesan-Rosemary Radishes

Prep time: 5 minutes | Cook time: 15 to 20 minutes | Serves 4

1 bunch radishes, stemmed, trimmed, and quartered	1 tablespoon chopped fresh rosemary
1 tablespoon avocado oil	Sea salt and freshly ground black pepper, to taste
2 tablespoons finely grated fresh Parmesan cheese	

1. Place the radishes in a medium bowl and toss them with the avocado oil, Parmesan cheese, rosemary, salt, and pepper. 2. Set the air fryer to 375ºF (191ºC). Arrange the radishes in a single layer in the air fryer basket. Roast for 15 to 20 minutes, until golden brown and tender. Let cool for 5 minutes before serving.

Per Serving:

calories: 58 | fat: 4g | protein: 1g | carbs: 4g | fiber: 2g | sodium: 63mg

Garlic Zucchini and Red Peppers

Prep time: 5 minutes | Cook time: 15 minutes | Serves 6

2 medium zucchini, cubed	2 tablespoons olive oil
1 red bell pepper, diced	½ teaspoon salt
2 garlic cloves, sliced	

1. Preheat the air fryer to 380°F(193ºC). 2. In a large bowl, mix together the zucchini, bell pepper, and garlic with the olive oil and salt. 3. Pour the mixture into the air fryer basket, and roast for 7 minutes. Shake or stir, then roast for 7 to 8 minutes more.

Per Serving:

calories: 59 | fat: 5g | protein: 1g | carbs: 4g | fiber: 1g | sodium: 200mg

Greek Garlic Dip

Prep time: 10 minutes | Cook time: 30 minutes | Serves 4

2 potatoes (about 1 pound / 454 g), peeled and quartered	juice
	4 garlic cloves, minced
½ cup olive oil	Sea salt
¼ cup freshly squeezed lemon	Freshly ground black pepper

1. Place the potatoes in a large saucepan and fill the pan three-quarters full with water. Bring the water to a boil over medium-high heat, then reduce the heat to medium and cook the potatoes until fork-tender, 20 to 30 minutes. 2. While the potatoes are boiling, in a medium bowl, stir together the olive oil, lemon juice, and garlic; set aside. 3. Drain the potatoes and return them to the saucepan. Pour in the oil mixture and mash with a potato masher or a fork until well combined and smooth. Taste and season with salt and pepper. Serve.

Per Serving:

calories: 334 | fat: 27g | protein: 3g | carbs: 22g | fiber: 3g | sodium: 47mg

Mini Moroccan Pumpkin Cakes

Prep time: 10 minutes | Cook time: 10 minutes | Serves 6

2 cups cooked brown rice	1 teaspoon ground cumin
1 cup pumpkin purée	Sea salt and freshly ground pepper, to taste
½ cup finely chopped walnuts	
3 tablespoons olive oil, divided	1 teaspoon hot paprika or a pinch of cayenne
½ medium onion, diced	
½ red bell pepper, diced	

1. Combine the rice, pumpkin, and walnuts in a large bowl; set aside. 2. In a medium skillet, heat the olive oil over medium heat, add the onion and bell pepper, and cook until soft, about 5 minutes. 3. Add the cumin to the onions and bell peppers. Add onion mixture to the rice mixture. 4. Mix thoroughly and season with sea salt, freshly ground pepper, and paprika or cayenne. 5. In a large skillet, heat 2 tablespoons of olive oil over medium heat. 6. Form the rice mixture into 1-inch patties and add them to the skillet. Cook until both sides are browned and crispy. 7. Serve with Greek yogurt or tzatziki on the side.

Per Serving:

calories: 193 | fat: 12g | protein: 3g | carbs: 20g | fiber: 3g | sodium: 6mg

Vibrant Green Beans

Prep time: 10 minutes | Cook time: 15 minutes | Serves 6

2 tablespoons olive oil	string beans, trimmed
2 leeks, white parts only, sliced	1 tablespoon Italian seasoning
Sea salt and freshly ground	2 tablespoons white wine
pepper, to taste	Zest of 1 lemon
1 pound (454 g) fresh green	

1. Heat the olive oil over medium heat in a large skillet. 2. Add leeks and cook, stirring often, until they start to brown and become lightly caramelized. 3. Season with sea salt and freshly ground pepper. 4. Add green beans and Italian seasoning, cooking for a few minutes until beans are tender but still crisp to the bite. 5. Add the wine and continue cooking until beans are done to your liking and leeks are crispy and browned. 6. Sprinkle with lemon zest before serving.

Per Serving:
calories: 87 | fat: 5g | protein: 2g | carbs: 11g | fiber: 3g | sodium: 114mg

Rice Pilaf with Dill

Prep time: 15 minutes | Cook time: 25 minutes | Serves 6

2 tablespoons olive oil	¼ teaspoon freshly ground
1 carrot, finely chopped (about	black pepper
¾ cup)	2 tablespoons chopped fresh
2 leeks, halved lengthwise,	dill
washed, well drained, and	1 cup low-sodium vegetable
sliced in half-moons	broth or water
½ teaspoon salt	½ cup basmati rice

1. In a 2-or 3-quart saucepan, heat the olive oil over medium heat. Add the carrot, leeks, salt, pepper, and 1 tablespoon of the dill. Cover and cook for 6 to 8 minutes, stirring once, to soften all the vegetables but not brown them. 2. Add the broth or water and bring to a boil. Stir in the rice, reduce the heat to maintain a simmer, cover, and cook for 15 minutes. Remove from the heat; let stand, covered, for 10 minutes. 3. Fluff the rice with fork. Stir in the remaining 1 tablespoon dill and serve.

Per Serving:
1 cup: calories: 100 | fat: 7g | protein: 2g | carbs: 11g | fiber: 4g | sodium: 209mg

Air-Fried Okra

Prep time: 10 minutes | Cook time: 10 minutes | Serves 4

1 egg	¼ teaspoon freshly ground
½ cup almond milk	black pepper
½ cup crushed pork rinds	½ pound (227 g) fresh okra,
¼ cup grated Parmesan cheese	stems removed and chopped
¼ cup almond flour	into 1-inch slices
1 teaspoon garlic powder	

1. Preheat the air fryer to 400°F (204°C). 2. In a shallow bowl, whisk together the egg and milk. 3. In a second shallow bowl, combine the pork rinds, Parmesan, almond flour, garlic powder, and black pepper. 4. Working with a few slices at a time, dip the okra into the egg mixture followed by the crumb mixture. Press lightly to ensure an even coating. 5. Working in batches if necessary, arrange the okra in a single layer in the air fryer basket and spray lightly with olive

oil. Pausing halfway through the cooking time to turn the okra, air fry for 10 minutes until tender and golden brown. Serve warm.

Per Serving:
calories: 200 | fat: 16g | protein: 6g | carbs: 8g | fiber: 2g | sodium: 228mg

Gorgonzola Sweet Potato Burgers

Prep time: 10 minutes |Cook time: 15 minutes| Serves: 4

1 large sweet potato (about 8 ounces / 227 g)	1 tablespoon dried oregano
	1 garlic clove
2 tablespoons extra-virgin olive oil, divided	¼ teaspoon kosher or sea salt
	½ cup crumbled Gorgonzola or
1 cup chopped onion (about ½ medium onion)	blue cheese (about 2 ounces / 57 g)
1 cup old-fashioned rolled oats	Salad greens or 4 whole-wheat
1 large egg	rolls, for serving (optional)
1 tablespoon balsamic vinegar	

1. Using a fork, pierce the sweet potato all over and microwave on high for 4 to 5 minutes, until tender in the center. Cool slightly, then slice in half. 2. While the sweet potato is cooking, in a large skillet over medium-high heat, heat 1 tablespoon of oil. Add the onion and cook for 5 minutes, stirring occasionally. 3. Using a spoon, carefully scoop the sweet potato flesh out of the skin and put the flesh in a food processor. Add the onion, oats, egg, vinegar, oregano, garlic, and salt. Process until smooth. Add the cheese and pulse four times to barely combine. With your hands, form the mixture into four (½-cup-size) burgers. Place the burgers on a plate, and press to flatten each to about ¾-inch thick. 4. Wipe out the skillet with a paper towel, then heat the remaining 1 tablespoon of oil over medium-high heat until very hot, about 2 minutes. Add the burgers to the hot oil, then turn the heat down to medium. Cook the burgers for 5 minutes, flip with a spatula, then cook an additional 5 minutes. Enjoy as is or serve on salad greens or whole-wheat rolls.

Per Serving:
calories: 337 | fat: 16g | protein: 13g | carbs: 38g | fiber: 6g | sodium: 378mg

Roasted Cauliflower with Lemon Tahini Sauce

Prep time: 10 minutes | Cook time: 20 minutes | Serves 2

½ large head cauliflower, stemmed and broken into florets (about 3 cups)	2 tablespoons freshly squeezed lemon juice
	1 teaspoon harissa paste
1 tablespoon olive oil	Pinch salt
2 tablespoons tahini	

1. Preheat the oven to 400°F(205°C) and set the rack to the lowest position. Line a sheet pan with parchment paper or foil. 2. Toss the cauliflower florets with the olive oil in a large bowl and transfer to the sheet pan. Reserve the bowl to make the tahini sauce. 3. Roast the cauliflower for 15 minutes, turning it once or twice, until it starts to turn golden. 4. In the same bowl, combine the tahini, lemon juice, harissa, and salt. 5. When the cauliflower is tender, remove it from the oven and toss it with the tahini sauce. Return to the sheet pan and roast for 5 minutes more.

Per Serving:
calories: 205 | fat: 15g | protein: 7g | carbs: 15g | fiber: 7g | sodium: 161mg

Stuffed Cucumbers

Prep time: 10 minutes | Cook time: 0 minutes | Serves 2

1 English cucumber	Sea salt and freshly ground
1 tomato, diced	pepper, to taste
1 avocado, diced	Small bunch cilantro, chopped
Dash of lime juice	

1. Cut the cucumber in half lengthwise and scoop out the flesh and seeds into a small bowl. 2. Without mashing too much, gently combine the cucumber flesh and seeds with the tomato, avocado, and lime juice. 3. Season with sea salt and freshly ground pepper to taste. 4. Put mixture back into cucumber halves and cut each piece in half. Garnish with the cilantro and serve.

Per Serving:

calories: 189 | fat: 15g | protein: 3g | carbs: 15g | fiber: 8g | sodium: 13mg

Spiced Honey-Walnut Carrots

Prep time: 5 minutes | Cook time: 12 minutes | Serves 6

1 pound (454 g) baby carrots	¼ teaspoon ground cinnamon
2 tablespoons olive oil	¼ cup black walnuts, chopped
¼ cup raw honey	

1. Preheat the air fryer to 360°F(182°C). 2. In a large bowl, toss the baby carrots with olive oil, honey, and cinnamon until well coated. 3. Pour into the air fryer and roast for 6 minutes. Shake the basket, sprinkle the walnuts on top, and roast for 6 minutes more. 4. Remove the carrots from the air fryer and serve.

Per Serving:

calories: 142 | fat: 8g | protein: 2g | carbs: 18g | fiber: 3g | sodium: 60mg

Stuffed Artichokes

Prep time: 20 minutes | Cook time: 5 to 7 hours | Serves 4 to 6

4 to 6 fresh large artichokes	black pepper
½ cup bread crumbs	¼ cup water
½ cup grated Parmesan cheese or Romano cheese	2 tablespoons extra-virgin olive oil
4 garlic cloves, minced	2 tablespoons chopped fresh
½ teaspoon sea salt	parsley for garnish (optional)
½ teaspoon freshly ground	

1. To trim and prepare the artichokes, cut off the bottom along with 1 inch from the top of each artichoke. Pull off and discard the lowest leaves nearest the stem end. Trim off any pointy tips of artichoke leaves that are poking out. Set aside. 2. In a small bowl, stir together the bread crumbs, Parmesan cheese, garlic, salt, and pepper. 3. Spread apart the artichoke leaves and stuff the bread-crumb mixture into the spaces, down to the base. 4. Pour the water into a slow cooker. 5. Place the artichokes in the slow cooker in a single layer. Drizzle the olive oil over the artichokes. 6. Cover the cooker and cook for 5 to 7 hours on Low heat, or until the artichokes are tender. 7. Garnish with fresh parsley if desired.

Per Serving:

calories: 224 | fat: 12g | protein: 12g | carbs: 23g | fiber: 8g | sodium: 883mg

Zucchini Fritters with Manchego and Smoked Paprika Yogurt

Prep time: 10 minutes | Cook time: 10 minutes | Serves 4 to 6

6 small zucchini, grated on the large holes of a box grater	parsley
1¼ teaspoons salt, divided	4 scallions, thinly sliced
1 cup plain Greek yogurt	3 eggs, beaten
2 teaspoons smoked paprika	½ cup all-purpose flour
Juice of ½ lemon	¼ teaspoon freshly ground black pepper
4 ounces (113 g) manchego cheese, grated	Neutral-flavored oil (such as grapeseed, safflower, or sunflower seed) for frying
¼ cup finely chopped fresh	

1. Put the grated zucchini in a colander. Sprinkle 1 teaspoon of salt over the top and then toss to combine. Let sit over the sink for at least 20 minutes to drain. Transfer the zucchini to a clean dishtowel and squeeze out as much of the water as you can. 2. Meanwhile, make the yogurt sauce. In a small bowl, stir together the yogurt, smoked paprika, lemon juice, and the remaining ¼ teaspoon of salt. 3. In a large bowl, combine the zucchini, cheese, parsley, scallions, eggs, flour, and pepper and stir to mix. 4. Fill a large saucepan with ½ inch of oil and heat over medium-high heat. When the oil is very hot, drop the batter in by rounded tablespoons, cooking 4 or 5 fritters at a time, flattening each dollop with the back of the spoon. Cook until golden on the bottom, about 2 minutes, then flip and cook on the second side until golden, about 2 minutes more. Transfer the cooked fritters to a plate lined with paper towels to drain and repeat until all of the batter has been cooked.

Per Serving:

calories: 237 | fat: 14g | protein: 11g | carbs: 18g | fiber: 3g | sodium: 655mg

Mediterranean Lentil Sloppy Joes

Prep time: 5 minutes |Cook time: 15 minutes| Serves: 4

1 tablespoon extra-virgin olive oil	sodium or no-salt-added diced tomatoes, undrained
1 cup chopped onion (about ½ medium onion)	1 teaspoon ground cumin
1 cup chopped bell pepper, any color (about 1 medium bell pepper)	1 teaspoon dried thyme
	¼ teaspoon kosher or sea salt
2 garlic cloves, minced (about 1 teaspoon)	4 whole-wheat pita breads, split open
1 (15-ounce / 425-g) can lentils, drained and rinsed	1½ cups chopped seedless cucumber (1 medium cucumber)
1 (14½-ounce / 411-g) can low-	1 cup chopped romaine lettuce

1. In a medium saucepan over medium-high heat, heat the oil. Add the onion and bell pepper and cook for 4 minutes, stirring frequently. Add the garlic and cook for 1 minute, stirring frequently. Add the lentils, tomatoes (with their liquid), cumin, thyme, and salt. Turn the heat to medium and cook, stirring occasionally, for 10 minutes, or until most of the liquid has evaporated. 2. Stuff the lentil mixture inside each pita. Lay the cucumbers and lettuce on top of the lentil mixture and serve.

Per Serving:

calories: 530 | fat: 6g | protein: 31g | carbs: 93g | fiber: 17g | sodium: 292mg

Green Veg & Macadamia Smash

Prep time: 25 minutes | Cook time: 15 minutes | Serves 6

⅔ cup macadamia nuts	2 cloves garlic, crushed
Enough water to cover and soak the macadamias	¼ cup extra-virgin olive oil
7 ounces (198 g) cavolo nero or kale, stalks removed and chopped	2 tablespoons fresh lemon juice
	4 medium spring onions, sliced
	¼ cup chopped fresh herbs, such as parsley, dill, basil, or mint
1 medium head broccoli, cut into florets, or broccolini	
Salt and black pepper, to taste	

1. Place the macadamias in a small bowl and add enough water to cover them. Soak for about 2 hours, then drain. Discard the water. 2. Fill a large pot with about 1½ cups (360 ml) of water, then insert a steamer colander. Bring to a boil over high heat, then reduce to medium-high. Add the cavolo nero and cook for 6 minutes. Add the broccoli and cook for 8 minutes or until fork-tender. Remove the lid, let the steam escape, and let cool slightly. 3. Place the cooked vegetables in a blender or a food processor. Add the soaked macadamias, garlic, olive oil, lemon juice, spring onions, and fresh herbs (you can reserve some for topping). 4. Process to the desired consistency (smooth or chunky). Season with salt and pepper to taste and serve. To store, let cool completely and store in a sealed container in the fridge for up to 5 days.

Per Serving:
calories: 250 | fat: 22g | protein: 5g | carbs: 12g | fiber: 5g | sodium: 44mg

Vegetable Terrine

Prep time: 30 minutes | Cook time: 5 to 7 hours | Serves 6

1 small eggplant, thinly sliced lengthwise	4 large tomatoes, sliced
	1 teaspoon sea salt
2 green bell peppers, halved, seeded, and sliced	¼ teaspoon freshly ground black pepper
2 red bell peppers, halved, seeded, and sliced	Nonstick cooking spray
1 portobello mushroom, cut into ¼-inch-thick slices	1 cup grated Parmesan cheese
	2 tablespoons extra-virgin olive oil
1 zucchini, thinly sliced lengthwise	1 tablespoon red wine vinegar
1 large red onion, cut into ¼-inch-thick rounds	2 teaspoons freshly squeezed lemon juice
	1 teaspoon dried basil
2 yellow squash, thinly sliced lengthwise	1 garlic clove, minced

1. Season the eggplant, green and red bell peppers, mushroom, zucchini, onion, squash, and tomatoes with salt and black pepper, but keep all the vegetables separate. 2. Generously coat a slow-cooker insert with cooking spray, or line the bottom and sides with parchment paper or aluminum foil. 3. Starting with half of the eggplant, line the bottom of the prepared slow cooker with overlapping slices. Sprinkle with 2 tablespoons of Parmesan cheese. 4. Add a second layer using half of the green and red bell peppers. Sprinkle with 2 more tablespoons of Parmesan cheese. 5. Add a third layer using half of the mushroom slices. Sprinkle with 2 more tablespoons of Parmesan cheese. 6. Add a fourth layer using half of the zucchini slices. Sprinkle with 2 more tablespoons of Parmesan cheese. 7. Add a fifth layer using half of the red onion slices. Sprinkle with another 2 tablespoons of Parmesan cheese. 8. Add a sixth layer using half of the yellow squash slices. Sprinkle with 2 more tablespoons of Parmesan cheese. 9. Add a final seventh layer with half of the tomato slices. Sprinkle with 2 more tablespoons of Parmesan cheese. 10. Repeat the layering with the remaining vegetables and Parmesan cheese in the same order until all of the vegetables have been used. 11. In a small bowl, whisk together the olive oil, vinegar, lemon juice, basil, and garlic until combined. Pour the mixture over the vegetables. Top with any remaining Parmesan cheese. 12. Cover the cooker and cook for 5 to 7 hours on Low heat. 13. Let cool to room temperature before slicing and serving.

Per Serving:
calories: 217 | fat: 11g | protein: 12g | carbs: 24g | fiber: 7g | sodium: 725mg

Roasted Brussels Sprouts with Orange and Garlic

Prep time: 5 minutes | Cook time: 10 minutes | Serves 4

1 pound (454 g) Brussels sprouts, quartered	2 tablespoons olive oil
	½ teaspoon salt
2 garlic cloves, minced	1 orange, cut into rings

1. Preheat the air fryer to 360°F(182ºC). 2. In a large bowl, toss the quartered Brussels sprouts with the garlic, olive oil, and salt until well coated. 3. Pour the Brussels sprouts into the air fryer, lay the orange slices on top of them, and roast for 10 minutes. 4. Remove from the air fryer and set the orange slices aside. Toss the Brussels sprouts before serving.

Per Serving:
calories: 127 | fat: 7g | protein: 4g | carbs: 15g | fiber: 5g | sodium: 319mg

Melitzanes Yiahni (Braised Eggplant)

Prep time: 15 minutes | Cook time: 30 minutes | Serves 6

2 large eggplants, cut into 1" pieces	minced
	2 cups diced fresh tomatoes
1¾ teaspoons salt, divided	1 cup water
3 tablespoons extra-virgin olive oil, divided	1 tablespoon dried oregano
	½ teaspoon ground black pepper
1 medium yellow onion, peeled and diced	2 tablespoons minced fresh basil
3 cloves garlic, peeled and	

1. Place eggplant in a colander and sprinkle with 1½ teaspoons salt. Place colander over a plate. Let stand 30 minutes to drain. 2. Press the Sauté button on the Instant Pot® and heat 2 tablespoons oil. Add onion and cook until soft, about 5 minutes. Add garlic and cook until fragrant, about 30 seconds. Add tomatoes and water. Press the Cancel button. 3. Rinse eggplant well and drain. Add to pot. Close lid, set steam release to Sealing, press the Manual button, and set time to 8 minutes. Once timer beeps, quick-release the pressure until the float valve drops, press the Cancel button, and open lid. Add oregano, pepper, and remaining ¼ teaspoon salt. 4. Add remaining 1 tablespoon oil to pot and stir well. Press the Sauté button and simmer for 15 minutes to thicken. Add basil and serve hot.

Per Serving:
calories: 121 | fat: 7g | protein: 2g | carbs: 14g | fiber: 7g | sodium: 107mg

Zucchini Fritters

Prep time: 10 minutes | Cook time: 10 minutes | Serves 4

2 zucchini, grated (about 1 pound / 454 g)	¼ teaspoon dried thyme
1 teaspoon salt	¼ teaspoon ground turmeric
¼ cup almond flour	¼ teaspoon freshly ground black pepper
¼ cup grated Parmesan cheese	1 tablespoon olive oil
1 large egg	½ lemon, sliced into wedges

1. Preheat the air fryer to 400°F (204°C). Cut a piece of parchment paper to fit slightly smaller than the bottom of the air fryer. 2. Place the zucchini in a large colander and sprinkle with the salt. Let sit for 5 to 10 minutes. Squeeze as much liquid as you can from the zucchini and place in a large mixing bowl. Add the almond flour, Parmesan, egg, thyme, turmeric, and black pepper. Stir gently until thoroughly combined. 3. Shape the mixture into 8 patties and arrange on the parchment paper. Brush lightly with the olive oil. Pausing halfway through the cooking time to turn the patties, air fry for 10 minutes until golden brown. Serve warm with the lemon wedges.

Per Serving:

calories: 78 | fat: 6g | protein: 4g | carbs: 2g | fiber: 0g | sodium: 712mg

Rosemary-Roasted Red Potatoes

Prep time: 5 minutes | Cook time: 20 minutes | Serves 6

1 pound (454 g) red potatoes, quartered	¼ teaspoon black pepper
¼ cup olive oil	1 garlic clove, minced
½ teaspoon kosher salt	4 rosemary sprigs

1. Preheat the air fryer to 360°F(182°C). 2. In a large bowl, toss the potatoes with the olive oil, salt, pepper, and garlic until well coated. 3. Pour the potatoes into the air fryer basket and top with the sprigs of rosemary. 4. Roast for 10 minutes, then stir or toss the potatoes and roast for 10 minutes more. 5. Remove the rosemary sprigs and serve the potatoes. Season with additional salt and pepper, if needed.

Per Serving:

calories: 134 | fat: 9g | protein: 1g | carbs: 12g | fiber: 1g | sodium: 208mg

Sautéed Fava Beans with Olive Oil, Garlic, and Chiles

Prep time: 10 minutes | Cook time: 7 minutes | Serves 4

3½ pounds (1.6 kg) fresh fava beans, shelled (4 cups)	zest
2 tablespoons olive oil	½ teaspoon crushed red pepper flakes
2 cloves garlic, minced	½ teaspoon salt
2 teaspoons fresh lemon juice	¼ teaspoon freshly ground black pepper
1 teaspoon finely grated lemon	

1. Bring a medium saucepan of lightly salted water to a boil. Add the shelled favas and cook for 3 to 4 minutes, until tender. Drain the favas and immediately place them in an ice water bath to stop their cooking. When cool, peel the tough outer skin off the beans. 2. Heat the olive oil in a large skillet over medium-high heat. Add the garlic and cook, stirring, until it is aromatic but not browned, about 30 seconds. Add the beans and cook, stirring, until heated through, about 2 minutes. Stir in the lemon juice, lemon zest, red pepper flakes, salt, and pepper and remove from the heat. Serve immediately.

Per Serving:

calories: 576 | fat: 9g | protein: 39g | carbs: 88g | fiber: 38g | sodium: 311mg

Spinach and Paneer Cheese

Prep time: 15 minutes | Cook time: 2 to 4 hours | Serves 6

2 pounds (907 g) fresh spinach	1 to 2 tablespoons cornstarch to thicken (if required)
1½-inch piece fresh ginger, roughly chopped	4 tablespoons butter
5 garlic cloves, whole	1 teaspoon cumin seeds
2 fresh green chiles, roughly chopped	3 garlic cloves, minced
1 onion, roughly chopped	1 tablespoon dried fenugreek leaves
1 teaspoon salt	2 tablespoons rapeseed oil
½ teaspoon turmeric	12 ounces (340 g) paneer, cut into cubes
4 tomatoes, finely chopped	

1. Heat the slow cooker to high and add the spinach, ginger, garlic, chiles, onion, salt, turmeric, and tomatoes. 2. Cover and cook on high for 3 hours, or on low for 6 hours. 3. Using your immersion blender or a food processor, purée the greens to a fine, glossy consistency. The aim is to have a thick and bright-green purée. If it's a little watery you may need to reduce it on the stove to thicken, or if your slow cooker has a boil function, use it to boil off a little of the liquid. You can also thicken it up by sprinkling with some cornstarch. 4. Heat the butter in a pan and add the cumin seeds until they sizzle. Then add the minced garlic and stir until it just browns. Remove from the heat. Add the dried fenugreek leaves and pour everything into the saag that's in the slow cooker. Whisk through. 5. Fry the cubes of paneer in a little oil in the same pan, until they are golden brown. Stir into the saag. Replace the lid and let everything sit for another 10 minutes before serving.

Per Serving:

calories: 252 | fat: 17g | protein: 10g | carbs: 20g | fiber: 6g | sodium: 682mg

Greek Fasolakia (Green Beans)

Prep time: 10 minutes | Cook time: 6 to 8 hours | Serves 6

2 pounds (907 g) green beans, trimmed	1 teaspoon dried dill
1 (15-ounce / 425-g) can no-salt-added diced tomatoes, with juice	1 teaspoon ground cumin
	1 teaspoon dried oregano
1 large onion, chopped	1 teaspoon sea salt
4 garlic cloves, chopped	½ teaspoon freshly ground black pepper
Juice of 1 lemon	¼ cup feta cheese, crumbled

1. In a slow cooker, combine the green beans, tomatoes and their juice, onion, garlic, lemon juice, dill, cumin, oregano, salt, and pepper. Stir to mix well. 2. Cover the cooker and cook for 6 to 8 hours on Low heat. 3. Top with feta cheese for serving.

Per Serving:

calories: 94 | fat: 2g | protein: 5g | carbs: 18g | fiber: 7g | sodium: 497mg

Corn Croquettes

Prep time: 10 minutes | Cook time: 12 to 14 minutes | Serves 4

½ cup leftover mashed potatoes	pepper
2 cups corn kernels (if frozen, thawed, and well drained)	¼ teaspoon salt
¼ teaspoon onion powder	½ cup panko bread crumbs
⅛ teaspoon ground black	Oil for misting or cooking spray

1. Place the potatoes and half the corn in food processor and pulse until corn is well chopped. 2. Transfer mixture to large bowl and stir in remaining corn, onion powder, pepper and salt. 3. Shape mixture into 16 balls. 4. Roll balls in panko crumbs, mist with oil or cooking spray, and place in air fryer basket. 5. Air fry at 360°F (182°C) for 12 to 14 minutes, until golden brown and crispy.

Per Serving:

calories: 149 | fat: 1g | protein: 5g | carbs: 33g | fiber: 3g | sodium: 250mg

Asparagus Fries

Prep time: 15 minutes | Cook time: 5 to 7 minutes per batch | Serves 4

12 ounces (340 g) fresh asparagus spears with tough ends trimmed off	¼ cup grated Parmesan cheese, plus 2 tablespoons
2 egg whites	¼ teaspoon salt
¼ cup water	Oil for misting or cooking spray
¾ cup panko bread crumbs	

1. Preheat the air fryer to 390°F (199°C). 2. In a shallow dish, beat egg whites and water until slightly foamy. 3. In another shallow dish, combine panko, Parmesan, and salt. 4. Dip asparagus spears in egg, then roll in crumbs. Spray with oil or cooking spray. 5. Place a layer of asparagus in air fryer basket, leaving just a little space in between each spear. Stack another layer on top, crosswise. Air fry at 390°F (199°C) for 5 to 7 minutes, until crispy and golden brown. 6. Repeat to cook remaining asparagus.

Per Serving:

calories: 132 | fat: 3g | protein: 8g | carbs: 19g | fiber: 3g | sodium: 436mg

Citrus-Roasted Broccoli Florets

Prep time: 5 minutes | Cook time: 12 minutes | Serves 6

4 cups broccoli florets (approximately 1 large head)	½ cup orange juice
2 tablespoons olive oil	1 tablespoon raw honey
½ teaspoon salt	Orange wedges, for serving (optional)

1. Preheat the air fryer to 360°F(182°C). 2. In a large bowl, combine the broccoli, olive oil, salt, orange juice, and honey. Toss the broccoli in the liquid until well coated. 3. Pour the broccoli mixture into the air fryer basket and roast for 6 minutes. Stir and roast for 6 minutes more. 4. Serve alone or with orange wedges for additional citrus flavor, if desired.

Per Serving:

calories: 73 | fat: 5g | protein: 2g | carbs: 8g | fiber: 0g | sodium: 207mg

Saffron Couscous with Almonds, Currants, and Scallions

Prep time: 5 minutes | Cook time: 35 minutes | Serves 8

2 cups whole wheat couscous	3 cups low-sodium chicken broth or vegetable broth
1 tablespoon olive oil	½ cup slivered almonds
5 scallions, thinly sliced, whites and greens kept separate	¼ cup dried currants
1 large pinch saffron threads, crumbled	Kosher salt and ground black pepper, to taste

1. In a medium saucepan over medium heat, toast the couscous, stirring occasionally, until lightly browned, about 5 minutes. Transfer to a bowl. 2. In the same saucepan, add the oil and scallion whites. Cook, stirring, until lightly browned, about 5 minutes. Sprinkle in the saffron and stir to combine. Pour in the broth and bring to a boil. 3. Remove the saucepan from the heat, stir in the couscous, cover, and let sit until all the liquid is absorbed and the couscous is tender, about 15 minutes. 4. Fluff the couscous with a fork. Fluff in the scallion greens, almonds, and currants. Season to taste with the salt and pepper.

Per Serving:

calories: 212 | fat: 6g | protein: 8g | carbs: 34g | fiber: 4g | sodium: 148mg

Caesar Whole Cauliflower

Prep time: 20 minutes | Cook time: 30 minutes | Serves 2 to 4

3 tablespoons olive oil	
2 tablespoons red wine vinegar	Kosher salt and freshly ground black pepper, to taste
2 tablespoons Worcestershire sauce	1 small head cauliflower (about 1 pound / 454 g), green leaves trimmed and stem trimmed flush with the bottom of the head
2 tablespoons grated Parmesan cheese	
1 tablespoon Dijon mustard	
4 garlic cloves, minced	
4 oil-packed anchovy fillets, drained and finely minced	1 tablespoon roughly chopped fresh flat-leaf parsley (optional)

1. In a liquid measuring cup, whisk together the olive oil, vinegar, Worcestershire, Parmesan, mustard, garlic, anchovies, and salt and pepper to taste. Place the cauliflower head upside down on a cutting board and use a paring knife to make an "x" through the full length of the core. Transfer the cauliflower head to a large bowl and pour half the dressing over it. Turn the cauliflower head to coat it in the dressing, then let it rest, stem-side up, in the dressing for at least 10 minutes and up to 30 minutes to allow the dressing to seep into all its nooks and crannies. 2. Transfer the cauliflower head, stem-side down, to the air fryer and air fry at 340°F (171°C) for 25 minutes. Drizzle the remaining dressing over the cauliflower and air fry at 400°F (204°C) until the top of the cauliflower is golden brown and the core is tender, about 5 minutes more. 3. Remove the basket from the air fryer and transfer the cauliflower to a large plate. Sprinkle with the parsley, if you like, and serve hot.

Per Serving:

calories: 187 | fat: 15g | protein: 5g | carbs: 9g | fiber: 2g | sodium: 453mg

Dinner Rolls

Prep time: 10 minutes | Cook time: 12 minutes | Serves 6

1 cup shredded Mozzarella cheese	almond flour
1 ounce (28 g) full-fat cream cheese	¼ cup ground flaxseed
	½ teaspoon baking powder
1 cup blanched finely ground	1 large egg

1. Place Mozzarella, cream cheese, and almond flour in a large microwave-safe bowl. Microwave for 1 minute. Mix until smooth. 2. Add flaxseed, baking powder, and egg until fully combined and smooth. Microwave an additional 15 seconds if it becomes too firm. 3. Separate the dough into six pieces and roll into balls. Place the balls into the air fryer basket. 4. Adjust the temperature to 320ºF (160ºC) and air fry for 12 minutes. 5. Allow rolls to cool completely before serving.

Per Serving:
calories: 223 | fat: 17g | protein: 13g | carbs: 7g | fiber: 4g | sodium: 175mg

Fried Zucchini Salad

Prep time: 10 minutes | Cook time: 5 to 7 minutes | Serves 4

2 medium zucchini, thinly sliced	Zest and juice of ½ lemon
5 tablespoons olive oil, divided	1 clove garlic, minced
¼ cup chopped fresh parsley	¼ cup crumbled feta cheese
2 tablespoons chopped fresh mint	Freshly ground black pepper, to taste

1. Preheat the air fryer to 400ºF (204ºC). 2. In a large bowl, toss the zucchini slices with 1 tablespoon of the olive oil. 3. Working in batches if necessary, arrange the zucchini slices in an even layer in the air fryer basket. Pausing halfway through the cooking time to shake the basket, air fry for 5 to 7 minutes until soft and lightly browned on each side. 4. Meanwhile, in a small bowl, combine the remaining 4 tablespoons olive oil, parsley, mint, lemon zest, lemon juice, and garlic. 5. Arrange the zucchini on a plate and drizzle with the dressing. Sprinkle the feta and black pepper on top. Serve warm or at room temperature.

Per Serving:
calories: 194 | fat: 19g | protein: 3g | carbs: 4g | fiber: 1g | sodium: 96mg

Root Vegetable Hash

Prep time: 20 minutes | Cook time: 8 hours | Makes 9 (¾-cup) servings

4 carrots, peeled and cut into 1-inch cubes	⅛ teaspoon freshly ground black pepper
3 large russet potatoes, peeled and cut into 1-inch cubes	½ teaspoon dried thyme leaves
1 onion, diced	1 sprig rosemary
3 garlic cloves, minced	½ cup vegetable broth
½ teaspoon salt	3 plums, cut into 1-inch pieces

1. In the slow cooker, combine the carrots, potatoes, onion, and garlic. Sprinkle with the salt, pepper, and thyme, and stir. 2. Imbed the rosemary sprig in the vegetables. 3. Pour the broth over everything. 4. Cover and cook on low for 7½ hours, or until the vegetables are tender. 5. Stir in the plums, cover, and cook on low for 30 minutes, until tender. 6. Remove and discard the rosemary sprig, and serve.

Per Serving:
calories: 137 | fat: 0g | protein: 3g | carbs: 32g | fiber: 4g | sodium: 204mg

Braised Radishes with Sugar Snap Peas and Dukkah

Prep time: 20 minutes | Cook time: 5 minutes | Serves 4

¼ cup extra-virgin olive oil, divided	peas, strings removed, sliced thin on bias
1 shallot, sliced thin	8 ounces (227 g) cremini mushrooms, trimmed and sliced thin
3 garlic cloves, sliced thin	
1½ pounds (680 g) radishes, 2 cups greens reserved, radishes trimmed and halved if small or quartered if large	2 teaspoons grated lemon zest plus 1 teaspoon juice
	1 cup plain Greek yogurt
½ cup water	½ cup fresh cilantro leaves
½ teaspoon table salt	3 tablespoons dukkah
8 ounces (227 g) sugar snap	

1. Using highest sauté function, heat 2 tablespoons oil in Instant Pot until shimmering. Add shallot and cook until softened, about 2 minutes. Stir in garlic and cook until fragrant, about 30 seconds. Stir in radishes, water, and salt. Lock lid in place and close pressure release valve. Select high pressure cook function and cook for 1 minute. 2. Turn off Instant Pot and quick-release pressure. Carefully remove lid, allowing steam to escape away from you. Stir in snap peas, cover, and let sit until heated through, about 3 minutes. Add radish greens, mushrooms, lemon zest and juice, and remaining 2 tablespoons oil and gently toss to combine. Season with salt and pepper to taste. 3. Spread ¼ cup yogurt over bottom of 4 individual serving plates. Using slotted spoon, arrange vegetable mixture on top and sprinkle with cilantro and dukkah. Serve.

Per Serving:
calories: 310 | fat: 23g | protein: 10g | carbs: 17g | fiber: 5g | sodium: 320mg

Crispy Lemon Artichoke Hearts

Prep time: 10 minutes | Cook time: 15 minutes | Serves 2

1 (15-ounce / 425-g) can artichoke hearts in water, drained	¼ cup whole wheat bread crumbs
1 egg	¼ teaspoon salt
1 tablespoon water	¼ teaspoon paprika
	½ lemon

1. Preheat the air fryer to 380°F(193ºC). 2. In a medium shallow bowl, beat together the egg and water until frothy. 3. In a separate medium shallow bowl, mix together the bread crumbs, salt, and paprika. 4. Dip each artichoke heart into the egg mixture, then into the bread crumb mixture, coating the outside with the crumbs. Place the artichokes hearts in a single layer of the air fryer basket. 5. Fry the artichoke hearts for 15 minutes. 6. Remove the artichokes from the air fryer, and squeeze fresh lemon juice over the top before serving.

Per Serving:
calories: 190 | fat: 3g | protein: 12g | carbs: 34g | fiber: 13g | sodium: 621mg

Mediterranean Zucchini Boats

Prep time: 5 minutes | Cook time: 10 minutes | Serves 4

1 large zucchini, ends removed, halved lengthwise	¼ cup feta cheese
6 grape tomatoes, quartered	1 tablespoon balsamic vinegar
¼ teaspoon salt	1 tablespoon olive oil

1. Use a spoon to scoop out 2 tablespoons from center of each zucchini half, making just enough space to fill with tomatoes and feta. 2. Place tomatoes evenly in centers of zucchini halves and sprinkle with salt. Place into ungreased air fryer basket. Adjust the temperature to 350ºF (177ºC) and roast for 10 minutes. When done, zucchini will be tender. 3. Transfer boats to a serving tray and sprinkle with feta, then drizzle with vinegar and olive oil. Serve warm.

Per Serving:
calories: 92 | fat: 6g | protein: 3g | carbs: 8g | fiber: 2g | sodium: 242mg

White Beans with Rosemary, Sage, and Garlic

Prep time: 10 minutes | Cook time: 10 minutes | Serves 2

1 tablespoon olive oil	1 teaspoon minced fresh rosemary (from 1 sprig) plus 1 whole fresh rosemary sprig
2 garlic cloves, minced	
1 (15-ounce / 425-g) can white cannellini beans, drained and rinsed	½ cup low-sodium chicken stock
¼ teaspoon dried sage	Salt

1. Heat the olive oil in a sauté pan over medium-high heat. Add the garlic and sauté for 30 seconds. 2. Add the beans, sage, minced and whole rosemary, and chicken stock and bring the mixture to a boil. 3. Reduce the heat to medium and simmer the beans for 10 minutes, or until most of the liquid is evaporated. If desired, mash some of the beans with a fork to thicken them. 4. Season with salt. Remove the rosemary sprig before serving

Per Serving:
calories: 155 | fat: 7g | protein: 6g | carbs: 17g | fiber: 8g | sodium: 153mg

Braised Greens with Olives and Walnuts

Prep time: 5 minutes | Cook time: 20 minutes | Serves 4

8 cups fresh greens (such as kale, mustard greens, spinach, or chard)	½ cup roughly chopped shelled walnuts
2 to 4 garlic cloves, finely minced	¼ cup extra-virgin olive oil
	2 tablespoons red wine vinegar
½ cup roughly chopped pitted green or black olives	1 to 2 teaspoons freshly chopped herbs such as oregano, basil, rosemary, or thyme

1. Remove the tough stems from the greens and chop into bite-size pieces. Place in a large rimmed skillet or pot. 2. Turn the heat to high and add the minced garlic and enough water to just cover the greens. Bring to a boil, reduce the heat to low, and simmer until the greens are wilted and tender and most of the liquid has evaporated, adding more if the greens start to burn. For more tender greens such as spinach, this may only take 5 minutes, while tougher greens such as chard may need up to 20 minutes. Once cooked, remove from the heat and add the chopped olives and walnuts. 3. In a small bowl, whisk together olive oil, vinegar, and herbs. Drizzle over the cooked greens and toss to coat. Serve warm.

Per Serving:
calories: 254 | fat: 25g | protein: 4g | carbs: 6g | fiber: 3g | sodium: 137mg

Superflax Tortillas

Prep time: 5 minutes | Cook time: 10 minutes | Serves 6

1 packed cup flax meal	1 teaspoon salt, or to taste
⅓ cup coconut flour	1 cup lukewarm water
¼ cup ground chia seeds	2 tablespoons extra-virgin avocado oil or ghee
2 tablespoons whole psyllium husks	

1. Place all the dry ingredients in a bowl and mix to combine. (For ground chia seeds, simply place whole seeds into a coffee grinder or food processor and pulse until smooth.) Add the water and mix until well combined. Place the dough in the refrigerator to rest for about 30 minutes. 2. When ready, remove the dough from the fridge and cut it into 4 equal pieces. You will make the remaining 2 tortillas using the excess dough. Place one piece of dough between two pieces of parchment paper and roll it out until very thin. Alternatively, use a silicone roller and a silicone mat. Remove the top piece of parchment paper. Press a large 8-inch (20 cm) lid into the dough (or use a piece of parchment paper cut into a circle of the same size). Press the lid into the dough or trace around it with your knife to cut out the tortilla. 3. Repeat for the remaining pieces of dough. Add the cut-off excess dough to the last piece and create the remaining 2 tortillas from it. If you have any dough left over, simply roll it out and cut it into tortilla-chip shapes. 4. Grease a large pan with the avocado oil and cook 1 tortilla at a time for 2 to 3 minutes on each side over medium heat until lightly browned. Don't overcook: the tortillas should be flexible, not too crispy. 5. Once cool, store the tortillas in a sealed container for up to 1 week and reheat them in a dry pan, if needed.

Per Serving:
calories: 182 | fat: 16g | protein: 4g | carbs: 8g | fiber: 7g | sodium: 396mg

Kohlrabi Fries

Prep time: 10 minutes | Cook time: 20 to 30 minutes | Serves 4

2 pounds (907 g) kohlrabi, peeled and cut into ¼ to ½-inch fries	2 tablespoons olive oil
	Salt and freshly ground black pepper, to taste

1. Preheat the air fryer to 400ºF (204ºC). 2. In a large bowl, combine the kohlrabi and olive oil. Season to taste with salt and black pepper. Toss gently until thoroughly coated. 3. Working in batches if necessary, spread the kohlrabi in a single layer in the air fryer basket. Pausing halfway through the cooking time to shake the basket, air fry for 20 to 30 minutes until the fries are lightly browned and crunchy.

Per Serving:
calories: 121 | fat: 7g | protein: 4g | carbs: 14g | fiber: 8g | sodium: 45mg

Mushroom-Stuffed Zucchini

Prep time: 15 minutes | Cook time: 46 minutes | Serves 2

2 tablespoons olive oil
2 cups button mushrooms, **finely** chopped
2 cloves garlic, finely chopped
2 tablespoons chicken broth

1 tablespoon flat-leaf parsley, finely chopped
1 tablespoon Italian seasoning
Sea salt and freshly ground pepper, to taste
2 medium zucchini, cut in half lengthwise

1. Preheat oven to 350°F (180°C). 2. Heat a large skillet over medium heat, and add the olive oil. Add the mushrooms and cook until tender, about 4 minutes. Add the **garlic and** cook for 2 more minutes. 3. Add the chicken broth and cook another 3–4 minutes. 4. Add the parsley and Italian seasoning, and season **with** sea salt and freshly ground pepper. 5. Stir and remove from heat. 6. Scoop out the insides of the halved zucchini and stuff with **mushroom** mixture. 7. Place zucchini in a casserole dish, and drizzle a tablespoon of water or broth in the bottom. 8. Cover with foil and bake for **30–40** minutes until zucchini are tender. Serve immediately.

Per Serving:
calories: 189 | fat: 14g | protein: 5g | carbs: 12g | fiber: 3g | sodium: 335mg

Chapter 8

Vegetarian Mains

Roasted Ratatouille Pasta

Prep time: 10 minutes | Cook time: 20 minutes | Serves 2

1 small eggplant (about 8 ounces / 227 g)	1 teaspoon Italian herb seasoning
1 small zucchini	1 tablespoon olive oil
1 portobello mushroom	2 cups farfalle pasta (about 8 ounces / 227 g)
1 Roma tomato, halved	
½ medium sweet red pepper, seeded	2 tablespoons minced sun-dried tomatoes in olive oil with herbs
½ teaspoon salt, plus additional for the pasta water	2 tablespoons prepared pesto

1. Slice the ends off the eggplant and zucchini. Cut them lengthwise into ½-inch slices. 2. Place the eggplant, zucchini, mushroom, tomato, and red pepper in a large bowl and sprinkle with ½ teaspoon of salt. Using your hands, toss the vegetables well so that they're covered evenly with the salt. Let them rest for about 10 minutes. 3. While the vegetables are resting, preheat the oven to 400°F (205°C) and set the rack to the bottom position. Line a baking sheet with parchment paper. 4. When the oven is hot, drain off any liquid from the vegetables and pat them dry with a paper towel. Add the Italian herb seasoning and olive oil to the vegetables and toss well to coat both sides. 5. Lay the vegetables out in a single layer on the baking sheet. Roast them for 15 to 20 minutes, flipping them over after about 10 minutes or once they start to brown on the underside. When the vegetables are charred in spots, remove them from the oven. 6. While the vegetables are roasting, fill a large saucepan with water. Add salt and cook the pasta according to package directions. Drain the pasta, reserving ½ cup of the pasta water. 7. When cool enough to handle, cut the vegetables into large chunks (about 2 inches) and add them to the hot pasta. 8. Stir in the sun-dried tomatoes and pesto and toss everything well.

Per Serving:

calories: 612 | fat: 16g | protein: 23g | carbs: 110g | fiber: 23g | sodium: 776mg

Orzo-Stuffed Tomatoes

Prep time: 15 minutes | Cook time: 30 minutes | Serves 2

1 tablespoon olive oil	to package instructions, or precooked)
1 small zucchini, minced	
½ medium onion, minced	½ teaspoon salt
1 garlic clove, minced	2 teaspoons dried oregano
⅔ cup cooked orzo (from ¼ cup dry orzo, cooked according	6 medium round tomatoes (not Roma)

1. Preheat the oven to 350°F (180°C). 2. Heat the olive oil in a large sauté pan over medium-high heat. Add the zucchini, onion, and garlic and sauté for 15 minutes, or until the vegetables turn golden. 3. Add the orzo, salt, and oregano and stir to heat through. Remove the pan from the heat and set aside. 4. Cut about ½ inch from the top of each tomato. With a paring knife, cut around the inner core of the tomato to remove about half of the flesh. Reserve for another recipe or a salad. 5. Stuff each tomato with the orzo mixture. 6. If serving hot, put the tomatoes in a baking dish, or, if they'll fit, a muffin tin. Roast the tomatoes for about 15 minutes, or until they're soft. Don't overcook them or they won't hold together. If desired, this can also be served without roasting the tomatoes.

Per Serving:

calories: 241 | fat: 8g | protein: 7g | carbs: 38g | fiber: 6g | sodium: 301mg

Balsamic Marinated Tofu with Basil and Oregano

Prep time: 10 minutes | Cook time: 30 minutes | Serves 4

¼ cup extra-virgin olive oil	1 teaspoon dried oregano
¼ cup balsamic vinegar	½ teaspoon dried thyme
2 tablespoons low-sodium soy sauce or gluten-free tamari	½ teaspoon dried sage
	¼ teaspoon kosher salt
3 garlic cloves, grated	¼ teaspoon freshly ground black pepper
2 teaspoons pure maple syrup	
Zest of 1 lemon	¼ teaspoon red pepper flakes (optional)
1 teaspoon dried basil	1 (16-ounce / 454-g) block extra firm tofu, drained and patted dry, cut into ½-inch or 1-inch cubes

1. In a bowl or gallon zip-top bag, mix together the olive oil, vinegar, soy sauce, garlic, maple syrup, lemon zest, basil, oregano, thyme, sage, salt, black pepper, and red pepper flakes, if desired. Add the tofu and mix gently. Put in the refrigerator and marinate for 30 minutes, or up to overnight if you desire. 2. Preheat the oven to 425°F (220°C). Line a baking sheet with parchment paper or foil. Arrange the marinated tofu in a single layer on the prepared baking sheet. Bake for 20 to 30 minutes, turning over halfway through, until slightly crispy on the outside and tender on the inside.

Per Serving:

calories: 225 | fat: 16g | protein: 13g | carbs: 9g | fiber: 2g | sodium: 265mg

Greek Frittata with Tomato-Olive Salad

Prep time: 10 minutes | Cook time: 25 minutes | Serves 4 to 6

Frittata:

2 tablespoons olive oil	2 tablespoons olive oil
6 scallions, thinly sliced	1 tablespoon lemon juice
4 cups (about 5 ounces / 142 g) baby spinach leaves	¼ teaspoon dried oregano
	½ teaspoon salt
8 eggs	¼ teaspoon freshly ground black pepper
¼ cup whole-wheat breadcrumbs, divided	
1 cup (about 3 ounces / 85 g) crumbled feta cheese	1 pint cherry, grape, or other small tomatoes, halved
¾ teaspoon salt	3 pepperoncini, stemmed and chopped
¼ teaspoon freshly ground black pepper	½ cup coarsely chopped pitted Kalamata olives
Tomato-Olive Salad:	

1. Preheat the oven to 450°F (235°C). 2. Heat the olive oil in an oven-safe skillet set over medium-high heat. Add the scallions and spinach and cook, stirring frequently, for about 4 minutes, until the spinach wilts. 3. In a medium bowl, whisk together the eggs, 2 tablespoons breadcrumbs, cheese, ¾ cup water, salt, and pepper. Pour the egg mixture into the skillet with the spinach and onions and stir to mix. Sprinkle the remaining 2 tablespoons of breadcrumbs evenly over the top. Bake the frittata in the preheated oven for about 20 minutes, until the egg is set and the top is lightly browned. 4. While the frittata is cooking, make the salad. In a medium bowl, whisk together the olive oil, lemon juice, oregano, salt, and pepper. Add the tomatoes, pepperoncini, and olives and toss to mix well. 5. Invert the frittata onto a serving platter and slice it into wedges. Serve warm or at room temperature with the tomato-olive salad.

Per Serving:

calories: 246 | fat: 19g | protein: 11g | carbs: 8g | fiber: 1g | sodium: 832mg

Broccoli-Cheese Fritters

Prep time: 5 minutes | Cook time: 20 to 25 minutes | Serves 4

1 cup broccoli florets	1 teaspoon garlic powder
1 cup shredded Mozzarella cheese	Salt and freshly ground black pepper, to taste
¾ cup almond flour	2 eggs, lightly beaten
½ cup flaxseed meal, divided	½ cup ranch dressing
2 teaspoons baking powder	

1. Preheat the air fryer to 400°F (204°C). 2. In a food processor fitted with a metal blade, pulse the broccoli until very finely chopped. 3. Transfer the broccoli to a large bowl and add the Mozzarella, almond flour, ¼ cup of the flaxseed meal, baking powder, and garlic powder. Stir until thoroughly combined. Season to taste with salt and black pepper. Add the eggs and stir again to form a sticky dough. Shape the dough into 1¼-inch fritters. 4. Place the remaining ¼ cup flaxseed meal in a shallow bowl and roll the fritters in the meal to form an even coating. 5. Working in batches if necessary, arrange the fritters in a single layer in the basket of the air fryer and spray generously with olive oil. Pausing halfway through the cooking time to shake the basket, air fry for 20 to 25 minutes until the fritters are golden brown and crispy. Serve with the ranch dressing for dipping.

Per Serving:

calories: 388 | fat: 30g | protein: 19g | carbs: 14g | fiber: 7g | sodium: 526mg

Quinoa with Almonds and Cranberries

Prep time: 15 minutes | Cook time: 0 minutes | Serves 4

2 cups cooked quinoa	½ teaspoon ground cumin
⅓ teaspoon cranberries or currants	½ teaspoon turmeric
¼ cup sliced almonds	¼ teaspoon ground cinnamon
2 garlic cloves, minced	¼ teaspoon freshly ground black pepper
1¼ teaspoons salt	

1. In a large bowl, toss the quinoa, cranberries, almonds, garlic, salt, cumin, turmeric, cinnamon, and pepper and stir to combine. Enjoy alone or with roasted cauliflower.

Per Serving:

calories: 194 | fat: 6g | protein: 7g | carbs: 31g | fiber: 4g | sodium: 727mg

Herbed Ricotta–Stuffed Mushrooms

Prep time: 10 minutes | Cook time: 30 minutes | Serves 4

6 tablespoons extra-virgin olive oil, divided	(such as basil, parsley, rosemary, oregano, or thyme)
4 portobello mushroom caps, cleaned and gills removed	2 garlic cloves, finely minced
1 cup whole-milk ricotta cheese	½ teaspoon salt
⅓ cup chopped fresh herbs	¼ teaspoon freshly ground black pepper

1. Preheat the oven to 400°F (205°C). 2. Line a baking sheet with parchment or foil and drizzle with 2 tablespoons olive oil, spreading evenly. Place the mushroom caps on the baking sheet, gill-side up. 3. In a medium bowl, mix together the ricotta, herbs, 2 tablespoons olive oil, garlic, salt, and pepper. Stuff each mushroom cap with one-quarter of the cheese mixture, pressing down if needed. Drizzle with remaining 2 tablespoons olive oil and bake until golden brown and the mushrooms are soft, 30 to 35 minutes, depending on the size of the mushrooms.

Per Serving:

calories: 308 | fat: 29g | protein: 9g | carbs: 6g | fiber: 1g | sodium: 351mg

Moroccan Vegetable Tagine

Prep time: 20 minutes | Cook time: 1 hour | Serves 6

½ cup extra-virgin olive oil	2 medium zucchini, cut into ½-inch-thick semicircles
2 medium yellow onions, sliced	2 cups cauliflower florets
6 celery stalks, sliced into ¼-inch crescents	1 (13¾-ounce / 390-g) can artichoke hearts, drained and quartered
6 garlic cloves, minced	1 cup halved and pitted green olives
1 teaspoon ground cumin	
1 teaspoon ginger powder	½ cup chopped fresh flat-leaf parsley, for garnish
1 teaspoon salt	
½ teaspoon paprika	½ cup chopped fresh cilantro leaves, for garnish
½ teaspoon ground cinnamon	
¼ teaspoon freshly ground black pepper	Greek yogurt, for garnish (optional)
2 cups vegetable stock	
1 medium eggplant, cut into 1-inch cubes	

1. In a large, thick soup pot or Dutch oven, heat the olive oil over medium-high heat. Add the onion and celery and sauté until softened, 6 to 8 minutes. Add the garlic, cumin, ginger, salt, paprika, cinnamon, and pepper and sauté for another 2 minutes. 2. Add the stock and bring to a boil. Reduce the heat to low and add the eggplant, zucchini, and cauliflower. Simmer on low heat, covered, until the vegetables are tender, 30 to 35 minutes. Add the artichoke hearts and olives, cover, and simmer for another 15 minutes. 3. Serve garnished with parsley, cilantro, and Greek yogurt (if using).

Per Serving:

calories: 265 | fat: 21g | protein: 5g | carbs: 19g | fiber: 9g | sodium: 858mg

Pesto Spinach Flatbread

Prep time: 10 minutes | Cook time: 8 minutes | Serves 4

1 cup blanched finely ground almond flour	cheese
2 ounces (57 g) cream cheese	1 cup chopped fresh spinach leaves
2 cups shredded Mozzarella	2 tablespoons basil pesto

1. Place flour, cream cheese, and Mozzarella in a large microwave-safe bowl and microwave on high 45 seconds, then stir. 2. Fold in spinach and microwave an additional 15 seconds. Stir until a soft dough ball forms. 3. Cut two pieces of parchment paper to fit air fryer basket. Separate dough into two sections and press each out on ungreased parchment to create 6-inch rounds. 4. Spread 1 tablespoon pesto over each flatbread and place rounds on parchment into ungreased air fryer basket. Adjust the temperature to 350°F (177°C) and air fry for 8 minutes, turning crusts halfway through cooking. Flatbread will be golden when done. 5. Let cool 5 minutes before slicing and serving.

Per Serving:

calories: 387 | fat: 28g | protein: 28g | carbs: 10g | fiber: 5g | sodium: 556mg

Pistachio Mint Pesto Pasta

Prep time: 10 minutes | Cook time: 10 minutes | Serves 4

8 ounces (227 g) whole-wheat pasta	shelled
1 cup fresh mint	1 garlic clove, peeled
½ cup fresh basil	½ teaspoon kosher salt
⅓ cup unsalted pistachios,	Juice of ½ lime
	⅓ cup extra-virgin olive oil

1. Cook the pasta according to the package directions. Drain, reserving ½ cup of the pasta water, and set aside. 2. In a food processor, add the mint, basil, pistachios, garlic, salt, and lime juice. Process until the pistachios are coarsely ground. Add the olive oil in a slow, steady stream and process until incorporated. 3. In a large bowl, mix the pasta with the pistachio pesto; toss well to incorporate. If a thinner, more saucy consistency is desired, add some of the reserved pasta water and toss well.

Per Serving:
calories: 420 | fat: 3g | protein: 11g | carbs: 48g | fiber: 2g | sodium: 150mg

Eggplant Parmesan

Prep time: 15 minutes | Cook time: 17 minutes | Serves 4

1 medium eggplant, ends trimmed, sliced into ½-inch rounds	1 ounce (28 g) 100% cheese crisps, finely crushed
¼ teaspoon salt	½ cup low-carb marinara sauce
2 tablespoons coconut oil	½ cup shredded Mozzarella cheese
½ cup grated Parmesan cheese	

1. Sprinkle eggplant rounds with salt on both sides and wrap in a kitchen towel for 30 minutes. Press to remove excess water, then drizzle rounds with coconut oil on both sides. 2. In a medium bowl, mix Parmesan and cheese crisps. Press each eggplant slice into mixture to coat both sides. 3. Place rounds into ungreased air fryer basket. Adjust the temperature to 350°F (177°C) and air fry for 15 minutes, turning rounds halfway through cooking. They will be crispy around the edges when done. 4. Spoon marinara over rounds and sprinkle with Mozzarella. Continue cooking an additional 2 minutes at 350°F (177°C) until cheese is melted. Serve warm.

Per Serving:
calories: 208 | fat: 13g | protein: 12g | carbs: 13g | fiber: 5g | sodium: 531mg

Freekeh, Chickpea, and Herb Salad

Prep time: 15 minutes | Cook time: 10 minutes | Serves 4 to 6

1 (15-ounce / 425-g) can chickpeas, rinsed and drained	3 tablespoons chopped celery leaves
1 cup cooked freekeh	½ teaspoon kosher salt
1 cup thinly sliced celery	⅓ cup extra-virgin olive oil
1 bunch scallions, both white and green parts, finely chopped	¼ cup freshly squeezed lemon juice
½ cup chopped fresh flat-leaf parsley	¼ teaspoon cumin seeds
¼ cup chopped fresh mint	1 teaspoon garlic powder

1. In a large bowl, combine the chickpeas, freekeh, celery, scallions, parsley, mint, celery leaves, and salt and toss lightly. 2. In a small bowl, whisk together the olive oil, lemon juice, cumin seeds, and garlic powder. Once combined, add to freekeh salad.

Per Serving:
calories: 350 | fat: 19g | protein: 9g | carbs: 38g | fiber: 9g | sodium: 329mg

Turkish Red Lentil and Bulgur Kofte

Prep time: 10 minutes | Cook time: 45 minutes | Serves 4

⅓ cup olive oil, plus 2 tablespoons, divided, plus more for brushing	2 tablespoons tomato paste
1 cup red lentils	1 teaspoon ground cumin
½ cup bulgur	¼ cup finely chopped flat-leaf parsley
1 teaspoon salt	3 scallions, thinly sliced
1 medium onion, finely diced	Juice of ½ lemon

1. Preheat the oven to 400°F(205°C). 2. Brush a large, rimmed baking sheet with olive oil. 3. In a medium saucepan, combine the lentils with 2 cups water and bring to a boil. Reduce the heat to low and cook, stirring occasionally, for about 15 minutes, until the lentils are tender and have soaked up most of the liquid. Remove from the heat, stir in the bulgur and salt, cover, and let sit for 15 minutes or so, until the bulgur is tender. 4. Meanwhile, heat ⅓ cup olive oil in a medium skillet over medium-high heat. Add the onion and cook, stirring frequently, until softened, about 5 minutes. Stir in the tomato paste and cook for 2 minutes more. Remove from the heat and stir in the cumin. 5. Add the cooked onion mixture to the lentil-bulgur mixture and stir to combine. Add the parsley, scallions, and lemon juice and stir to mix well. 6. Shape the mixture into walnut-sized balls and place them on the prepared baking sheet. Brush the balls with the remaining 2 tablespoons of olive oil and bake for 15 to 20 minutes, until golden brown. Serve hot.

Per Serving:
calories: 460 | fat: 25g | protein: 16g | carbs: 48g | fiber: 19g | sodium: 604mg

Mozzarella and Sun-Dried Portobello Mushroom Pizza

Prep time: 10 minutes | Cook time: 10 minutes | Serves 4

4 large portobello mushroom caps	4 sun-dried tomatoes
3 tablespoons extra-virgin olive oil	1 cup mozzarella cheese, divided
Salt	½ to ¾ cup low-sodium tomato sauce
Freshly ground black pepper	

1. Preheat the broiler on high. 2. On a baking sheet, drizzle the mushroom caps with the olive oil and season with salt and pepper. Broil the portobello mushrooms for 5 minutes on each side, flipping once, until tender. 3. Fill each mushroom cap with 1 sun-dried tomato, 2 tablespoons of cheese, and 2 to 3 tablespoons of sauce. Top each with 2 tablespoons of cheese. Place the caps back under the broiler for a final 2 to 3 minutes, then quarter the mushrooms and serve.

Per Serving:
calories: 218| fat: 16g | protein: 11g | carbs: 12g | fiber: 2g | sodium: 244mg

Parmesan Artichokes

Prep time: 10 minutes | Cook time: 10 minutes | Serves 4

2 medium artichokes, trimmed and quartered, center removed	Parmesan cheese
2 tablespoons coconut oil	¼ cup blanched finely ground almond flour
1 large egg, beaten	½ teaspoon crushed red pepper flakes
½ cup grated vegetarian	

1. In a large bowl, toss artichokes in coconut oil and then dip each piece into the egg. 2. Mix the Parmesan and almond flour in a large bowl. Add artichoke pieces and toss to cover as completely as possible, sprinkle with pepper flakes. Place into the air fryer basket. 3. Adjust the temperature to 400ºF (204ºC) and air fry for 10 minutes. 4. Toss the basket two times during cooking. Serve warm.

Per Serving:
calories: 207 | fat: 13g | protein: 10g | carbs: 15g | fiber: 5g | sodium: 211mg

Cauliflower Rice-Stuffed Peppers

Prep time: 10 minutes | Cook time: 15 minutes | Serves 4

2 cups uncooked cauliflower rice	cheese
¾ cup drained canned petite diced tomatoes	¼ teaspoon salt
	¼ teaspoon ground black pepper
2 tablespoons olive oil	4 medium green bell peppers, tops removed, seeded
1 cup shredded Mozzarella	

1. In a large bowl, mix all ingredients except bell peppers. Scoop mixture evenly into peppers. 2. Place peppers into ungreased air fryer basket. Adjust the temperature to 350ºF (177ºC) and air fry for 15 minutes. Peppers will be tender and cheese will be melted when done. Serve warm.

Per Serving:
calories: 144 | fat: 7g | protein: 11g | carbs: 11g | fiber: 5g | sodium: 380mg

Stuffed Portobellos

Prep time: 10 minutes | Cook time: 8 minutes | Serves 4

3 ounces (85 g) cream cheese, softened	leaves
½ medium zucchini, trimmed and chopped	4 large portobello mushrooms, stems removed
¼ cup seeded and chopped red bell pepper	2 tablespoons coconut oil, melted
1½ cups chopped fresh spinach	½ teaspoon salt

1. In a medium bowl, mix cream cheese, zucchini, pepper, and spinach. 2. Drizzle mushrooms with coconut oil and sprinkle with salt. Scoop ¼ zucchini mixture into each mushroom. 3. Place mushrooms into ungreased air fryer basket. Adjust the temperature to 400ºF (204ºC) and air fry for 8 minutes. Portobellos will be tender and tops will be browned when done. Serve warm.

Per Serving:
calories: 151 | fat: 13g | protein: 4g | carbs: 6g | fiber: 2g | sodium: 427mg

Eggs Poached in Moroccan Tomato Sauce

Prep time: 10 minutes | Cook time: 35 minutes | Serves 4

1 tablespoon olive oil	1 teaspoon salt
1 medium yellow onion, diced	¼ cup tomato paste
2 red bell peppers, seeded and diced	1 (28-ounce / 794-g) can diced tomatoes, drained
1¾ teaspoons sweet paprika	8 eggs
1 teaspoon ras al hanout	¼ cup chopped cilantro
½ teaspoon cayenne pepper	

1. Heat the olive oil in a skillet over medium-high heat. Add the onion and bell peppers and cook, stirring frequently, until softened, about 5 minutes. Stir in the paprika, ras al hanout, cayenne, salt, and tomato paste and cook, stirring occasionally, for 5 minutes. 2. Stir in the diced tomatoes, reduce the heat to medium-low, and simmer for about 15 minutes, until the tomatoes break down and the sauce thickens. 3. Make 8 wells in the sauce and drop one egg into each. Cover the pan and cook for about 10 minutes, until the whites are fully set, but the yolks are still runny. 4. Spoon the sauce and eggs into serving bowls and serve hot, garnished with cilantro.

Per Serving:
calories: 238 | fat: 13g | protein: 15g | carbs: 18g | fiber: 5g | sodium: 735mg

Mushroom Ragù with Parmesan Polenta

Prep time: 20 minutes | Cook time: 30 minutes | Serves 2

½ ounce (14 g) dried porcini mushrooms (optional but recommended)	½ cup red wine
	1 cup mushroom stock (or reserved liquid from soaking the porcini mushrooms, if using)
2 tablespoons olive oil	
1 pound (454 g) baby bella (cremini) mushrooms, quartered	½ teaspoon dried thyme
	1 fresh rosemary sprig
1 large shallot, minced (about ⅓ cup)	1½ cups water
	½ teaspoon salt
1 garlic clove, minced	⅓ cup instant polenta
1 tablespoon flour	2 tablespoons grated Parmesan cheese
2 teaspoons tomato paste	

1. If using the dried porcini mushrooms, soak them in 1 cup of hot water for about 15 minutes to soften them. When they're softened, scoop them out of the water, reserving the soaking liquid. (I strain it through a coffee filter to remove any possible grit.) Mince the porcini mushrooms. 2. Heat the olive oil in a large sauté pan over medium-high heat. Add the mushrooms, shallot, and garlic, and sauté for 10 minutes, or until the vegetables are wilted and starting to caramelize. 3. Add the flour and tomato paste, and cook for another 30 seconds. Add the red wine, mushroom stock or porcini soaking liquid, thyme, and rosemary. Bring the mixture to a boil, stirring constantly until it thickens. Reduce the heat and let it simmer for 10 minutes. 4. While the mushrooms are simmering, bring the water to a boil in a saucepan and add salt. 5. Add the instant polenta and stir quickly while it thickens. Stir in the Parmesan cheese. Taste and add additional salt if needed.

Per Serving:
calories: 451 | fat: 16g | protein: 14g | carbs: 58g | fiber: 5g | sodium: 165mg

Provençal Ratatouille with Herbed Breadcrumbs and Goat Cheese

Prep time: 10 minutes | Cook time: 1 hour 5 minutes | Serves 4

6 tablespoons olive oil, divided	tomatoes, drained
2 medium onions, diced	1 teaspoon salt
2 cloves garlic, minced	½ teaspoon freshly ground
2 medium eggplants, halved	black pepper
lengthwise and cut into ¾-inch	8 ounces (227 g) fresh
thick half rounds	breadcrumbs
3 medium zucchini, halved	1 tablespoon chopped fresh
lengthwise and cut into ¾-inch	parsley
thick half rounds	1 tablespoon chopped fresh
2 red bell peppers, seeded and	basil
cut into 1½-inch pieces	1 tablespoon chopped fresh
1 green bell pepper, seeded and	chives
cut into 1½-inch pieces	6 ounces (170 g) soft, fresh
1 (14-ounce / 397-g) can diced	goat cheese

1. Preheat the oven to 375°F(190°C). 2. Heat 5 tablespoons of the olive oil in a large skillet over medium heat. Add the onions and garlic and cook, stirring frequently, until the onions are soft and beginning to turn golden, about 8 minutes. Add the eggplant, zucchini, and bell peppers and cook, turning the vegetables occasionally, for another 10 minutes. Stir in the tomatoes, salt, and pepper and let simmer for 15 minutes. 3. While the vegetables are simmering, stir together the breadcrumbs, the remaining tablespoon of olive oil, the parsley, basil, and chives. 4. Transfer the vegetable mixture to a large baking dish, spreading it out into an even layer. Crumble the goat cheese over the top, then sprinkle the breadcrumb mixture evenly over the top. Bake in the preheated oven for about 30 minutes, until the topping is golden brown and crisp. Serve hot.

Per Serving:

calories: 644 | fat: 37g | protein: 21g | carbs: 63g | fiber: 16g | sodium: 861mg

Eggplants Stuffed with Walnuts and Feta

Prep time: 10 minutes | Cook time: 55 minutes | Serves 6

3 medium eggplants, halved	pieces
lengthwise	2¼ teaspoons ground cinnamon
2 teaspoons salt, divided	1½ teaspoons dried oregano
¼ cup olive oil, plus 2	½ teaspoon freshly ground
tablespoons, divided	black pepper
2 medium onions, diced	¼ cup whole-wheat
1½ pints cherry or grape	breadcrumbs
tomatoes, halved	⅔ cup (about 3 ounces / 85 g)
¾ cup roughly chopped walnut	crumbled feta cheese

1. Scoop out the flesh of the eggplants, leaving a ½-inch thick border of flesh in the skins. Dice the flesh that you removed and place it in a colander set over the sink. Sprinkle 1½ teaspoons of salt over the diced eggplant and inside the eggplant shells and let stand for 30 minutes. Rinse the shells and the pieces and pat dry with paper towels. 2. Heat ¼ cup of olive oil in a large skillet over medium heat. Add the eggplant shells, skin-side down, and cook for about 4 minutes, until browned and softened. Turn over and cook on the cut side until golden brown and soft, about 4 minutes more. Transfer to a plate lined with paper towel to drain. 3. Drain off all but about 1 to 2 tablespoons of the oil in the skillet and heat over medium-high heat. Add the onions and cook, stirring, until beginning to soften, about 3 minutes. Add the diced eggplant, tomatoes, walnuts, cinnamon, oregano, ¼ cup water, the remaining ½ teaspoon of salt, and the pepper. Cook, stirring occasionally, until the vegetables are golden brown and softened, about 8 minutes. 4. Preheat the broiler to high. 5. In a small bowl, toss together the breadcrumbs and 1 tablespoon olive oil. 6. Arrange the eggplant shells cut-side up on a large, rimmed baking sheet. Brush each shell with about ½ teaspoon of olive oil. Cook under the broiler until tender and just starting to turn golden brown, about 5 minutes. Remove the eggplants from the broiler and reduce the heat of the oven to 375°F (190°C). 7. Spoon the sautéed vegetable mixture into the eggplant shells, dividing equally. Sprinkle the breadcrumbs over the tops of the filled eggplants, dividing equally. Sprinkle the cheese on top, again dividing equally. Bake in the oven until the filling and shells are heated through and the topping is nicely browned and crisp, about 35 minutes.

Per Serving:

calories: 274 | fat: 15g | protein: 7g | carbs: 34g | fiber: 13g | sodium: 973mg

Beet and Carrot Fritters with Yogurt Sauce

Prep time: 15 minutes | Cook time: 15 minutes | Serves 2

For the Yogurt Sauce:	
⅓ cup plain Greek yogurt	Zest of ½ lemon
1 tablespoon freshly squeezed	¼ teaspoon garlic powder
lemon juice	¼ teaspoon salt

For the Fritters:	
1 large carrot, peeled	unseasoned bread crumbs
1 small potato, peeled	¼ teaspoon garlic powder
1 medium golden or red beet,	¼ teaspoon salt
peeled	1 large egg, beaten
1 scallion, minced	¼ cup feta cheese, crumbled
2 tablespoons fresh minced	2 tablespoons olive oil (more if
parsley	needed)
¼ cup brown rice flour or	

Make the Yogurt Sauce: In a small bowl, mix together the yogurt, lemon juice and zest, garlic powder, and salt. Set aside. Make the Fritters: 1. Shred the carrot, potato, and beet in a food processor with the shredding blade. You can also use a mandoline with a julienne shredding blade or a vegetable peeler. Squeeze out any moisture from the vegetables and place them in a large bowl. 2. Add the scallion, parsley, rice flour, garlic powder, salt, and egg. Stir the mixture well to combine. Add the feta cheese and stir briefly, leaving chunks of feta cheese throughout. 3. Heat a large nonstick sauté pan over medium-high heat and add 1 tablespoon of the olive oil. 4. Make the fritters by scooping about 3 tablespoons of the vegetable mixture into your hands and flattening it into a firm disc about 3 inches in diameter. 5. Place 2 fritters at a time in the pan and let them cook for about two minutes. Check to see if the underside is golden, and then flip and repeat on the other side. Remove from the heat, add the rest of the olive oil to the pan, and repeat with the remaining vegetable mixture. 6. To serve, spoon about 1 tablespoon of the yogurt sauce on top of each fritter.

Per Serving:

calories: 295 | fat: 14g | protein: 6g | carbs: 44g | fiber: 5g | sodium: 482mg

Vegetable Burgers

Prep time: 10 minutes | Cook time: 12 minutes | Serves 4

8 ounces (227 g) cremini mushrooms	yellow onion
2 large egg yolks	1 clove garlic, peeled and finely minced
½ medium zucchini, trimmed and chopped	½ teaspoon salt
¼ cup peeled and chopped	¼ teaspoon ground black pepper

1. Place all ingredients into a food processor and pulse twenty times until finely chopped and combined. 2. Separate mixture into four equal sections and press each into a burger shape. Place burgers into ungreased air fryer basket. Adjust the temperature to 375ºF (191ºC) and air fry for 12 minutes, turning burgers halfway through cooking. Burgers will be browned and firm when done. 3. Place burgers on a large plate and let cool 5 minutes before serving.

Per Serving:
calories: 50 | fat: 3g | protein: 3g | carbs: 4g | fiber: 1g | sodium: 299mg

Cauliflower Steaks with Olive Citrus Sauce

Prep time: 15 minutes | Cook time: 30 minutes | Serves 4

1 or 2 large heads cauliflower (at least 2 pounds / 907 g, enough for 4 portions)	Zest of 1 orange
⅓ cup extra-virgin olive oil	¼ cup black olives, pitted and chopped
¼ teaspoon kosher salt	1 tablespoon Dijon or grainy mustard
⅛ teaspoon ground black pepper	1 tablespoon red wine vinegar
Juice of 1 orange	½ teaspoon ground coriander

1. Preheat the oven to 400ºF (205ºC). Line a baking sheet with parchment paper or foil. 2. Cut off the stem of the cauliflower so it will sit upright. Slice it vertically into four thick slabs. Place the cauliflower on the prepared baking sheet. Drizzle with the olive oil, salt, and black pepper. Bake for about 30 minutes, turning over once, until tender and golden brown. 3. In a medium bowl, combine the orange juice, orange zest, olives, mustard, vinegar, and coriander; mix well. 4. Serve the cauliflower warm or at room temperature with the sauce.

Per Serving:
calories: 265 | fat: 21g | protein: 5g | carbs: 19g | fiber: 4g | sodium: 310mg

Crispy Eggplant Rounds

Prep time: 15 minutes | Cook time: 10 minutes | Serves 4

1 large eggplant, ends trimmed, cut into ½-inch slices	ground
½ teaspoon salt	½ teaspoon paprika
2 ounces (57 g) Parmesan 100% cheese crisps, finely	¼ teaspoon garlic powder
	1 large egg

1. Sprinkle eggplant rounds with salt. Place rounds on a kitchen towel for 30 minutes to draw out excess water. Pat rounds dry. 2. In a medium bowl, mix cheese crisps, paprika, and garlic powder. In a separate medium bowl, whisk egg. Dip each eggplant round in egg, then gently press into cheese crisps to coat both sides. 3.

Place eggplant rounds into ungreased air fryer basket. Adjust the temperature to 400ºF (204ºC) and air fry for 10 minutes, turning rounds halfway through cooking. Eggplant will be golden and crispy when done. Serve warm.

Per Serving:
calories: 113 | fat: 5g | protein: 7g | carbs: 10g | fiber: 4g | sodium: 567mg

Cheesy Cauliflower Pizza Crust

Prep time: 15 minutes | Cook time: 11 minutes | Serves 2

1 (12-ounce / 340-g) steamer bag cauliflower	2 tablespoons blanched finely ground almond flour
½ cup shredded sharp Cheddar cheese	1 teaspoon Italian blend seasoning
1 large egg	

1. Cook cauliflower according to package instructions. Remove from bag and place into cheesecloth or paper towel to remove excess water. Place cauliflower into a large bowl. 2. Add cheese, egg, almond flour, and Italian seasoning to the bowl and mix well. 3. Cut a piece of parchment to fit your air fryer basket. Press cauliflower into 6-inch round circle. Place into the air fryer basket. 4. Adjust the temperature to 360ºF (182ºC) and air fry for 11 minutes. 5. After 7 minutes, flip the pizza crust. 6. Add preferred toppings to pizza. Place back into air fryer basket and cook an additional 4 minutes or until fully cooked and golden. Serve immediately.

Per Serving:
calories: 251 | fat: 17g | protein: 15g | carbs: 12g | fiber: 5g | sodium: 375mg

One-Pan Mushroom Pasta with Mascarpone

Prep time: 10 minutes | Cook time: 20 minutes | Serves 2

2 tablespoons olive oil	stock
1 large shallot, minced	6 ounces (170 g) dry pappardelle pasta
8 ounces (227 g) baby bella (cremini) mushrooms, sliced	2 tablespoons mascarpone cheese
¼ cup dry sherry	Salt
1 teaspoon dried thyme	Freshly ground black pepper
2 cups low-sodium vegetable	

1. Heat olive oil in a large sauté pan over medium-high heat. Add the shallot and mushrooms and sauté for 10 minutes, or until the mushrooms have given up much of their liquid. 2. Add the sherry, thyme, and vegetable stock. Bring the mixture to a boil. 3. Add the pasta, breaking it up as needed so it fits into the pan and is covered by the liquid. Return the mixture to a boil. Cover, and reduce the heat to medium-low. Let the pasta cook for 10 minutes, or until al dente. Stir it occasionally so it doesn't stick. If the sauce gets too dry, add some water or additional chicken stock. 4. When the pasta is tender, stir in the mascarpone cheese and season with salt and pepper. 5. The sauce will thicken up a bit when it's off the heat.

Per Serving:
calories: 517 | fat: 18g | protein: 16g | carbs: 69g | fiber: 3g | sodium: 141mg

Chapter 9

Desserts

Crispy Apple Phyllo Tart

Prep time: 15 minutes | Cook time: 30 minutes | Serves 4

5 teaspoons extra virgin olive oil 2 teaspoons fresh lemon juice ¼ teaspoon ground cinnamon 1½ teaspoons granulated sugar, divided	1 large apple (any variety), peeled and cut into ⅛-inch thick slices 5 phyllo sheets, defrosted 1 teaspoon all-purpose flour 1½ teaspoons apricot jam

1. Preheat the oven to 350°F (180°C). Line a baking sheet with parchment paper, and pour the olive oil into a small dish. Set aside. 2. In a separate small bowl, combine the lemon juice, cinnamon, 1 teaspoon of the sugar, and the apple slices. Mix well to ensure the apple slices are coated in the seasonings. Set aside. 3. On a clean working surface, stack the phyllo sheets one on top of the other. Place a large bowl with an approximate diameter of 15 inches on top of the sheets, then draw a sharp knife around the edge of the bowl to cut out a circle through all 5 sheets. Discard the remaining phyllo. 4. Working quickly, place the first sheet on the lined baking sheet and then brush with the olive oil. Repeat the process by placing a second sheet on top of the first sheet, then brushing the second sheet with olive oil. Repeat until all the phyllo sheets are in a single stack. 5. Sprinkle the flour and remaining sugar over the top of the sheets. Arrange the apples in overlapping circles 4 inches from the edge of the phyllo. 6. Fold the edges of the phyllo in and then twist them all around the apple filling to form a crust edge. Brush the edge with the remaining olive oil. Bake for 30 minutes or until the crust is golden and the apples are browned on the edges. 7. While the tart is baking, heat the apricot jam in a small sauce pan over low heat until it's melted. 8. When the tart is done baking, brush the apples with the jam sauce. Slice the tart into 4 equal servings and serve warm. Store at room temperature, covered in plastic wrap, for up to 2 days.

Per Serving:

calories: 165 | fat: 7g | protein: 2g | carbs: 24g | fiber: 2g | sodium: 116mg

Chocolate Pudding

Prep time: 10 minutes | Cook time: 0 minutes | Serves 4

2 ripe avocados, halved and pitted ¼ cup unsweetened cocoa powder ¼ cup heavy whipping cream, plus more if needed 2 teaspoons vanilla extract	1 to 2 teaspoons liquid stevia or monk fruit extract (optional) ½ teaspoon ground cinnamon (optional) ¼ teaspoon salt Whipped cream, for serving (optional)

1. Using a spoon, scoop out the ripe avocado into a blender or large bowl, if using an immersion blender. Mash well with a fork. 2. Add the cocoa powder, heavy whipping cream, vanilla, sweetener (if using), cinnamon (if using), and salt. Blend well until smooth and creamy, adding additional cream, 1 tablespoon at a time, if the mixture is too thick. 3. Cover and refrigerate for at least 1 hour before serving. Serve chilled with additional whipped cream, if desired.

Per Serving:

calories: 205 | fat: 18g | protein: 3g | carbs: 12g | fiber: 9g | sodium: 156mg

Strawberry Ricotta Parfaits

Prep time: 10 minutes | Cook time: 0 minutes | Serves 4

2 cups ricotta cheese ¼ cup honey 2 cups sliced strawberries 1 teaspoon sugar	Toppings such as sliced almonds, fresh mint, and lemon zest (optional)

1. In a medium bowl, whisk together the ricotta and honey until well blended. Place the bowl in the refrigerator for a few minutes to firm up the mixture. 2. In a medium bowl, toss together the strawberries and sugar. 3. In each of four small glasses, layer 1 tablespoon of the ricotta mixture, then top with a layer of the strawberries and finally another layer of the ricotta. 4. Finish with your preferred toppings, if desired, then serve.

Per Serving:

calories: 311 | fat: 16g | protein: 14g | carbs: 29g | fiber: 2g | sodium: 106mg

Banana Cream Pie Parfaits

Prep time: 10 minutes | Cook time: 0 minutes | Serves 2

1 cup nonfat vanilla pudding 2 low-sugar graham crackers, crushed	1 banana, peeled and sliced ¼ cup walnuts, chopped Honey for drizzling

1. In small parfait dishes or glasses, layer the ingredients, starting with the pudding and ending with chopped walnuts. 2. You can repeat the layers, depending on the size of the glass and your preferences. 3. Drizzle with the honey. Serve chilled.

Per Serving:

calories: 312 | fat: 11g | protein: 7g | carbs: 50g | fiber: 3g | sodium: 273mg

Poached Pears with Greek Yogurt and Pistachio

Prep time: 10 minutes | Cook time: 3 minutes | Serves 8

2 cups water 1¾ cups apple cider ¼ cup lemon juice 1 cinnamon stick 1 teaspoon vanilla bean paste 4 large Bartlett pears, peeled	1 cup low-fat plain Greek yogurt ½ cup unsalted roasted pistachio meats

1. Add water, apple cider, lemon juice, cinnamon, vanilla, and pears to the Instant Pot®. Close lid, set steam release to Sealing, press the Manual button, and set time to 3 minutes. 2. When the timer beeps, quick-release the pressure until the float valve drops. Press the Cancel button and open lid. With a slotted spoon remove pears to a plate and allow to cool to room temperature. 3. To serve, carefully slice pears in half with a sharp paring knife and scoop out core with a melon baller. Lay pear halves on dessert plates or in shallow bowls. Top with yogurt and garnish with pistachios. Serve immediately.

Per Serving:

calories: 181 | fat: 7g | protein: 7g | carbs: 23g | fiber: 4g | sodium: 11mg

Blueberry Compote

Prep time: 10 minutes | Cook time: 5 minutes | Serves 8

1 (16-ounce/ 454-g) bag frozen blueberries, thawed	2 tablespoons cornstarch
¼ cup sugar	2 tablespoons water
1 tablespoon lemon juice	¼ teaspoon vanilla extract
	¼ teaspoon grated lemon zest

1. Add blueberries, sugar, and lemon juice to the Instant Pot®. Close lid, set steam release to Sealing, press the Manual button, and set time to 1 minute. 2. When the timer beeps, quick-release the pressure until the float valve drops. Press the Cancel button and open lid. 3. Press the Sauté button. In a small bowl, combine cornstarch and water. Stir into blueberry mixture and cook until mixture comes to a boil and thickens, about 3–4 minutes. Press the Cancel button and stir in vanilla and lemon zest. Serve immediately or refrigerate until ready to serve.

Per Serving:

calories: 57 | fat: 0g | protein: 0g | carbs: 14g | fiber: 2g | sodium: 0mg

Cinnamon-Stewed Dried Plums with Greek Yogurt

Prep time: 5 minutes | Cook time: 3 minutes | Serves 6

3 cups dried plums	2 cinnamon sticks
2 cups water	3 cups low-fat plain Greek yogurt
2 tablespoons sugar	

1. Add dried plums, water, sugar, and cinnamon to the Instant Pot®. Close lid, set steam release to Sealing, press the Manual button, and set time to 3 minutes. 2. When the timer beeps, quick-release the pressure until the float valve drops. Press the Cancel button and open lid. Remove and discard cinnamon sticks. Serve warm over Greek yogurt.

Per Serving:

calories: 301 | fat: 2g | protein: 14g | carbs: 61g | fiber: 4g | sodium: 50mg

Crunchy Sesame Cookies

Prep time: 10 minutes | Cook time: 15 minutes | Yield 14 to 16

1 cup sesame seeds, hulled	butter, softened
1 cup sugar	2 large eggs
8 tablespoons (1 stick) salted	1¼ cups flour

1. Preheat the oven to 350°F(180°C). Toast the sesame seeds on a baking sheet for 3 minutes. Set aside and let cool. 2. Using a mixer, cream together the sugar and butter. 3. Add the eggs one at a time until well-blended. 4. Add the flour and toasted sesame seeds and mix until well-blended. 5. Drop spoonfuls of cookie dough onto a baking sheet and form them into round balls, about 1-inch in diameter, similar to a walnut. 6. Put in the oven and bake for 5 to 7 minutes or until golden brown. 7. Let the cookies cool and enjoy.

Per Serving:

calories: 218 | fat: 12g | protein: 4g | carbs: 25g | fiber: 2g | sodium: 58mg

Orange–Olive Oil Cupcakes

Prep time: 15 minutes | Cook time: 20 minutes | Makes 6 cupcakes

1 large egg	Zest of 1 orange
2 tablespoons powdered sugar-free sweetener (such as stevia or monk fruit extract)	1 cup almond flour
	¾ teaspoon baking powder
½ cup extra-virgin olive oil	⅛ teaspoon salt
1 teaspoon almond extract	1 tablespoon freshly squeezed orange juice

1. Preheat the oven to 350°F (180ºC). Place muffin liners into 6 cups of a muffin tin. 2. In a large bowl, whisk together the egg and powdered sweetener. Add the olive oil, almond extract, and orange zest and whisk to combine well. 3. In a small bowl, whisk together the almond flour, baking powder, and salt. Add to wet ingredients along with the orange juice and stir until just combined. 4. Divide the batter evenly into 6 muffin cups and bake until a toothpick inserted in the center of the cupcake comes out clean, 15 to 18 minutes. 5. Remove from the oven and cool for 5 minutes in the tin before transferring to a wire rack to cool completely.

Per Serving:

1 cupcake: calories: 280 | fat: 27g | protein: 4g | carbs: 8g | fiber: 2g | sodium: 65mg

Pomegranate-Quinoa Dark Chocolate Bark

Prep time: 10 minutes |Cook time: 10 minutes| Serves: 6

Nonstick cooking spray	8 ounces (227 g) dark chocolate or 1 cup dark chocolate chips
½ cup uncooked tricolor or regular quinoa	½ cup fresh pomegranate seeds
½ teaspoon kosher or sea salt	

1. In a medium saucepan coated with nonstick cooking spray over medium heat, toast the uncooked quinoa for 2 to 3 minutes, stirring frequently. Do not let the quinoa burn. Remove the pan from the stove, and mix in the salt. Set aside 2 tablespoons of the toasted quinoa to use for the topping. 2. Break the chocolate into large pieces, and put it in a gallon-size zip-top plastic bag. Using a metal ladle or a meat pounder, pound the chocolate until broken into smaller pieces. (If using chocolate chips, you can skip this step.) Dump the chocolate out of the bag into a medium, microwave-safe bowl and heat for 1 minute on high in the microwave. Stir until the chocolate is completely melted. Mix the toasted quinoa (except the topping you set aside) into the melted chocolate. 3. Line a large, rimmed baking sheet with parchment paper. Pour the chocolate mixture onto the sheet and spread it evenly until the entire pan is covered. Sprinkle the remaining 2 tablespoons of quinoa and the pomegranate seeds on top. Using a spatula or the back of a spoon, press the quinoa and the pomegranate seeds into the chocolate. 4. Freeze the mixture for 10 to 15 minutes, or until set. Remove the bark from the freezer, and break it into about 2-inch jagged pieces. Store in a sealed container or zip-top plastic bag in the refrigerator until ready to serve.

Per Serving:

calories: 290 | fat: 17g | protein: 5g | carbs: 29g | fiber: 6g | sodium: 202mg

Dried Fruit Compote

Prep time: 15 minutes | Cook time: 8 minutes | Serves 6

8 ounces (227 g) dried apricots, quartered	1 cup golden raisins
8 ounces (227 g) dried peaches, quartered	1½ cups orange juice
	1 cinnamon stick
	4 whole cloves

1. Place all ingredients in the Instant Pot®. Stir to combine. Close lid, set steam release to Sealing, press the Manual button, and set time to 3 minutes. When the timer beeps, let pressure release naturally, about 20 minutes. Press the Cancel button and open lid. 2. Remove and discard cinnamon stick and cloves. Press the Sauté button and simmer for 5–6 minutes. Serve warm or allow to cool, and then cover and refrigerate for up to a week.

Per Serving:

calories: 258 | fat: 0g | protein: 4g | carbs: 63g | fiber: 5g | sodium: 7mg

Individual Apple Pockets

Prep time: 5 minutes | Cook time: 15 minutes | Serves 6

1 organic puff pastry, rolled out, at room temperature	⅛ teaspoon ground cinnamon
1 Gala apple, peeled and sliced	⅛ teaspoon ground cardamom
¼ cup brown sugar	Nonstick cooking spray
	Honey, for topping

1. Preheat the oven to 350°F(180°C). 2. Cut the pastry dough into 4 even discs. Peel and slice the apple. In a small bowl, toss the slices with brown sugar, cinnamon, and cardamom. 3. Spray a muffin tin very well with nonstick cooking spray. Be sure to spray only the muffin holders you plan to use. 4. Once sprayed, line the bottom of the muffin tin with the dough and place 1 or 2 broken apple slices on top. Fold the remaining dough over the apple and drizzle with honey. 5. Bake for 15 minutes or until brown and bubbly.

Per Serving:

calories: 250 | fat: 15g | protein: 3g | carbs: 30g | fiber: 1g | sodium: 98mg

Chocolate-Dipped Fruit Bites

Prep time: 10 minutes | Cook time: 0 minutes | Serves 4 to 6

½ cup semisweet chocolate chips	2 kiwis, peeled and sliced
¼ cup low-fat milk	1 cup honeydew melon chunks (about 2-inch chunks)
½ teaspoon pure vanilla extract	1 pound (454 g) whole strawberries
½ teaspoon ground nutmeg	
¼ teaspoon salt	

1. Place the chocolate chips in a small bowl. 2. In another small bowl, microwave the milk until hot, about 30 seconds. Pour the milk over the chocolate chips and let sit for 1 minute, then whisk until the chocolate is melted and smooth. Stir in the vanilla, nutmeg, and salt and allow to cool for 5 minutes. 3. Line a baking sheet with wax paper. Dip each piece of fruit halfway into the chocolate, tap gently to remove excess chocolate, and place the fruit on the baking sheet. 4. Once all the fruit has been dipped, allow it to sit until dry, about 30 minutes. Arrange on a platter and serve.

Per Serving:

calories: 125 | fat: 5g | protein: 2g | carbs: 21g | fiber: 3g | sodium:

110mg

Creamy Spiced Almond Milk

Prep time: 5 minutes | Cook time: 1 minute | Serves 6

1 cup raw almonds	1 teaspoon vanilla bean paste
5 cups filtered water, divided	½ teaspoon pumpkin pie spice

1. Add almonds and 1 cup water to the Instant Pot®. Close lid, set steam release to Sealing, press the Manual button, and set time to 1 minute. 2. When the timer beeps, quick-release the pressure until the float valve drops. Press the Cancel button and open lid. Strain almonds and rinse under cool water. Transfer to a high-powered blender with remaining 3.cups water. Purée for 2 minutes on high speed. 4. Pour mixture into a nut milk bag set over a large bowl. Squeeze bag to extract all liquid. Stir in vanilla and pumpkin pie spice. Transfer to a Mason jar or sealed jug and refrigerate for 8 hours. Stir or shake gently before serving.

Per Serving:

calories: 86 | fat: 8g | protein: 3g | carbs: 3g | fiber: 2g | sodium: 0mg

Chocolate Lava Cakes

Prep time: 5 minutes | Cook time: 15 minutes | Serves 2

2 large eggs, whisked	½ teaspoon vanilla extract
¼ cup blanched finely ground almond flour	2 ounces (57 g) low-carb chocolate chips, melted

1. In a medium bowl, mix eggs with flour and vanilla. Fold in chocolate until fully combined. 2. Pour batter into two ramekins greased with cooking spray. Place ramekins into air fryer basket. Adjust the temperature to 320°F (160°C) and bake for 15 minutes. Cakes will be set at the edges and firm in the center when done. Let cool 5 minutes before serving.

Per Serving:

calories: 313 | fat: 23g | protein: 11g | carbs: 16g | fiber: 5g | sodium: 77mg

Grilled Fruit Kebabs with Honey Labneh

Prep time: 15 minutes | Cook time: 10 minutes | Serves 2

⅔ cup prepared labneh, or, if making your own, ⅔ cup full-fat plain Greek yogurt	Pinch salt
2 tablespoons honey	3 cups fresh fruit cut into 2-inch chunks (pineapple, cantaloupe, nectarines, strawberries, plums, or mango)
1 teaspoon vanilla extract	

1. If making your own labneh, place a colander over a bowl and line it with cheesecloth. Place the Greek yogurt in the cheesecloth and wrap it up. Put the bowl in the refrigerator and let sit for at least 12 to 24 hours, until it's thick like soft cheese. 2. Mix honey, vanilla, and salt into labneh. Stir well to combine and set it aside. 3. Heat the grill to medium (about 300°F/ 150°C) and oil the grill grate. Alternatively, you can cook these on the stovetop in a heavy grill pan (cast iron works well). 4. Thread the fruit onto skewers and grill for 4 minutes on each side, or until fruit is softened and has grill marks on each side. 5. Serve the fruit with labneh to dip.

Per Serving:

calories: 292 | fat: 6g | protein: 5g | carbs: 60g | fiber: 4g | sodium: 131mg

Cherry-Stuffed Apples

Prep time: 15 minutes | Cook time: 4 hours | Serves 2

3 apples	2 tablespoons apple cider
1 tablespoon freshly squeezed	2 tablespoons honey
lemon juice	¼ cup water
⅓ cup dried cherries	

1. Cut about half an inch off the top of each of the apples, and peel a small strip of the skin away around the top. 2. Using a small serrated spoon or melon baller, core the apples, making sure not to go through the bottom. Drizzle with the lemon juice. 3. Fill the apples with the dried cherries. Carefully spoon the cider and honey into the apples. 4. Place the apples in the slow cooker. Pour the water around the apples. 5. Cover and cook on low for 4 hours, or until the apples are soft, and serve.

Per Serving:

calories: 227 | fat: 1g | protein: 1g | carbs: 60g | fiber: 7g | sodium: 6mg

Creamy Rice Pudding

Prep time: 5 minutes | Cook time: 45 minutes | Serves 6

1¼ cups long-grain rice	1 tablespoon rose water or
5 cups whole milk	orange blossom water
1 cup sugar	1 teaspoon cinnamon

1. Rinse the rice under cold water for 30 seconds. 2. Put the rice, milk, and sugar in a large pot. Bring to a gentle boil while continually stirring. 3. Turn the heat down to low and let simmer for 40 to 45 minutes, stirring every 3 to 4 minutes so that the rice does not stick to the bottom of the pot. 4. Add the rose water at the end and simmer for 5 minutes. 5. Divide the pudding into 6 bowls. Sprinkle the top with cinnamon. Cool for at least 1 hour before serving. Store in the fridge.

Per Serving:

calories: 394 | fat: 7g | protein: 9g | carbs: 75g | fiber: 1g | sodium: 102mg

Lemon Berry Cream Pops

Prep time: 10 minutes | Cook time: 5 minutes | Makes 8 ice pops

Cream Pops:

2 cups coconut cream	to taste
1 tablespoon unsweetened	2 cups raspberries, fresh or
vanilla extract	frozen and defrosted
Optional: low-carb sweetener,	

Coating:

1⅓ cups coconut butter	tablespoons
¼ cup virgin coconut oil	1 teaspoon unsweetened vanilla
Zest from 2 lemons, about 2	extract

1. To make the cream pops: In a bowl, whisk the coconut cream with the vanilla and optional sweetener until smooth and creamy. In another bowl, crush the raspberries using a fork, then add them to the bowl with the coconut cream and mix to combine. 2. Divide the mixture among eight ⅓-cup ice pop molds. Freeze until solid for 3 hours, or until set. 3. To easily remove the ice pops from the molds, fill a pot as tall as the ice pops with warm (not hot) water and dip the ice pop molds in for 15 to 20 seconds. Remove the ice pops from the molds and then freeze again. 4. Meanwhile, prepare the coating: Place the coconut butter and coconut oil in a small saucepan over low heat. Stir until smooth, remove from the heat, and add the lemon zest and vanilla. Let cool to room temperature. 5. Remove the ice pops from the freezer, two at a time, and, holding the ice pops over the saucepan, use a spoon to drizzle the coating all over. Return to the freezer until fully set, about 10 minutes. Store in the freezer in a resealable bag for up to 3 months.

Per Serving:

calories: 549 | fat: 8g | protein: 3g | carbs: 58g | fiber: 3g | sodium: 7mg

Red-Wine Poached Pears

Prep time: 10 minutes | Cook time: 20 minutes | Serves 2

2 cups red wine, such as Merlot	1 cinnamon stick
or Zinfandel, more if necessary	2 peppercorns
2 firm pears, peeled	1 bay leaf
2 to 3 cardamom pods, split	

1. Put all ingredients in a large pot and bring to a boil. Make sure the pears are submerged in the wine. 2. Reduce heat and simmer for 15–20 minutes until the pears are tender when poked with a fork. 3. Remove the pears from the wine, and allow to cool. 4. Bring the wine to a boil, and cook until it reduces to a syrup. 5. Strain and drizzle the pears with the warmed syrup before serving.

Per Serving:

calories: 268 | fat: 0g | protein: 1g | carbs: 22g | fiber: 6g | sodium: 0mg

Honeyed Roasted Apples with Walnuts

Prep time: 5 minutes | Cook time: 12 to 15 minutes | Serves 4

2 Granny Smith apples	½ teaspoon ground cinnamon
¼ cup certified gluten-free	2 tablespoons chopped walnuts
rolled oats	Pinch salt
2 tablespoons honey	1 tablespoon olive oil

1. Preheat the air fryer to 380°F (193°C). 2. Core the apples and slice them in half. 3. In a medium bowl, mix together the oats, honey, cinnamon, walnuts, salt, and olive oil. 4. Scoop a quarter of the oat mixture onto the top of each half apple. 5. Place the apples in the air fryer basket, and roast for 12 to 15 minutes, or until the apples are fork-tender.

Per Serving:

calories: 144 | fat: 6g | protein: 1g | carbs: 22g | fiber: 3g | sodium: 2mg

Cucumber-Lime Popsicles

Prep time: 5 minutes | Cook time: 0 minutes | Serves 4 to 6

2 cups cold water	¼ cup honey
1 cucumber, peeled	Juice of 1 lime

1. In a blender, purée the water, cucumber, honey, and lime juice. Pour into popsicle molds, freeze, and enjoy on a hot summer day!

Per Serving:

calories: 49 | fat: 0g | protein: 0g | carbs: 13g | fiber: 0g | sodium: 3mg

Halva Protein Slices

Prep time: 5 minutes | Cook time: 0 minutes | Serves 16

¾ cup tahini	vanilla extract
⅓ cup coconut butter	½ teaspoon cinnamon
¼ cup virgin coconut oil	⅛ teaspoon salt
1 cup collagen powder	Optional: low-carb sweetener,
½ teaspoon vanilla powder or	to taste
1½ teaspoons unsweetened	

1. To soften the tahini and the coconut butter, place them in a small saucepan over low heat with the coconut oil. Remove from the heat and set aside to cool for a few minutes. 2. Add the remaining ingredients and optional sweetener. Stir to combine, then pour the mixture into an 8 × 8–inch (20 × 20 cm) parchment-lined pan or a silicone pan, or any pan or container lined with parchment paper. Place in the fridge for at least 1 hour or until fully set. 3. Cut into 16 pieces and serve. To store, keep refrigerated for up to 2 weeks or freeze to up to 3 months.

Per Serving:
calories: 131 | fat: 13g | protein: 2g | carbs: 3g | fiber: 1g | sodium: 33mg

Peaches Poached in Rose Water

Prep time: 15 minutes | Cook time: 1 minute | Serves 6

1 cup water	1 teaspoon vanilla bean paste
1 cup rose water	6 large yellow peaches, pitted
¼ cup wildflower honey	and quartered
8 green cardamom pods, lightly	½ cup chopped unsalted roasted
crushed	pistachio meats

1. Add water, rose water, honey, cardamom, and vanilla to the Instant Pot®. Whisk well, then add peaches. Close lid, set steam release to Sealing, press the Manual button, and set time to 1 minute. 2. When the timer beeps, quick-release the pressure until the float valve drops. Press the Cancel button and open lid. Allow peaches to stand for 10 minutes. Carefully remove peaches from poaching liquid with a slotted spoon. 3. Slip skins from peach slices. Arrange slices on a plate and garnish with pistachios. Serve warm or at room temperature.

Per Serving:
calories: 145 | fat: 3g | protein: 2g | carbs: 28g | fiber: 2g | sodium: 8mg

Pears Poached in Pomegranate and Wine

Prep time: 5 minutes | Cook time: 60 minutes | Serves 4

4 ripe, firm Bosc pears, peeled,	wine, such as vin santo
left whole, and stems left intact	½ cup pomegranate seeds
1½ cups pomegranate juice	(seeds from about ½ whole
1 cup sweet, white dessert	fruit)

1. Slice off a bit of the bottom of each pear to create a flat surface so that the pears can stand upright. If desired, use an apple corer to remove the cores of the fruit, working from the bottom. 2. Lay the pears in a large saucepan on their sides and pour the juice and wine over the top. Set over medium-high heat and bring to a simmer. Cover the pan, reduce the heat, and let the pears simmer, turning twice, for about 40 minutes, until the pears are tender. Transfer the pears to a shallow bowl, leaving the cooking liquid in the saucepan. 3. Turn the heat under the saucepan to high and bring the poaching liquid to a boil. Cook, stirring frequently, for about 15 to 20 minutes, until the liquid becomes thick and syrupy and is reduced to about ½ cup. 4. Spoon a bit of the syrup onto each of 4 serving plates and top each with a pear, sitting it upright. Drizzle a bit more of the sauce over the pears and garnish with the pomegranate seeds. Serve immediately.

Per Serving:
calories: 208 | fat: 0g | protein: 1g | carbs: 46g | fiber: 7g | sodium: 7mg

Spanish Cream

Prep time: 5 minutes | Cook time: 0 minutes | Serves 6

3 large eggs	tablespoon unsweetened vanilla
1¼ cups unsweetened almond	extract
milk, divided	1 teaspoon cinnamon, plus
1 tablespoon gelatin powder	more for dusting
1¼ cups goat's cream, heavy	½ ounce (14 g) grated 100%
whipping cream, or coconut	chocolate, for topping
cream	Optional: low-carb sweetener,
1 teaspoon vanilla powder or 1	to taste

1. Separate the egg whites from the egg yolks. Place ½ cup (120 ml) of the almond milk in a small bowl, then add the gelatin and let it bloom. 2. Place the yolks, cream, and the remaining ¾ cup (180 ml) almond milk in a heatproof bowl placed over a small saucepan filled with 1 cup (240 ml) of water, placed over medium heat, ensuring that the bottom of the bowl doesn't touch the water. Whisk while heating until the mixture is smooth and thickened. 3. Stir in the vanilla, cinnamon, sweetener (if using), and the bloomed gelatin. Cover with plastic wrap pressed to the surface, and chill for 30 minutes. At this point the mixture will look runny. Don't panic! This is absolutely normal. It will firm up. 4. In a bowl with a hand mixer, or in a stand mixer, whisk the egg whites until stiff, then fold them through the cooled custard. Divide among six serving glasses and chill until fully set, 3 to 4 hours. Sprinkle with the grated chocolate and, optionally, add the sweetener and a dusting of cinnamon. Store covered in the refrigerator for up to 5 days.

Per Serving:
calories: 172 | fat: 13g | protein: 5g | carbs: 7g | fiber: 1g | sodium: 83mg

Dark Chocolate Lava Cake

Prep time: 5 minutes | Cook time: 10 minutes | Serves 4

Olive oil cooking spray	½ teaspoon baking powder
¼ cup whole wheat flour	¼ cup raw honey
1 tablespoon unsweetened dark	1 egg
chocolate cocoa powder	2 tablespoons olive oil
⅛ teaspoon salt	

1. Preheat the air fryer to 380°F(193ºC). Lightly coat the insides of four ramekins with olive oil cooking spray. 2. In a medium bowl, combine the flour, cocoa powder, salt, baking powder, honey, egg, and olive oil. 3. Divide the batter evenly among the ramekins. 4. Place the filled ramekins inside the air fryer and bake for 10 minutes. 5. Remove the lava cakes from the air fryer and slide a knife around the outside edge of each cake. Turn each ramekin upside down on a saucer and serve.

Per Serving:
calories: 179 | fat: 8g | protein: 3g | carbs: 26g | fiber: 1g | sodium: 95mg

Chapter 10

Salads

Citrus Fennel Salad

Prep time: 15 minutes | Cook time: 0 minutes | Serves 2

For the Dressing:

2 tablespoons fresh orange juice
3 tablespoons olive oil
1 tablespoon blood orange vinegar, other orange vinegar,

or cider vinegar
1 tablespoon honey
Salt
Freshly ground black pepper

For the Salad:

2 cups packed baby kale
1 medium navel or blood orange, segmented
½ small fennel bulb, stems and leaves removed, sliced into

matchsticks
3 tablespoons toasted pecans, chopped
2 ounces (57 g) goat cheese, crumbled

Make the Dressing: Combine the orange juice, olive oil, vinegar, and honey in a small bowl and whisk to combine. Season with salt and pepper. Set the dressing aside. Make the Salad: 1. Divide the baby kale, orange segments, fennel, pecans, and goat cheese evenly between two plates. 2. Drizzle half of the dressing over each salad.

Per Serving:

calories: 502 | fat: 39g | protein: 13g | carbs: 31g | fiber: 6g | sodium: 158mg

Pear-Fennel Salad with Pomegranate

Prep time: 15 minutes | Cook time: 5 minutes | Serves 6

Dressing:

2 tablespoons red wine vinegar
1½ tablespoons pomegranate molasses
2 teaspoons finely chopped shallot

½ teaspoon Dijon mustard
½ teaspoon kosher salt
¼ teaspoon ground black pepper
¼ cup extra-virgin olive oil

Salad:

¼ cup walnuts, coarsely chopped, or pine nuts
2 red pears, halved, cored, and very thinly sliced
1 bulb fennel, halved, cored, and very thinly sliced, fronds reserved

1 tablespoon fresh lemon juice
4 cups baby arugula
½ cup pomegranate seeds
⅓ cup crumbled feta cheese or shaved Parmigiano-Reggiano cheese

1. Make the Dressing: In a small bowl or jar with a lid, combine the vinegar, pomegranate molasses, shallot, mustard, salt, and pepper. Add the oil and whisk until emulsified (or cap the jar and shake vigorously). Set aside. 2. Make the Salad: In a small skillet over medium heat, toast the nuts until golden and fragrant, 4 to 5 minutes. Remove from the skillet to cool. 3. In a large bowl, combine the pears and fennel. Sprinkle with the lemon juice and toss gently. 4. Add the arugula and toss again to evenly distribute. Pour over 3 to 4 tablespoons of the dressing, just enough to moisten the arugula, and toss. Add the pomegranate seeds, cheese, and nuts and toss again. Add more dressing, if necessary, or store remainder in the refrigerator for up to 1 week. Serve the salad topped with the reserved fennel fronds.

Per Serving:

calories: 165 | fat: 10g | protein:31g | carbs: 18g | fiber: 4g | sodium: 215mg

Orange-Tarragon Chicken Salad Wrap

Prep time: 15 minutes | Cook time: 0 minutes | Serves 4

½ cup plain whole-milk Greek yogurt
2 tablespoons Dijon mustard
2 tablespoons extra-virgin olive oil
2 tablespoons chopped fresh tarragon or 1 teaspoon dried tarragon
½ teaspoon salt
¼ teaspoon freshly ground black pepper

2 cups cooked shredded chicken
½ cup slivered almonds
4 to 8 large Bibb lettuce leaves, tough stem removed
2 small ripe avocados, peeled and thinly sliced
Zest of 1 clementine, or ½ small orange (about 1 tablespoon)

1. In a medium bowl, combine the yogurt, mustard, olive oil, tarragon, orange zest, salt, and pepper and whisk until creamy. 2. Add the shredded chicken and almonds and stir to coat. 3. To assemble the wraps, place about ½ cup chicken salad mixture in the center of each lettuce leaf and top with sliced avocados.

Per Serving:

calories: 491 | fat: 38g | protein: 28g | carbs: 14g | fiber: 9g | sodium: 454mg

Zucchini and Ricotta Salad

Prep time: 5 minutes | Cook time: 2 minutes | Serves 1

2 teaspoons raw pine nuts
5 ounces (142 g) whole-milk ricotta cheese
1 tablespoon chopped fresh mint
1 teaspoon chopped fresh basil
1 tablespoon chopped fresh parsley
Pinch of fine sea salt
1 medium zucchini, very thinly sliced horizontally with a

mandoline slicer
Pinch of freshly ground black pepper
For the Dressing:
1½ tablespoons extra virgin olive oil
1 tablespoon fresh lemon juice
Pinch of fine sea salt
Pinch of freshly ground black pepper

1. Add the pine nuts to a small pan placed over medium heat. Toast the nuts, turning them frequently, for 2 minutes or until golden. Set aside. 2. In a food processor, combine the ricotta, mint, basil, parsley, and a pinch of sea salt. Process until smooth and then set aside. 3. Make the dressing by combining the olive oil and lemon juice in a small bowl. Use a fork to stir rapidly until the mixture thickens, then add a pinch of sea salt and a pinch of black pepper. Stir again. 4. Place the sliced zucchini in a medium bowl. Add half of the dressing, and toss to coat the zucchini. 5. To serve, place half of the ricotta mixture in the center of a serving plate, then layer the zucchini in a circle, covering the cheese. Add the rest of the cheese in the center and on top of the zucchini, then sprinkle the toasted pine nuts over the top. Drizzle the remaining dressing over the top, and finish with a pinch of black pepper. Store covered in the refrigerator for up to 1 day.

Per Serving:

calories: 504 | fat: 43g | protein: 19g | carbs: 13g | fiber: 3g | sodium: 136mg

Chopped Greek Antipasto Salad

**Prep time: 20 minutes |Cook time: 0 minutes|
Serves: 6**

For the Salad:

1 head Bibb lettuce or ½ head romaine lettuce, chopped (about 2½ cups)	halved
	1 pint grape tomatoes, halved (about 1½ cups)
¼ cup loosely packed chopped basil leaves	1 seedless cucumber, peeled and chopped (about 1½ cups)
1 (15-ounce / 425-g) can chickpeas, drained and rinsed	½ cup cubed feta cheese (about 2 ounces / 57 g)
1 (14-ounce / 397-g) can artichoke hearts, drained and	1 (2¼-ounce / 35-g) can sliced black olives (about ½ cup)

For the Dressing:

3 tablespoons extra-virgin olive oil	1 tablespoon chopped fresh oregano or ½ teaspoon dried oregano
1 tablespoon red wine vinegar	
1 tablespoon freshly squeezed lemon juice (from about ½ small lemon)	1 teaspoon honey
	¼ teaspoon freshly ground black pepper

1. In a medium bowl, toss the lettuce and basil together. Spread out on a large serving platter or in a large salad bowl. Arrange the chickpeas, artichoke hearts, tomatoes, cucumber, feta, and olives in piles next to each other on top of the lettuce layer. 2. In a small pitcher or bowl, whisk together the oil, vinegar, lemon juice, oregano, honey, and pepper. Serve on the side with the salad, or drizzle over all the ingredients right before serving.

Per Serving:

calories: 267 | fat: 13g | protein: 11g | carbs: 31g | fiber: 11g | sodium: 417mg

Italian Summer Vegetable Barley Salad

**Prep time: 1 minutes | Cook time: 25 to 45 minutes |
Serves 4**

1 cup uncooked barley (hulled or pearl)	chopped
3 cups water	15 Kalamata olives, pitted and sliced or chopped
¾ teaspoon fine sea salt, divided	¼ cup chopped fresh parsley
1 teaspoon plus 3 tablespoons extra virgin olive oil, divided	¼ cup chopped fresh basil
3 tablespoons fresh lemon juice	1 cup cherry tomatoes, halved
2 medium zucchini, washed and	½ teaspoon freshly ground black pepper

1. Place the barley in a medium pot and add 3 cups of water and ¼ teaspoon of the sea salt. Bring to a boil over high heat, then reduce the heat to low. Simmer for 25–40 minutes, depending on the type of barley you're using, adding small amounts of hot water if the barley appears to be drying out. Cook until the barley is soft but still chewy, then transfer to a mesh strainer and rinse with cold water. 2. Empty the rinsed barley into a large bowl, drizzle 1 teaspoon of the olive oil over the top, fluff with a fork, and then set aside. 3. In a small bowl, combine the remaining 3 tablespoons of olive oil and the lemon juice. Whisk until the dressing thickens. 4. In a large bowl, combine the barley, zucchini, olives, parsley, and basil. Toss and then add the cherry tomatoes, remaining ½ teaspoon of sea salt, and black pepper. Toss gently, drizzle the dressing over the top, and continue tossing until the ingredients are coated with the dressing. Serve promptly. Store covered in the refrigerator for up to 3 days.

Per Serving:

calories: 308 | fat: 13g | protein: 7g | carbs: 45g | fiber: 10g | sodium: 614mg

Panzanella (Tuscan Bread and Tomatoes Salad)

**Prep time: 10 minutes | Cook time: 20 minutes |
Serves 6**

4 ounces (113 g) sourdough bread, cut into 1' slices	Few grinds of ground black pepper
3 tablespoons extra-virgin olive oil, divided	2 pounds (907 g) ripe tomatoes (mixed colors)
2 tablespoons red wine vinegar	6 ounces (170 g) fresh mozzarella pearls
2 cloves garlic, mashed to a paste	1 cucumber, cut into ½'-thick half-moons
1 teaspoon finely chopped fresh oregano or ½ teaspoon dried	1 small red onion, thinly sliced
1 teaspoon fresh thyme leaves	1 cup baby arugula
½ teaspoon Dijon mustard	½ cup torn fresh basil
Pinch of kosher salt	

1. Coat a grill rack or grill pan with olive oil and prepare to medium-high heat. 2. Brush 1 tablespoon of the oil all over the bread slices. Grill the bread on both sides until grill marks appear, about 2 minutes per side. Cut the bread into 1' cubes. 3. In a large bowl, whisk together the vinegar, garlic, oregano, thyme, mustard, salt, pepper, and the remaining 2 tablespoons oil until emulsified. 4. Add the bread, tomatoes, mozzarella, cucumber, onion, arugula, and basil. Toss to combine and let sit for 10 minutes to soak up the flavors.

Per Serving:

calories: 219 | fat: 12g | protein: 10g | carbs: 19g | fiber: 3g | sodium: 222mg

Arugula Salad with Grapes, Goat Cheese, and Za'atar Croutons

**Prep time: 10 minutes | Cook time: 10 minutes |
Serves 4**

Croutons:

2 slices whole wheat bread, cubed	2 teaspoons olive oil, divided
	1 teaspoon za'atar

Vinaigrette:

2 tablespoons olive oil	¼ teaspoon kosher salt
1 tablespoon red wine vinegar	⅛ teaspoon ground black pepper
½ teaspoon chopped fresh rosemary	

Salad:

4 cups baby arugula	2 ounces (57 g) goat cheese, crumbled
1 cup grapes, halved	
½ red onion, thinly sliced	

1. Make the Croutons: Toss the bread cubes with 1 teaspoon of the oil and the za'atar. In a medium skillet over medium heat, warm the remaining 1 teaspoon oil. Cook the bread cubes, stirring frequently, until browned and crispy, 8 to 10 minutes. 2. Make the Vinaigrette: In a small bowl, whisk together the oil, vinegar, rosemary, salt, and pepper. 3. Make the Salad: In a large bowl, toss the arugula, grapes, and onion with the vinaigrette. Top with the cheese and croutons.

Per Serving:

calories: 204 | fat: 14g | protein: 6g | carbs: 15g | fiber: 2g | sodium: 283mg

Raw Zucchini Salad

Prep time: 15 minutes | Cook time: 0 minutes | Serves 2

1 medium zucchini, shredded or sliced paper thin	Sea salt and freshly ground pepper, to taste
6 cherry tomatoes, halved	3–4 basil leaves, thinly sliced
3 tablespoons olive oil	2 tablespoons freshly grated, low-fat Parmesan cheese
Juice of 1 lemon	

1. Layer the zucchini slices on 2 plates in even layers. Top with the tomatoes. 2. Drizzle with the olive oil and lemon juice. Season to taste. 3. Top with the basil and sprinkle with cheese before serving.

Per Serving:

calories: 256 | fat: 21g | protein: 2g | carbs: 19g | fiber: 3g | sodium: 3mg

Citrus Avocado Salad

Prep time: 5 minutes | Cook time: 0 minutes | Serves 2

½ medium orange (any variety), peeled and cut into bite-sized chunks	Pinch of freshly ground black pepper
1 medium tangerine, peeled and sectioned	For the Dressing:
	3 tablespoons extra virgin olive oil
½ medium white grapefruit, peeled and cut into bite-sized chunks	1 tablespoon fresh lemon juice
	½ teaspoon ground cumin
2 thin slices red onion	½ teaspoon coarse sea salt
1 medium avocado, peeled, pitted, and sliced	Pinch of freshly ground black pepper

1. Make the dressing by combining the olive oil, lemon juice, cumin, sea salt, and black pepper in a small jar or bowl. Whisk or shake to combine. 2. Toss the orange, tangerine, and grapefruit in a medium bowl, then place the sliced onion on top. Drizzle half the dressing over the salad. 3. Fan the avocado slices over the top of the salad. Drizzle the remaining dressing over the salad and then sprinkle a pinch of black pepper over the top. 4. Toss gently before serving. (This salad is best eaten fresh, but can be stored in the refrigerator for up to 1 day.)

Per Serving:

calories: 448 | fat: 36g | protein: 4g | carbs: 35g | fiber: 11g | sodium: 595mg

Cauliflower Tabbouleh Salad

Prep time: 15 minutes | Cook time: 0 minutes | Serves 4

¼ cup extra-virgin olive oil	⅛ teaspoon ground cinnamon
¼ cup lemon juice	1 pound (454 g) riced cauliflower
Zest of 1 lemon	1 English cucumber, diced
¾ teaspoon kosher salt	12 cherry tomatoes, halved
½ teaspoon ground turmeric	1 cup fresh parsley, chopped
¼ teaspoon ground coriander	½ cup fresh mint, chopped
¼ teaspoon ground cumin	
¼ teaspoon black pepper	

1. In a large bowl, whisk together the olive oil, lemon juice, lemon zest, salt, turmeric, coriander, cumin, black pepper, and cinnamon. 2. Add the riced cauliflower to the bowl and mix well. Add in the cucumber, tomatoes, parsley, and mint and gently mix together.

Per Serving:

calories: 180 | fat: 15g | protein: 4g | carbs: 12g | fiber: 5g | sodium:260 mg

Wild Greens Salad with Fresh Herbs

Prep time: 10 minutes | Cook time: 20 minutes | Serves 6 to 8

¼ cup olive oil	or apple cider vinegar
2 pounds (907 g) dandelion greens, tough stems removed and coarsely chopped	1 tablespoon fresh thyme, chopped
1 small bunch chicory, trimmed and coarsely chopped	2 cloves garlic, minced
	½ teaspoon kosher salt
1 cup chopped fresh flat-leaf parsley, divided	½ teaspoon ground black pepper
1 cup chopped fresh mint, divided	¼ cup almonds or walnuts, coarsely chopped
½ cup water	2 tablespoons chopped fresh chives or scallion greens
2 tablespoons red wine vinegar	1 tablespoon chopped fresh dill

1. In a large pot over medium heat, warm the oil. Add the greens, half of the parsley, half of the mint, the water, vinegar, thyme, garlic, salt, and pepper. Reduce the heat to a simmer and cook until the greens are very tender, about 20 minutes. 2. Meanwhile, in a small skillet over medium heat, toast the nuts until golden and fragrant, 5 to 8 minutes. Remove from the heat. 3. If serving immediately, stir the chives or scallion greens, dill, and the remaining parsley and mint into the pot. If serving as a cool or cold salad, allow to come to room temperature or refrigerate until cold before stirring in the fresh herbs. Top with the toasted nuts before serving.

Per Serving:

calories: 190 | fat: 13g | protein: 6g | carbs: 17g | fiber: 7g | sodium: 279mg

Arugula Spinach Salad with Shaved Parmesan

Prep time: 10 minutes | Cook time: 2 minutes | Serves 3

3 tablespoons raw pine nuts	5 dried figs, pitted and chopped
3 cups arugula	2½ ounces (71 g) shaved Parmesan cheese
3 cups baby leaf spinach	
For the Dressing:	
4 teaspoons balsamic vinegar	5 tablespoons extra virgin olive oil
1 teaspoon Dijon mustard	
1 teaspoon honey	

1. In a small pan over low heat, toast the pine nuts for 2 minutes or until they begin to brown. Promptly remove them from the heat and transfer to a small bowl. 2. Make the dressing by combining the balsamic vinegar, Dijon mustard, and honey in a small bowl. Using a fork to whisk, gradually add the olive oil while continuously mixing. 3. In a large bowl, toss the arugula and baby spinach and then top with the figs, Parmesan cheese, and toasted pine nuts. Drizzle the dressing over the top and toss until the ingredients are thoroughly coated with the dressing. Serve promptly. (This salad is best served fresh.)

Per Serving:

calories: 416 | fat: 35g | protein: 10g | carbs: 18g | fiber: 3g | sodium: 478mg

Mediterranean Potato Salad

**Prep time: 10 minutes |Cook time: 20 minutes|
Serves: 6**

2 pounds (907 g) Yukon Gold baby potatoes, cut into 1-inch cubes
3 tablespoons freshly squeezed lemon juice (from about 1 medium lemon)
3 tablespoons extra-virgin olive oil
1 tablespoon olive brine

¼ teaspoon kosher or sea salt
1 (2¼-ounce / 35-g) can sliced olives (about ½ cup)
1 cup sliced celery (about 2 stalks) or fennel
2 tablespoons chopped fresh oregano
2 tablespoons torn fresh mint

1. In a medium saucepan, cover the potatoes with cold water until the waterline is one inch above the potatoes. Set over high heat, bring the potatoes to a boil, then turn down the heat to medium-low. Simmer for 12 to 15 minutes, until the potatoes are just fork tender. 2. While the potatoes are cooking, in a small bowl, whisk together the lemon juice, oil, olive brine, and salt. 3. Drain the potatoes in a colander and transfer to a serving bowl. Immediately pour about 3 tablespoons of the dressing over the potatoes. Gently mix in the olives and celery. 4. Before serving, gently mix in the oregano, mint, and the remaining dressing.

Per Serving:
calories: 192 | fat: 8g | protein: 3g | carbs: 28g | fiber: 4g | sodium: 195mg

Greek Village Salad

**Prep time: 10 minutes | Cook time: 0 minutes |
Serves 4**

5 large tomatoes, cut into medium chunks
2 red onions, cut into medium chunks or sliced
1 English cucumber, peeled and cut into medium chunks
2 green bell peppers, cut into medium chunks
¼ cup extra-virgin olive oil,

plus extra for drizzling
1 cup kalamata olives, for topping
¼ teaspoon dried oregano, plus extra for garnish
¼ lemon
4 ounces (113 g) Greek feta cheese, sliced

1. In a large bowl, mix the tomatoes, onions, cucumber, bell peppers, olive oil, olives, and oregano. 2. Divide the vegetable mixture evenly among four bowls and top each with a squirt of lemon juice and 1 slice of feta. Drizzle with olive oil, garnish with oregano, and serve.

Per Serving:
calories: 315 | fat: 24g | protein: 8g | carbs: 21g | fiber: 6g | sodium: 524mg

Tabbouleh

**Prep time: 15 minutes | Cook time: 12 minutes |
Serves 4 to 6**

1 cup water
½ cup dried bulgur
½ English cucumber, quartered lengthwise and sliced
2 tomatoes on the vine, diced
2 scallions, chopped
Juice of 1 lemon
2 cups coarsely chopped fresh

Italian parsley
⅓ cup coarsely chopped fresh mint leaves
1 garlic clove
¼ cup extra-virgin olive oil
Sea salt
Freshly ground black pepper

1. In a medium saucepan, combine the water and bulgur and bring to a boil over medium heat. Reduce the heat to low, cover, and cook until the bulgur is tender, about 12 minutes. Drain off any excess liquid, fluff the bulgur with a fork, and set aside to cool. 2. In a large bowl, toss together the bulgur, cucumber, tomatoes, scallions, and lemon juice. 3. In a food processor, combine the parsley, mint, and garlic and process until finely chopped. 4. Add the chopped herb mixture to the bulgur mixture and stir to combine. Add the olive oil and stir to incorporate. 5. Season with salt and pepper and serve.

Per Serving:
calories: 215 | fat: 14g | protein: 4g | carbs: 21g | fiber: 5g | sodium: 66mg

Beets with Goat Cheese and Chermoula

**Prep time: 10 minutes | Cook time: 40 minutes |
Serves 4**

6 beets, trimmed
Chermoula:
1 cup fresh cilantro leaves
1 cup fresh flat-leaf parsley leaves
¼ cup fresh lemon juice
3 cloves garlic, minced
2 teaspoons ground cumin

1 teaspoon smoked paprika
½ teaspoon kosher salt
¼ teaspoon chili powder (optional)
¼ cup extra-virgin olive oil
2 ounces (57 g) goat cheese, crumbled

1. Preheat the oven to 400°F(205ºC). 2. Wrap the beets in a piece of foil and place on a baking sheet. Roast until the beets are tender enough to be pierced with a fork, 30 to 40 minutes. When cool enough to handle, remove the skins and slice the beets into ¼' rounds. Arrange the beet slices on a large serving platter. 3. To make the chermoula: In a food processor, pulse the cilantro, parsley, lemon juice, garlic, cumin, paprika, salt, and chili powder (if using) until the herbs are just coarsely chopped and the ingredients are combined. Stir in the oil. 4. To serve, dollop the chermoula over the beets and scatter the cheese on top.

Per Serving:
calories: 249 | fat: 19g | protein: 6g | carbs: 15g | fiber: 5g | sodium: 472mg

Grain-Free Kale Tabbouleh

**Prep time: 15 minutes | Cook time: 0 minutes |
Serves 8**

2 plum tomatoes, seeded and chopped
½ cup finely chopped fresh parsley
4 scallions (green onions), finely chopped
1 head kale, finely chopped (about 2 cups)

1 cup finely chopped fresh mint
1 small Persian cucumber, peeled, seeded, and diced
3 tablespoons extra-virgin olive oil
2 tablespoons fresh lemon juice
Coarsely ground black pepper (optional)

1. Place the tomatoes in a strainer set over a bowl and set aside to drain as much liquid as possible. 2. In a large bowl, stir to combine the parsley, scallions, kale, and mint. 3. Shake any remaining liquid from the tomatoes and add them to the kale mixture. Add the cucumber. 4. Add the olive oil and lemon juice and toss to combine. Season with pepper, if desired.

Per Serving:
1 cup: calories: 65 | fat: 5g | protein: 1g | carbs: 4g | fiber: 1g | sodium: 21mg

Sicilian Salad

Prep time: 5 minutes | Cook time: 0 minutes | Serves 2

2 tablespoons extra virgin olive oil	sliced
1 tablespoon red wine vinegar	2 tablespoons capers, drained
2 medium tomatoes (preferably beefsteak variety), sliced	6 green olives, halved
½ medium red onion, thinly	1 teaspoon dried oregano
	Pinch of fine sea salt

1. Make the dressing by combining the olive oil and vinegar in a small bowl. Use a fork to whisk until the mixture thickens slightly. Set aside. 2. Arrange the sliced tomatoes on a large plate and then scatter the onions, capers, and olives over the tomatoes. 3. Sprinkle the oregano and sea salt over the top, then drizzle the dressing over the salad. Serve promptly. (This salad is best served fresh, but can be stored covered in the refrigerator for up to 1 day.)

Per Serving:

calories: 169 | fat: 15g | protein: 2g | carbs: 8g | fiber: 3g | sodium: 336mg

Pipirrana (Spanish Summer Salad)

Prep time: 15 minutes | Cook time: 0 minutes | Serves 2

1 medium red onion, diced	Pinch of ground cumin
2 large tomatoes, cut into small cubes	½ teaspoon salt plus a pinch for the garlic paste
1 large Persian or mini cucumber, cut into small cubes	3 tablespoons extra virgin olive oil plus a few drops for the garlic paste
1 large green bell pepper, seeded and diced	2 tablespoons red wine vinegar
2 garlic cloves, minced	

1. Place the onions in a small bowl filled with water. Set aside to soak. 2. Place the tomatoes, cucumber, and bell pepper in a medium bowl. Drain the onions and then combine them with the rest of the vegetables. Mix well. 3. In a mortar or small bowl, combine the garlic, cumin, a pinch of salt, and a few drops of olive oil, then roll or mash the ingredients until a paste is formed. 4. In another small bowl, combine 3 tablespoons of the olive oil, vinegar, and ½ teaspoon of the salt. Add the garlic paste and mix well. 5. Add the dressing to the salad and mix well. 6. Cover and refrigerate for 30 minutes before serving. Store in the refrigerator for up to 2 days.

Per Serving:

calories: 274 | fat: 21g | protein: 4g | carbs: 20g | fiber: 6g | sodium: 600mg

Tomato and Pepper Salad

Prep time: 10 minutes | Cook time: 0 minutes | Serves 6

3 large yellow peppers	4 large tomatoes, seeded and diced
¼ cup olive oil	
1 small bunch fresh basil leaves	Sea salt and freshly ground pepper, to taste
2 cloves garlic, minced	

1. Preheat broiler to high heat and broil the peppers until blackened on all sides. 2. Remove from heat and place in a paper bag. Seal and allow peppers to cool. 3. Once cooled, peel the skins off the peppers, then seed and chop them. 4. Add half of the peppers to a food processor along with the olive oil, basil, and garlic, and pulse several times to make the dressing. 5. Combine the rest of the peppers with the tomatoes and toss with the dressing. 6. Season the salad with sea salt and freshly ground pepper. Allow salad to come to room temperature before serving.

Per Serving:

calories: 129 | fat: 9g | protein: 2g | carbs: 11g | fiber: 2g | sodium: 8mg

Traditional Greek Salad

Prep time: 10 minutes | Cook time: 0 minutes | Serves 4

2 large English cucumbers	lemon juice
4 Roma tomatoes, quartered	1 tablespoon red wine vinegar
1 green bell pepper, cut into 1- to 1½-inch chunks	1 tablespoon chopped fresh oregano or 1 teaspoon dried oregano
¼ small red onion, thinly sliced	
4 ounces (113 g) pitted Kalamata olives	¼ teaspoon freshly ground black pepper
¼ cup extra-virgin olive oil	4 ounces (113 g) crumbled traditional feta cheese
2 tablespoons freshly squeezed	

1. Cut the cucumbers in half lengthwise and then into ½-inch-thick half-moons. Place in a large bowl. 2. Add the quartered tomatoes, bell pepper, red onion, and olives. 3. In a small bowl, whisk together the olive oil, lemon juice, vinegar, oregano, and pepper. Drizzle over the vegetables and toss to coat. 4. Divide between salad plates and top each with 1 ounce (28 g) of feta.

Per Serving:

calories: 256 | fat: 22g | protein: 6g | carbs: 11g | fiber: 3g | sodium: 476mg

Yellow and White Hearts of Palm Salad

Prep time: 10 minutes | Cook time: 0 minutes | Serves 4

2 (14-ounce / 397-g) cans hearts of palm, drained and cut into ½-inch-thick slices	leaf parsley
	2 tablespoons low-fat mayonnaise
1 avocado, cut into ½-inch pieces	2 tablespoons extra-virgin olive oil
1 cup halved yellow cherry tomatoes	¼ teaspoon salt
½ small shallot, thinly sliced	⅛ teaspoon freshly ground black pepper
¼ cup coarsely chopped flat-	

1. In a large bowl, toss the hearts of palm, avocado, tomatoes, shallot, and parsley. 2. In a small bowl, whisk the mayonnaise, olive oil, salt, and pepper, then mix into the large bowl.

Per Serving:

calories: 192 | fat: 15g | protein: 5g | carbs: 14g | fiber: 7g | sodium: 841mg

Watermelon Burrata Salad

Prep time: 10 minutes | Cook time: 0 minutes | Serves 4

2 cups cubes or chunks watermelon
1½ cups small burrata cheese balls, cut into medium chunks
1 small red onion or 2 shallots, thinly sliced into half-moons
¼ cup olive oil
¼ cup balsamic vinegar

4 fresh basil leaves, sliced chiffonade-style (roll up leaves of basil, and slice into thin strips)
1 tablespoon lemon zest
Salt and freshly ground black pepper, to taste

1. In a large bowl, mix all the ingredients. Refrigerate until chilled before serving.
Per Serving:
1 cup: calories: 224 | fat: 14g | protein: 14g | carbs: 12g | fiber: 1g | sodium: 560mg

Melon Caprese Salad

Prep time: 20 minutes |Cook time: 0 minutes| Serves: 6

1 cantaloupe, quartered and seeded
½ small seedless watermelon
1 cup grape tomatoes
2 cups fresh mozzarella balls (about 8 ounces / 227 g)
⅓ cup fresh basil or mint leaves, torn into small pieces

2 tablespoons extra-virgin olive oil
1 tablespoon balsamic vinegar
¼ teaspoon freshly ground black pepper
¼ teaspoon kosher or sea salt

1. Using a melon baller or a metal, teaspoon-size measuring spoon, scoop balls out of the cantaloupe. You should get about 2½ to 3 cups from one cantaloupe. (If you prefer, cut the melon into bite-size pieces instead of making balls.) Put them in a large colander over a large serving bowl. 2. Using the same method, ball or cut the watermelon into bite-size pieces; you should get about 2 cups. Put the watermelon balls in the colander with the cantaloupe. 3. Let the fruit drain for 10 minutes. Pour the juice from the bowl into a container to refrigerate and save for drinking or adding to smoothies. Wipe the bowl dry, and put in the cut fruit. 4. Add the tomatoes, mozzarella, basil, oil, vinegar, pepper, and salt to the fruit mixture. Gently mix until everything is incorporated and serve.
Per Serving:
calories: 297 | fat: 12g | protein: 14g | carbs: 39g | fiber: 3g | sodium: 123mg

Chapter 11

Pizzas, Wraps, and Sandwiches

Moroccan Lamb Wrap with Harissa

Prep time: 10 minutes | Cook time: 10 minutes | Serves 4

1 clove garlic, minced	1 medium eggplant, sliced
2 teaspoons ground cumin	½-inch thick
2 teaspoons chopped fresh	1 medium zucchini, sliced
thyme	lengthwise into 4 slices
¼ cup olive oil, divided	1 bell pepper (any color),
1 lamb leg steak, about 12	roasted and skinned
ounces (340 g)	6 to 8 Kalamata olives, sliced
4 (8-inch) pocketless pita	Juice of 1 lemon
rounds or naan, preferably	2 to 4 tablespoons harissa
whole-wheat	2 cups arugula

1. In a large bowl, combine the garlic, cumin, thyme, and 1 tablespoon of the olive oil. Add the lamb, turn to coat, cover, refrigerate, and marinate for at least an hour. 2. Preheat the oven to 400°F(205°C). 3. Heat a grill or grill pan to high heat. Remove the lamb from the marinade and grill for about 4 minutes per side, until medium-rare. Transfer to a plate and let rest for about 10 minutes before slicing thinly across the grain. 4. While the meat is resting, wrap the bread rounds in aluminum foil and heat in the oven for about 10 minutes. 5. Meanwhile, brush the eggplant and zucchini slices with the remaining olive oil and grill until tender, about 3 minutes. Dice them and the bell pepper. Toss in a large bowl with the olives and lemon juice. 6. Spread some of the harissa onto each warm flatbread round and top each evenly with roasted vegetables, a few slices of lamb, and a handful of the arugula. 7. Roll up the wraps, cut each in half crosswise, and serve immediately.

Per Serving:

calories: 553 | fat: 24g | protein: 33g | carbs: 53g | fiber: 11g | sodium: 531mg

Grilled Chicken Salad Pita

Prep time: 15 minutes | Cook time: 16 minutes | Serves 1

1 boneless, skinless chicken	½ small red onion, thinly sliced
breast	½ small cucumber, chopped
Sea salt and freshly ground	1 tablespoon olive oil
pepper, to taste	Juice of 1 lemon
1 cup baby spinach	1 whole-wheat pita pocket
1 roasted red pepper, sliced	2 tablespoons crumbled feta
1 tomato, chopped	cheese

1. Preheat a gas or charcoal grill to medium-high heat. 2. Season the chicken breast with sea salt and freshly ground pepper, and grill until cooked through, about 7–8 minutes per side. 3. Allow chicken to rest for 5 minutes before slicing into strips. 4. While the chicken is cooking, put all the chopped vegetables into a medium-mixing bowl and season with sea salt and freshly ground pepper. 5. Chop the chicken into cubes and add to salad. Add the olive oil and lemon juice and toss well. 6. Stuff the mixture onto a pita pocket and top with the feta cheese. Serve immediately.

Per Serving:

calories: 653 | fat: 26g | protein: 71g | carbs: 34g | fiber: 6g | sodium: 464mg

Roasted Vegetable Bocadillo with Romesco Sauce

Prep time: 10 minutes | Cook time: 20 minutes | Serves 4

2 small yellow squash, sliced	2 roasted red peppers from a
lengthwise	jar, drained
2 small zucchini, sliced	2 tablespoons blanched
lengthwise	almonds
1 medium red onion, thinly	1 tablespoon sherry vinegar
sliced	1 small clove garlic
4 large button mushrooms,	4 crusty multigrain rolls
sliced	4 ounces (113 g) goat cheese, at
2 tablespoons olive oil	room temperature
1 teaspoon salt, divided	1 tablespoon chopped fresh
½ teaspoon freshly ground	basil
black pepper, divided	

1. Preheat the oven to 400°F(205°C). 2. In a medium bowl, toss the yellow squash, zucchini, onion, and mushrooms with the olive oil, ½ teaspoon salt, and ¼ teaspoon pepper. Spread on a large baking sheet. Roast the vegetables in the oven for about 20 minutes, until softened. 3. Meanwhile, in a food processor, combine the roasted peppers, almonds, vinegar, garlic, the remaining ½ teaspoon salt, and the remaining ¼ teaspoon pepper and process until smooth. 4. Split the rolls and spread ¼ of the goat cheese on the bottom of each. Place the roasted vegetables on top of the cheese, dividing equally. Top with chopped basil. Spread the top halves of the rolls with the roasted red pepper sauce and serve immediately.

Per Serving:

calories: 379 | fat: 21g | protein: 17g | carbs: 32g | fiber: 4g | sodium: 592mg

Margherita Open-Face Sandwiches

Prep time: 10 minutes |Cook time: 5 minutes| Serves: 4

2 (6- to 7-inch) whole-wheat	¼ teaspoon dried oregano
submarine or hoagie rolls,	1 cup fresh mozzarella (about 4
sliced open horizontally	ounces / 113 g), patted dry and
1 tablespoon extra-virgin olive	sliced
oil	¼ cup lightly packed fresh basil
1 garlic clove, halved	leaves, torn into small pieces
1 large ripe tomato, cut into 8	¼ teaspoon freshly ground
slices	black pepper

1. Preheat the broiler to high with the rack 4 inches under the heating element. 2. Place the sliced bread on a large, rimmed baking sheet. Place under the broiler for 1 minute, until the bread is just lightly toasted. Remove from the oven. 3. Brush each piece of the toasted bread with the oil, and rub a garlic half over each piece. 4. Place the toasted bread back on the baking sheet. Evenly distribute the tomato slices on each piece, sprinkle with the oregano, and layer the cheese on top. 5. Place the baking sheet under the broiler. Set the timer for 1½ minutes, but check after 1 minute. When the cheese is melted and the edges are just starting to get dark brown, remove the sandwiches from the oven (this can take anywhere from 1½ to 2 minutes). 6. Top each sandwich with the fresh basil and pepper.

Per Serving:

calories: 176 | fat: 9g | protein: 10g | carbs: 14g | fiber: 2g | sodium: 119mg

Grilled Eggplant and Chopped Greek Salad Wraps

Prep time: 10 minutes | Cook time: 20 minutes | Serves 4

15 small tomatoes, such as cherry or grape tomatoes, halved	2 tablespoons olive oil, plus 2 teaspoons, divided
10 pitted Kalamata olives, chopped	¾ teaspoon salt, divided
1 medium red onion, halved and thinly sliced	1 medium cucumber, peeled, halved lengthwise, seeded, and diced
¾ cup crumbled feta cheese (about 4 ounces / 113 g)	1 large eggplant, sliced ½-inch thick
2 tablespoons balsamic vinegar	½ teaspoon freshly ground black pepper
1 tablespoon chopped fresh parsley	4 whole-wheat sandwich wraps or whole-wheat flour tortillas
1 clove garlic, minced	

1. In a medium bowl, toss together the tomatoes, olives, onion, cheese, vinegar, parsley, garlic, 2 teaspoons olive oil, and ¼ teaspoon of salt. Let sit at room temperature for 20 minutes. Add the cucumber, toss to combine, and let sit another 10 minutes. 2. While the salad is resting, grill the eggplant. Heat a grill or grill pan to high heat. Brush the remaining 2 tablespoons olive oil onto both sides of the eggplant slices. Grill for about 8 to 10 minutes per side, until grill marks appear and the eggplant is tender and cooked through. Transfer to a plate and season with the remaining ½ teaspoon of salt and the pepper. 3. Heat the wraps in a large, dry skillet over medium heat just until warm and soft, about 1 minute on each side. Place 2 or 3 eggplant slices down the center of each wrap. Spoon some of the salad mixture on top of the eggplant, using a slotted spoon so that any excess liquid is drained off. Fold in the sides of the wrap and roll up like a burrito. Serve immediately.

Per Serving:

calories: 233 | fat: 10g | protein: 8g | carbs: 29g | fiber: 7g | sodium: 707mg

Barbecue Chicken Pita Pizza

Prep time: 5 minutes | Cook time: 5 to 7 minutes per batch | Makes 4 pizzas

1 cup barbecue sauce, divided	cheese
4 pita breads	½ small red onion, thinly sliced
2 cups shredded cooked chicken	2 tablespoons finely chopped fresh cilantro
2 cups shredded Mozzarella	

1. Measure ½ cup of the barbecue sauce in a small measuring cup. Spread 2 tablespoons of the barbecue sauce on each pita. 2. In a medium bowl, mix together the remaining ½ cup of barbecue sauce and chicken. Place ½ cup of the chicken on each pita. Top each pizza with ½ cup of the Mozzarella cheese. Sprinkle the tops of the pizzas with the red onion. 3. Place one pizza in the air fryer. Air fry at 400ºF (204ºC) for 5 to 7 minutes. Repeat this process with the remaining pizzas. 4. Top the pizzas with the cilantro.

Per Serving:

calories: 530 | fat: 19g | protein: 40g | carbs: 47g | fiber: 2g | sodium: 672mg

Beans and Greens Pizza

Prep time: 11 minutes | Cook time: 14 to 19 minutes | Serves 4

¾ cup whole-wheat pastry flour	1 cup canned no-salt-added cannellini beans, rinsed and drained
½ teaspoon low-sodium baking powder	
1 tablespoon olive oil, divided	½ teaspoon dried thyme
1 cup chopped kale	1 piece low-sodium string cheese, torn into pieces
2 cups chopped fresh baby spinach	

1. In a small bowl, mix the pastry flour and baking powder until well combined. 2. Add ¼ cup of water and 2 teaspoons of olive oil. Mix until a dough forms. 3. On a floured surface, press or roll the dough into a 7-inch round. Set aside while you cook the greens. 4. In a baking pan, mix the kale, spinach, and remaining teaspoon of the olive oil. Air fry at 350ºF (177ºC) for 3 to 5 minutes, until the greens are wilted. Drain well. 5. Put the pizza dough into the air fryer basket. Top with the greens, cannellini beans, thyme, and string cheese. Air fry for 11 to 14 minutes, or until the crust is golden brown and the cheese is melted. Cut into quarters to serve.

Per Serving:

calories: 181 | fat: 6g | protein: 8g | carbs: 27g | fiber: 6g | sodium: 103mg

Flatbread Pizza with Roasted Cherry Tomatoes, Artichokes, and Feta

Prep time: 5 minutes | Cook time: 20 minutes | Serves 4

1½ pounds (680 g) cherry or grape tomatoes, halved	1 can artichoke hearts, rinsed, well drained, and cut into thin wedges
3 tablespoons olive oil, divided	
½ teaspoon salt	8 ounces (227 g) crumbled feta cheese
½ teaspoon freshly ground black pepper	¼ cup chopped fresh Greek oregano
4 Middle Eastern–style flatbread rounds	

1. Preheat the oven to 500°F(260ºC). 2. In a medium bowl, toss the tomatoes with 1 tablespoon olive oil, the salt, and the pepper. Spread out on a large baking sheet. Roast in the preheated oven until the tomato skins begin to blister and crack, about 10 to 12 minutes. Remove the tomatoes from the oven and reduce the heat to 450°F(235ºC). 3. Place the flatbreads on a large baking sheet (or two baking sheets if necessary) and brush the tops with the remaining 2 tablespoons of olive oil. Top with the artichoke hearts, roasted tomatoes, and cheese, dividing equally. 4. Bake the flatbreads in the oven for about 8 to 10 minutes, until the edges are lightly browned and the cheese is melted. Sprinkle the oregano over the top and serve immediately.

Per Serving:

calories: 436 | fat: 27g | protein: 16g | carbs: 34g | fiber: 6g | sodium: 649mg

Dill Salmon Salad Wraps

**Prep time: 10 minutes |Cook time: 10 minutes|
Serves:6**

1 pound (454 g) salmon filet, cooked and flaked, or 3 (5-ounce / 142-g) cans salmon	2 tablespoons capers
½ cup diced carrots (about 1 carrot)	1½ tablespoons extra-virgin olive oil
½ cup diced celery (about 1 celery stalk)	1 tablespoon aged balsamic vinegar
3 tablespoons chopped fresh dill	½ teaspoon freshly ground black pepper
3 tablespoons diced red onion (a little less than ⅛ onion)	¼ teaspoon kosher or sea salt
	4 whole-wheat flatbread wraps or soft whole-wheat tortillas

1. In a large bowl, mix together the salmon, carrots, celery, dill, red onion, capers, oil, vinegar, pepper, and salt. 2. Divide the salmon salad among the flatbreads. Fold up the bottom of the flatbread, then roll up the wrap and serve.

Per Serving:
calories: 185 | fat: 8g | protein: 17g | carbs: 12g | fiber: 2g | sodium: 237mg

Pesto Chicken Mini Pizzas

**Prep time: 5 minutes | Cook time: 10 minutes |
Serves 4**

2 cups shredded cooked chicken	4 English muffins, split
¾ cup pesto	2 cups shredded Mozzarella cheese

1. In a medium bowl, toss the chicken with the pesto. Place one-eighth of the chicken on each English muffin half. Top each English muffin with ¼ cup of the Mozzarella cheese. 2. Put four pizzas at a time in the air fryer and air fry at 350°F (177°C) for 5 minutes. Repeat this process with the other four pizzas.

Per Serving:
calories: 617 | fat: 36g | protein: 45g | carbs: 29g | fiber: 3g | sodium: 544mg

Mediterranean-Pita Wraps

**Prep time: 5 minutes | Cook time: 14 minutes |
Serves 4**

1 pound (454 g) mackerel fish fillets	Sea salt and freshly ground black pepper, to taste
2 tablespoons olive oil	2 ounces (57 g) feta cheese, crumbled
1 tablespoon Mediterranean seasoning mix	4 tortillas
½ teaspoon chili powder	

1. Toss the fish fillets with the olive oil; place them in the lightly oiled air fryer basket. 2. Air fry the fish fillets at 400°F (204°C) for about 14 minutes, turning them over halfway through the cooking time. 3. Assemble your pitas with the chopped fish and remaining ingredients and serve warm.

Per Serving:
calories: 275 | fat: 13g | protein: 27g | carbs: 13g | fiber: 2g | sodium: 322mg

Classic Margherita Pizza

**Prep time: 10 minutes | Cook time: 10 minutes |
Serves 4**

All-purpose flour, for dusting	1 teaspoon Italian seasoning
1 pound (454 g) premade pizza dough	Pinch sea salt, plus more as needed
1 (15-ounce / 425-g) can crushed San Marzano tomatoes, with their juices	1½ teaspoons olive oil, for drizzling
2 garlic cloves	10 slices mozzarella cheese
	12 to 15 fresh basil leaves

1. Preheat the oven to 475°F (245°C). 2. On a floured surface, roll out the dough to a 12-inch round and place it on a lightly floured pizza pan or baking sheet. 3. In a food processor, combine the tomatoes with their juices, garlic, Italian seasoning, and salt and process until smooth. Taste and adjust the seasoning. 4. Drizzle the olive oil over the pizza dough, then spoon the pizza sauce over the dough and spread it out evenly with the back of the spoon, leaving a 1-inch border. Evenly distribute the mozzarella over the pizza. 5. Bake until the crust is cooked through and golden, 8 to 10 minutes. Remove from the oven and let sit for 1 to 2 minutes. Top with the basil right before serving.

Per Serving:
calories: 570 | fat: 21g | protein: 28g | carbs: 66g | fiber: 4g | sodium: 570mg

Turkish Pizza

**Prep time: 20 minutes | Cook time: 10 minutes |
Serves 4**

4 ounces (113 g) ground lamb or 85% lean ground beef	2 teaspoons tomato paste
¼ cup finely chopped green bell pepper	¼ teaspoon sweet paprika
¼ cup chopped fresh parsley	¼ teaspoon ground cumin
1 small plum tomato, seeded and finely chopped	⅛ to ¼ teaspoon red pepper flakes
2 tablespoons finely chopped yellow onion	⅛ teaspoon ground allspice
1 garlic clove, minced	⅛ teaspoon kosher salt
	⅛ teaspoon black pepper
	4 (6-inch) flour tortillas
For Serving:	
Chopped fresh mint	Lemon wedges
Extra-virgin olive oil	

1. In a medium bowl, gently mix the ground lamb, bell pepper, parsley, chopped tomato, onion, garlic, tomato paste, paprika, cumin, red pepper flakes, allspice, salt, and black pepper until well combined. 2. Divide the meat mixture evenly among the tortillas, spreading it all the way to the edge of each tortilla. 3. Place 1 tortilla in the air fryer basket. Set the air fryer to 400°F (204°C) for 10 minutes, or until the meat topping has browned and the edge of the tortilla is golden. Transfer to a plate and repeat to cook the remaining tortillas. 4. Serve the pizzas warm, topped with chopped fresh mint and a drizzle of extra-virgin olive oil and with lemon wedges alongside.

Per Serving:
calories: 172 | fat: 8g | protein: 8g | carbs: 18g | fiber: 2g | sodium: 318mg

Bocadillo with Herbed Tuna and Piquillo Peppers

Prep time: 5 minutes | Cook time: 20 minutes | Serves 4

2 tablespoons olive oil, plus more for brushing	3 tablespoons sherry vinegar
1 medium onion, finely chopped	1 carrot, finely diced
2 leeks, white and tender green parts only, finely chopped	2 (8-ounce / 227-g) jars Spanish tuna in olive oil
1 teaspoon chopped thyme	4 crusty whole-wheat sandwich rolls, split
½ teaspoon dried marjoram	1 ripe tomato, grated on the large holes of a box grater
½ teaspoon salt	4 piquillo peppers, cut into thin strips
¼ teaspoon freshly ground black pepper	

1. Heat 2 tablespoons olive oil in a medium skillet over medium heat. Add the onion, leeks, thyme, marjoram, salt, and pepper. Stir frequently until the onions are softened, about 10 minutes. Stir in the vinegar and carrot and cook until the liquid has evaporated, 5 minutes. Transfer the mixture to a bowl and let cool to room temperature or refrigerate for 15 minutes or so. 2. In a medium bowl, combine the tuna, along with its oil, with the onion mixture, breaking the tuna chunks up with a fork. 3. Brush the rolls lightly with oil and toast under the broiler until lightly browned, about 2 minutes. Spoon the tomato pulp onto the bottom half of each roll, dividing equally and spreading it with the back of the spoon. Divide the tuna mixture among the rolls and top with the piquillo pepper slices. Serve immediately.

Per Serving:

calories: 416 | fat: 18g | protein: 35g | carbs: 30g | fiber: 5g | sodium: 520mg

Turkey and Provolone Panini with Roasted Peppers and Onions

Prep time: 15 minutes | Cook time: 1 hour 5 minutes | Serves 4

For the peppers and onions	black pepper
2 red bell pepper, seeded and quartered	For the panini
2 red onions, peeled and quartered	2 tablespoons olive oil
2 tablespoons olive oil	8 slices whole-wheat bread
½ teaspoon salt	8 ounces (227 g) thinly sliced provolone cheese
½ teaspoon freshly ground	8 ounces (227 g) sliced roasted turkey or chicken breast

1. Preheat the oven to 375°F(190°C). 2. To roast the peppers and onions, toss them together with the olive oil, salt, and pepper on a large, rimmed baking sheet. Spread them out in a single layer and then bake in the preheated oven for 45 to 60 minutes, turning occasionally, until they are tender and beginning to brown. Remove the peppers and onions from the oven and let them cool for a few minutes until they are cool enough to handle. Skin the peppers and thinly slice them. Thinly slice the onions. 3. Preheat a skillet or grill pan over medium-high heat. 4. To make the panini, brush one side of each of the 8 slices of bread with olive oil. Place 4 of the bread slices, oiled side down, on your work surface. Top each with ¼ of

the cheese and ¼ of the turkey, and top with some of the roasted peppers and onions. Place the remaining 4 bread slices on top of the sandwiches, oiled side up. 5. Place the sandwiches in the skillet or grill pan (you may have to cook them in two batches), cover the pan, and cook until the bottoms have golden brown grill marks and the cheese is beginning to melt, about 2 minutes. Turn the sandwiches over and cook, covered, until the second side is golden brown and the cheese is melted, another 2 minutes or so. Cut each sandwich in half and serve immediately.

Per Serving:

calories: 603 | fat: 32g | protein: 41g | carbs: 37g | fiber: 6g | sodium: 792mg

Turkey Burgers with Feta and Dill

Prep time: 5 minutes | Cook time: 15 minutes | Serves 4

1 pound (454 g) ground turkey breast	½ teaspoon kosher salt
1 small red onion, ½ finely chopped, ½ sliced	¼ teaspoon ground black pepper
½ cup crumbled feta cheese	4 whole grain hamburger rolls
¼ cup chopped fresh dill	4 thick slices tomato
1 clove garlic, minced	4 leaves lettuce

1. Coat a grill rack or grill pan with olive oil and prepare to medium-high heat. 2. In a large bowl, use your hands to combine the turkey, chopped onion, cheese, dill, garlic, salt, and pepper. Do not overmix. Divide into 4 patties, 4' in diameter. 3. Grill the patties, covered, until a thermometer inserted in the center registers 165°F(74°C), 5 to 6 minutes per side. 4. Serve each patty on a roll with the sliced onion, 1 slice of the tomato, and 1 leaf of the lettuce.

Per Serving:

calories: 305 | fat: 7g | protein: 35g | carbs: 26g | fiber: 3g | sodium: 708mg

Grilled Eggplant and Feta Sandwiches

Prep time: 10 minutes | Cook time: 8 minutes | Serves 2

1 medium eggplant, sliced into ½-inch-thick slices	4 slices whole-wheat bread, toasted
2 tablespoons olive oil	1 cup baby spinach leaves
Sea salt and freshly ground pepper, to taste	2 ounces (57 g) feta cheese, softened
5 to 6 tablespoons hummus	

1. Preheat a gas or charcoal grill to medium-high heat. 2. Salt both sides of the sliced eggplant, and let sit for 20 minutes to draw out the bitter juices. 3. Rinse the eggplant and pat dry with a paper towel. 4. Brush the eggplant slices with olive oil and season with sea salt and freshly ground pepper. 5. Grill the eggplant until lightly charred on both sides but still slightly firm in the middle, about 3–4 minutes a side. 6. Spread the hummus on the bread and top with the spinach leaves, feta, and eggplant. Top with the other slice of bread and serve warm.

Per Serving:

calories: 516 | fat: 27g | protein: 14g | carbs: 59g | fiber: 14g | sodium: 597mg

Avocado and Asparagus Wraps

Prep time: 10 minutes | Cook time: 10 minutes | Serves 6

12 spears asparagus
1 ripe avocado, mashed slightly
Juice of 1 lime
2 cloves garlic, minced
2 cups brown rice, cooked and chilled

3 tablespoons Greek yogurt
Sea salt and freshly ground pepper, to taste
3 (8-inch) whole-grain tortillas
½ cup cilantro, diced
2 tablespoons red onion, diced

1. Steam asparagus in microwave or stove top steamer until tender. Mash the avocado, lime juice, and garlic in a medium mixing bowl. In a separate bowl, mix the rice and yogurt. 2. Season both mixtures with sea salt and freshly ground pepper to taste. Heat the tortillas in a dry nonstick skillet. 3. Spread each tortilla with the avocado mixture, and top with the rice, cilantro, and onion, followed by the asparagus. 4. Fold up both sides of the tortilla, and roll tightly to close. Cut in half diagonally before serving.

Per Serving:
calories: 361 | fat: 9g | protein: 9g | carbs: 63g | fiber: 7g | sodium: 117mg

Jerk Chicken Wraps

Prep time: 30 minutes | Cook time: 15 minutes | Serves 4

1 pound (454 g) boneless, skinless chicken tenderloins
1 cup jerk marinade
Olive oil
4 large low-carb tortillas

1 cup julienned carrots
1 cup peeled cucumber ribbons
1 cup shredded lettuce
1 cup mango or pineapple chunks

1. In a medium bowl, coat the chicken with the jerk marinade, cover, and refrigerate for 1 hour. 2. Spray the air fryer basket lightly with olive oil. 3. Place the chicken in the air fryer basket in a single layer and spray lightly with olive oil. You may need to cook the chicken in batches. Reserve any leftover marinade. 4. Air fry at 375ºF (191ºC) for 8 minutes. Turn the chicken over and brush with some of the remaining marinade. Cook until the chicken reaches an internal temperature of at least 165ºF (74ºC), an additional 5 to 7 minutes. 5. To assemble the wraps, fill each tortilla with ¼ cup carrots, ¼ cup cucumber, ¼ cup lettuce, and ¼ cup mango. Place one quarter of the chicken tenderloins on top and roll up the tortilla. These are great served warm or cold.

Per Serving:
calories: 241 | fat: 4g | protein: 28g | carbs: 23g | fiber: 4g | sodium: 85mg

Chapter 12

Pasta

Orzo with Feta and Marinated Peppers

Prep time:1 hour 25 minutes | Cook time: 37 minutes | Serves 2

2 medium red bell peppers
¼ cup extra virgin olive oil
1 tablespoon balsamic vinegar plus 1 teaspoon for serving
¼ teaspoon ground cumin
Pinch of ground cinnamon
Pinch of ground cloves
¼ teaspoon fine sea salt plus a

pinch for the orzo
1 cup uncooked orzo
3 ounces (85 g) crumbled feta
1 tablespoon chopped fresh basil
¼ teaspoon freshly ground black pepper

1. Preheat the oven at 350°F (180°C). Place the peppers on a baking pan and roast in the oven for 25 minutes or until they're soft and can be pierced with a fork. Set aside to cool for 10 minutes. 2. While the peppers are roasting, combine the olive oil, 1 tablespoon of the balsamic vinegar, cumin, cinnamon, cloves, and ¼ teaspoon of the sea salt. Stir to combine, then set aside. 3. Peel the cooled peppers, remove the seeds, and then chop into large pieces. Place the peppers in the olive oil and vinegar mixture and then toss to coat, ensuring the peppers are covered in the marinade. Cover and place in the refrigerator to marinate for 20 minutes. 4. While the peppers are marinating, prepare the orzo by bringing 3 cups of water and a pinch of salt to a boil in a large pot over high heat. When the water is boiling, add the orzo, reduce the heat to medium, and cook, stirring occasionally, for 10–12 minutes or until soft, then drain and transfer to a serving bowl. 5. Add the peppers and marinade to the orzo, mixing well, then place in the refrigerator and to cool for at least 1 hour. 6. To serve, top with the feta, basil, black pepper, and 1 teaspoon of the balsamic vinegar. Mix well, and serve promptly. Store covered in the refrigerator for up to 3 days.

Per Serving:
calories: 600 | fat: 37g | protein: 15g | carbs: 51g | fiber: 4g | sodium: 690mg

Rotini with Spinach, Cherry Tomatoes, and Feta

Prep time: 5 minutes | Cook time: 30 minutes | Serves 2

6 ounces (170 g) uncooked rotini pasta (penne pasta will also work)
1 garlic clove, minced
3 tablespoons extra virgin olive oil, divided
1½ cups cherry tomatoes, halved and divided

9 ounces (255 g) baby leaf spinach, washed and chopped
1½ ounces (43 g) crumbled feta, divided
Kosher salt, to taste
Freshly ground black pepper, to taste

1. Cook the pasta according to the package instructions, reserving ½ cup of the cooking water. Drain and set aside. 2. While the pasta is cooking, combine the garlic with 2 tablespoons of the olive oil in a small bowl. Set aside. 3. Add the remaining tablespoon of olive oil to a medium pan placed over medium heat and then add 1 cup of the tomatoes. Cook for 2–3 minutes, then use a fork to mash lightly. 4. Add the spinach to the pan and continue cooking, stirring occasionally, until the spinach is wilted and the liquid is absorbed, about 4–5 minutes. 5. Transfer the cooked pasta to the pan with the spinach and tomatoes. Add 3 tablespoons of the pasta water, the garlic and olive oil mixture, and 1 ounce (28 g) of the crumbled feta. Increase the heat to high and cook for 1 minute. 6. Top with

the remaining cherry tomatoes and feta, and season to taste with kosher salt and black pepper. Store covered in the refrigerator for up to 2 days.

Per Serving:
calories: 602 | fat: 27g | protein: 19g | carbs: 74g | fiber: 7g | sodium: 307mg

Rigatoni with Lamb Meatballs

Prep time: 15 minutes | Cook time: 3 to 5 hours | Serves 4

8 ounces (227 g) dried rigatoni pasta
2 (28-ounce / 794-g) cans no-salt-added crushed tomatoes or no-salt-added diced tomatoes
1 small onion, diced
1 bell pepper, any color, seeded and diced
3 garlic cloves, minced, divided
1 pound (454 g) raw ground

lamb
1 large egg
2 tablespoons bread crumbs
1 tablespoon dried parsley
1 teaspoon dried oregano
1 teaspoon sea salt
½ teaspoon freshly ground black pepper

1. In a slow cooker, combine the pasta, tomatoes, onion, bell pepper, and 1 clove of garlic. Stir to mix well. 2. In a large bowl, mix together the ground lamb, egg, bread crumbs, the remaining 2 garlic cloves, parsley, oregano, salt, and black pepper until all of the ingredients are evenly blended. Shape the meat mixture into 6 to 9 large meatballs. Nestle the meatballs into the pasta and tomato sauce. 3. Cover the cooker and cook for 3 to 5 hours on Low heat, or until the pasta is tender.

Per Serving:
calories: 653 | fat: 29g | protein: 32g | carbs: 69g | fiber: 10g | sodium: 847mg

Toasted Orzo Salad

Prep time: 15 minutes | Cook time: 8 minutes | Serves 6

2 tablespoons light olive oil
1 clove garlic, peeled and crushed
2 cups orzo
3 cups vegetable broth
½ cup sliced black olives
3 scallions, thinly sliced
1 medium Roma tomato, seeded and diced

1 medium red bell pepper, seeded and diced
¼ cup crumbled feta cheese
1 tablespoon extra-virgin olive oil
1 tablespoon red wine vinegar
½ teaspoon ground black pepper
¼ teaspoon salt

1. Press the Sauté button on the Instant Pot® and heat light olive oil. Add garlic and orzo and cook, stirring frequently, until orzo is light golden brown, about 5 minutes. Press the Cancel button. 2. Add broth and stir. Close lid, set steam release to Sealing, press the Manual button, and set time to 3 minutes. When the timer beeps, let pressure release naturally for 5 minutes, then quick-release the remaining pressure until the float valve drops and open lid. 3. Transfer orzo to a medium bowl, then set aside to cool to room temperature, about 30 minutes. Add olives, scallions, tomato, bell pepper, feta, extra-virgin olive oil, vinegar, black pepper, and salt, and stir until combined. Serve at room temperature or refrigerate for at least 2 hours.

Per Serving:
calories: 120 | fat: 4g | protein: 4g | carbs: 17g | fiber: 1g | sodium: 586mg

Simple Pesto Pasta

Prep time: 10 minutes | Cook time: 10 minutes | Serves 4 to 6

1 pound (454 g) spaghetti	black pepper
4 cups fresh basil leaves, stems removed	¼ cup lemon juice
3 cloves garlic	½ cup pine nuts, toasted
1 teaspoon salt	½ cup grated Parmesan cheese
½ teaspoon freshly ground	1 cup extra-virgin olive oil

1. Bring a large pot of salted water to a boil. Add the spaghetti to the pot and cook for 8 minutes. 2. Put basil, garlic, salt, pepper, lemon juice, pine nuts, and Parmesan cheese in a food processor bowl with chopping blade and purée. 3. While the processor is running, slowly drizzle the olive oil through the top opening. Process until all the olive oil has been added. 4. Reserve ½ cup of the pasta water. Drain the pasta and put it into a bowl. Immediately add the pesto and pasta water to the pasta and toss everything together. Serve warm.

Per Serving:

calories: 1067 | fat: 72g | protein: 23g | carbs: 91g | fiber: 6g | sodium: 817mg

Bowtie Pesto Pasta Salad

Prep time: 5 minutes | Cook time: 4 minutes | Serves 8

1 pound (454 g) whole-wheat bowtie pasta	2 cups baby spinach
4 cups water	½ cup chopped fresh basil
1 tablespoon extra-virgin olive oil	½ cup prepared pesto
2 cups halved cherry tomatoes	½ teaspoon ground black pepper
	½ cup grated Parmesan cheese

1. Add pasta, water, and olive oil to the Instant Pot®. Close lid, set steam release to Sealing, press the Manual button, and set time to 4 minutes. 2. When the timer beeps, quick-release the pressure until the float valve drops and open lid. Drain off any excess liquid. Allow pasta to cool to room temperature, about 30 minutes. Stir in tomatoes, spinach, basil, pesto, pepper, and cheese. Refrigerate for 2 hours. Stir well before serving.

Per Serving:

calories: 360 | fat: 13g | protein: 16g | carbs: 44g | fiber: 7g | sodium: 372mg

Creamy Spring Vegetable Linguine

Prep time: 10 minutes | Cook time: 10 minutes | Serves 4 to 6

1 pound (454 g) linguine	1 cup frozen peas, thawed
5 cups water, plus extra as needed	4 ounces (113 g) finely grated Pecorino Romano (2 cups), plus extra for serving
1 tablespoon extra-virgin olive oil	½ teaspoon pepper
1 teaspoon table salt	2 teaspoons grated lemon zest
1 cup jarred whole baby artichokes packed in water, quartered	2 tablespoons chopped fresh tarragon

1. Loosely wrap half of pasta in dish towel, then press bundle against corner of counter to break noodles into 6-inch lengths; repeat with remaining pasta. 2. Add pasta, water, oil, and salt to Instant Pot, making sure pasta is completely submerged. Lock lid in place and close pressure release valve. Select high pressure cook function and cook for 4 minutes. Turn off Instant Pot and quick-release pressure. Carefully remove lid, allowing steam to escape away from you. 3. Stir artichokes and peas into pasta, cover, and let sit until heated through, about 3 minutes. Gently stir in Pecorino and pepper until cheese is melted and fully combined, 1 to 2 minutes. Adjust consistency with extra hot water as needed. Stir in lemon zest and tarragon, and season with salt and pepper to taste. Serve, passing extra Pecorino separately.

Per Serving:

calories: 390 | fat: 8g | protein: 17g | carbs: 59g | fiber: 4g | sodium: 680mg

Israeli Pasta Salad

Prep time: 15 minutes | Cook time: 4 minutes | Serves 6

½ pound (227 g) whole-wheat penne pasta	½ medium red onion, peeled and chopped
4 cups water	½ cup crumbled feta cheese
1 tablespoon plus ¼ cup extra-virgin olive oil, divided	1 teaspoon fresh thyme leaves
1 cup quartered cherry tomatoes	1 teaspoon chopped fresh oregano
½ English cucumber, chopped	½ teaspoon ground black pepper
½ medium orange bell pepper, seeded and chopped	¼ cup lemon juice

1. Add pasta, water, and 1 tablespoon oil to the Instant Pot®. Close lid, set steam release to Sealing, press the Manual button, and set time to 4 minutes. 2. When the timer beeps, quick-release the pressure until the float valve drops and open lid. Drain and set aside to cool for 30 minutes. Stir in tomatoes, cucumber, bell pepper, onion, feta, thyme, oregano, black pepper, lemon juice, and remaining ¼ cup oil. Refrigerate for 2 hours.

Per Serving:

calories: 243 | fat: 16g | protein: 7g | carbs: 20g | fiber: 3g | sodium: 180mg

Creamy Chicken Pasta

Prep time: 10 minutes | Cook time: 4 to 6 hours | Serves 4

¼ cup water	1 small red onion, diced
2 tablespoons arrowroot flour	2 garlic cloves, minced
2 pounds (907 g) boneless, skinless chicken breasts or thighs	1 teaspoon dried oregano
	1 teaspoon dried parsley
1 (28-ounce / 794-g) can no-salt-added diced tomatoes, plus more as needed	1 teaspoon sea salt
	½ teaspoon freshly ground black pepper
1 green or red bell pepper, seeded and diced	8 ounces (227 g) dried pasta
	1 cup low-sodium chicken broth (optional)

1. In a small bowl, whisk together the water and arrowroot flour until the flour dissolves. 2. In a slow cooker, combine the chicken, tomatoes, bell pepper, onion, garlic, oregano, parsley, salt, black pepper, and arrowroot mixture. Stir to mix well. 3. Cover the cooker and cook for 4 to 6 hours on Low heat. 4. Stir in the pasta, making sure it is completely submerged. If it is not, add an additional 1 cup of diced tomatoes or 1 cup of chicken broth. Replace the cover on the cooker and cook for 15 to 30 minutes on Low heat, or until the pasta is tender.

Per Serving:

calories: 555 | fat: 12g | protein: 52g | carbs: 61g | fiber: 11g | sodium: 623mg

Zucchini with Bow Ties

**Prep time: 5 minutes |Cook time: 25 minutes|
Serves: 4**

3 tablespoons extra-virgin olive
oil
2 garlic cloves, minced (about 1
teaspoon)
3 large or 4 medium zucchini,
diced (about 4 cups)
½ teaspoon freshly ground
black pepper
¼ teaspoon kosher or sea salt
½ cup 2% milk
¼ teaspoon ground nutmeg
8 ounces (227 g) uncooked
farfalle (bow ties) or other
small pasta shape
½ cup grated Parmesan or
Romano cheese (about 2
ounces / 57 g)
1 tablespoon freshly squeezed
lemon juice (from ½ medium
lemon)

1. In a large skillet over medium heat, heat the oil. Add the garlic and cook for 1 minute, stirring frequently. Add the zucchini, pepper, and salt. Stir well, cover, and cook for 15 minutes, stirring once or twice. 2. In a small, microwave-safe bowl, warm the milk in the microwave on high for 30 seconds. Stir the milk and nutmeg into the skillet and cook uncovered for another 5 minutes, stirring occasionally. 3. While the zucchini is cooking, in a large stockpot, cook the pasta according to the package directions. 4. Drain the pasta in a colander, saving about 2 tablespoons of pasta water. Add the pasta and pasta water to the skillet. Mix everything together and remove from the heat. Stir in the cheese and lemon juice and serve.
Per Serving:
calories: 405 | fat: 16g | protein: 12g | carbs: 57g | fiber: 9g | sodium: 407mg

Toasted Orzo with Shrimp and Feta

**Prep time: 10 minutes | Cook time: 15 minutes |
Serves 4 to 6**

1 pound (454 g) large shrimp
(26 to 30 per pound), peeled
and deveined
1 tablespoon grated lemon zest
plus 1 tablespoon juice
¼ teaspoon table salt
¼ teaspoon pepper
2 tablespoons extra-virgin olive
oil, plus extra for serving
1 onion, chopped fine
2 garlic cloves, minced
2 cups orzo
2 cups chicken broth, plus extra
as needed
1¼ cups water
½ cup pitted kalamata olives,
chopped coarse
1 ounce (28 g) feta cheese,
crumbled (¼ cup), plus extra
for serving
1 tablespoon chopped fresh dill

1. Toss shrimp with lemon zest, salt, and pepper in bowl; refrigerate until ready to use. 2. Using highest sauté function, heat oil in Instant Pot until shimmering. Add onion and cook until softened, about 5 minutes. Stir in garlic and cook until fragrant, about 30 seconds. Add orzo and cook, stirring frequently, until orzo is coated with oil and lightly browned, about 5 minutes. Stir in broth and water, scraping up any browned bits. 3. Lock lid in place and close pressure release valve. Select high pressure cook function and cook for 2 minutes. Turn off Instant Pot and quick-release pressure. Carefully remove lid, allowing steam to escape away from you. 4. Stir shrimp, olives, and feta into orzo. Cover and let sit until shrimp are opaque throughout, 5 to 7 minutes. Adjust consistency with extra hot broth as needed. Stir in dill and lemon juice, and season with salt and pepper to taste. Sprinkle individual portions with extra feta and drizzle with extra oil before serving.
Per Serving:
calories: 320 | fat: 8g | protein: 18g | carbs: 46g | fiber: 2g | sodium:

670mg

Toasted Couscous with Feta, Cucumber, and Tomato

**Prep time: 15 minutes | Cook time: 10 minutes |
Serves 8**

1 tablespoon plus ¼ cup light
olive oil, divided
2 cups Israeli couscous
3 cups vegetable broth
2 large tomatoes, seeded and
diced
1 large English cucumber, diced
1 medium red onion, peeled
and chopped
½ cup crumbled feta cheese
¼ cup red wine vinegar
½ teaspoon ground black
pepper
¼ cup chopped flat-leaf parsley
¼ cup chopped fresh basil

1. Press the Sauté button on the Instant Pot® and heat 1 tablespoon oil. Add couscous and cook, stirring frequently, until couscous is light golden brown, about 7 minutes. Press the Cancel button. 2. Add broth and stir. Close lid, set steam release to Sealing, press the Manual button, and set time to 2 minutes. When the timer beeps, let pressure release naturally for 5 minutes, then quick-release the remaining pressure until the float valve drops and open lid. 3. Fluff couscous with a fork, then transfer to a medium bowl and set aside to cool to room temperature, about 30 minutes. Add remaining ¼ cup oil, tomatoes, cucumber, onion, feta, vinegar, pepper, parsley, and basil, and stir until combined. Serve at room temperature or refrigerate for at least 2 hours.
Per Serving:
calories: 286 | fat: 11g | protein: 9g | carbs: 38g | fiber: 3g | sodium: 438mg

Rotini with Walnut Pesto, Peas, and Cherry Tomatoes

**Prep time: 10 minutes | Cook time: 4 minutes |
Serves 8**

1 cup packed fresh basil leaves
⅓ cup chopped walnuts
¼ cup grated Parmesan cheese
¼ cup plus 1 tablespoon extra-
virgin olive oil, divided
1 clove garlic, peeled
1 tablespoon lemon juice
¼ teaspoon salt
1 pound (454 g) whole-wheat
rotini pasta
4 cups water
1 pint cherry tomatoes
1 cup fresh or frozen green peas
½ teaspoon ground black
pepper

1. In a food processor, add basil and walnuts. Pulse until finely chopped, about 12 pulses. Add cheese, ¼ cup oil, garlic, lemon juice, and salt, and pulse until a rough paste forms, about 10 pulses. Refrigerate until ready to use. 2. Add pasta, water, and remaining 1 tablespoon oil to the Instant Pot®. Close lid, set steam release to Sealing, press the Manual button, and set time to 4 minutes. 3. When the timer beeps, quick-release the pressure until the float valve drops and open lid. Drain off any excess liquid. Allow pasta to cool to room temperature, about 30 minutes. Stir in basil mixture until pasta is well coated. Add tomatoes, peas, and pepper and toss to coat. Refrigerate for 2 hours. Stir well before serving.
Per Serving:
calories: 371 | fat: 15g | protein: 12g | carbs: 47g | fiber: 7g | sodium: 205mg

Linguine with Avocado Pesto

Prep time: 10 minutes | Cook time: 10 minutes | Serves 4

1 pound (454 g) dried linguine	1 tablespoon packed sun-dried
2 avocados, coarsely chopped	tomatoes
½ cup olive oil	⅛ teaspoon Italian seasoning
½ cup packed fresh basil	⅛ teaspoon red pepper flakes
½ cup pine nuts	Sea salt
Juice of 1 lemon	Freshly ground black pepper
3 garlic cloves	

1. Fill a large stockpot three-quarters full with water and bring to a boil over high heat. Add the pasta and cook according to the package instructions until al dente, about 15 minutes. 2. While the pasta is cooking, in a food processor, combine the avocados, olive oil, basil, pine nuts, lemon juice, garlic, sun-dried tomatoes, Italian seasoning, and red pepper flakes and process until a paste forms. Taste and season with salt and black pepper. 3. When the pasta is done, drain it and return it to the pot. Add half the pesto and mix. Add more pesto as desired and serve.

Per Serving:

calories: 694 | fat: 29g | protein: 17g | carbs: 93g | fiber: 8g | sodium: 11mg

Avgolemono

Prep time: 10 minutes | Cook time: 3 minutes | Serves 6

6 cups chicken stock	pepper
½ cup orzo	¼ cup lemon juice
1 tablespoon olive oil	2 large eggs
12 ounces (340 g) cooked	2 tablespoons chopped fresh
chicken breast, shredded	dill
½ teaspoon salt	1 tablespoon chopped fresh
½ teaspoon ground black	flat-leaf parsley

1. Add stock, orzo, and olive oil to the Instant Pot®. Close lid, set steam release to Sealing, press the Manual button, and set time to 3 minutes. When the timer beeps, quick-release the pressure until the float valve drops. Open lid and stir in chicken, salt, and pepper. 2. In a medium bowl, combine lemon juice and eggs, then slowly whisk in hot cooking liquid from the pot, ¼ cup at a time, until 1 cup of liquid has been added. Immediately add egg mixture to soup and stir well. Let stand on the Keep Warm setting, stirring occasionally, for 10 minutes. Add dill and parsley. Serve immediately.

Per Serving:

calories: 193 | fat: 5g | protein: 21g | carbs: 15g | fiber: 1g | sodium: 552mg

Couscous with Tomatoes and Olives

Prep time: 5 minutes | Cook time: 3 minutes | Serves 4

1 tablespoon tomato paste	oregano
2 cups vegetable broth	2 tablespoons minced fresh
1 cup couscous	chives
1 cup halved cherry tomatoes	1 tablespoon extra-virgin olive
½ cup halved mixed olives	oil
¼ cup minced fresh flat-leaf	1 tablespoon red wine vinegar
parsley	½ teaspoon ground black
2 tablespoons minced fresh	pepper

1. Pour tomato paste and broth into the Instant Pot® and stir until completely dissolved. Stir in couscous. Close lid, set steam release to Sealing, press the Manual button, and set time to 3 minutes. When the timer beeps, let pressure release naturally for 10 minutes, then quick-release the remaining pressure and open lid. 2. Fluff couscous with a fork. Add tomatoes, olives, parsley, oregano, chives, oil, vinegar, and pepper, and stir until combined. Serve warm or at room temperature.

Per Serving:

calories: 232 | fat: 5g | protein: 7g | carbs: 37g | fiber: 2g | sodium: 513mg

Couscous with Crab and Lemon

Prep time: 10 minutes | Cook time: 7 minutes | Serves 4

1 cup couscous	1 tablespoon minced fresh dill
1 clove garlic, peeled and	8 ounces (227 g) jumbo lump
minced	crabmeat
2 cups water	3 tablespoons lemon juice
3 tablespoons extra-virgin olive	½ teaspoon ground black
oil, divided	pepper
¼ cup minced fresh flat-leaf	¼ cup grated Parmesan cheese
parsley	

1. Place couscous, garlic, water, and 1 tablespoon oil in the Instant Pot® and stir well. Close lid, set steam release to Sealing, press the Manual button, and set time to 7 minutes. When the timer beeps, let pressure release naturally for 10 minutes, then quick-release the remaining pressure and open lid. 2. Fluff couscous with a fork. Add parsley, dill, crabmeat, lemon juice, pepper, and remaining 2 tablespoons oil, and stir until combined. Top with cheese and serve immediately.

Per Serving:

calories: 360 | fat: 15g | protein: 22g | carbs: 34g | fiber: 2g | sodium: 388mg

Spaghetti with Fresh Mint Pesto and Ricotta Salata

Prep time: 5 minutes | Cook time: 15 minutes | Serves 4

1 pound (454 g) spaghetti	lemon
¼ cup slivered almonds	⅓ cup olive oil
2 cups packed fresh mint	¼ teaspoon freshly ground
leaves, plus more for garnish	black pepper
3 medium garlic cloves	½ cup freshly grated ricotta
1 tablespoon lemon juice and	salata, plus more for garnish
½ teaspoon lemon zest from 1	

1. Set a large pot of salted water over high heat to boil for the pasta. 2. In a food processor, combine the almonds, mint leaves, garlic, lemon juice and zest, olive oil, and pepper and pulse to a smooth paste. Add the cheese and pulse to combine. 3. When the water is boiling, add the pasta and cook according to the package instructions. Drain the pasta and return it to the pot. Add the pesto to the pasta and toss until the pasta is well coated. Serve hot, garnished with additional mint leaves and cheese, if desired.

Per Serving:

calories: 619 | fat: 31g | protein: 21g | carbs: 70g | fiber: 4g | sodium: 113mg

Fettuccine with Tomatoes and Pesto

Prep time: 15 minutes | Cook time: 10 minutes | Serves 4

1 pound (454 g) whole-grain fettuccine
4 Roma tomatoes, diced
2 teaspoons tomato paste
1 cup vegetable broth
2 garlic cloves, minced
1 tablespoon chopped fresh oregano

½ teaspoon salt
1 packed cup fresh basil leaves
¼ cup extra-virgin olive oil
¼ cup grated Parmesan cheese
¼ cup pine nuts

1. Bring a large stockpot of water to a boil over high heat, and cook the fettuccine according to the package instructions until al dente (still slightly firm). Drain but do not rinse. 2. Meanwhile, in a large, heavy skillet, combine the tomatoes, tomato paste, broth, garlic, oregano, and salt and stir well. Cook over medium heat for 10 minutes. 3. In a blender or food processor, combine the basil, olive oil, Parmesan cheese, and pine nuts and blend until smooth. 4. Stir the pesto into the tomato mixture. Add the pasta and cook, stirring frequently, just until the pasta is well coated and heated through. 5. Serve immediately.

Per Serving:
calories: 636 | fat: 22g | protein: 11g | carbs: 96g | fiber: 3g | sodium: 741mg

Pasta with Marinated Artichokes and Spinach

Prep time: 10 minutes | Cook time: 5 minutes | Serves 6

1 pound (454 g) whole-wheat spaghetti, broken in half
3½ cups water
4 tablespoons extra-virgin olive oil, divided
¼ teaspoon salt
2 cups baby spinach

1 cup drained marinated artichoke hearts
2 tablespoons chopped fresh oregano
2 tablespoons chopped fresh flat-leaf parsley
1 teaspoon ground black pepper
½ cup grated Parmesan cheese

1. Add pasta, water, 2 tablespoons oil, and salt to the Instant Pot®. Close lid, set steam release to Sealing, press the Manual button, and set time to 5 minutes. 2. When the timer beeps, quick-release the pressure until the float valve drops and open lid. Drain off any excess liquid. Stir in remaining 2 tablespoons oil and spinach. Toss until spinach is wilted. Stir in artichokes, oregano, and parsley until well mixed. Sprinkle with pepper and cheese, and serve immediately.

Per Serving:
calories: 414 | fat: 16g | protein: 16g | carbs: 56g | fiber: 9g | sodium: 467mg

Mediterranean Pasta Salad

Prep time: 20 minutes | Cook time: 15 minutes | Serves 4

4 cups dried farfalle (bow-tie) pasta
1 cup canned chickpeas, drained and rinsed
⅔ cup water-packed artichoke hearts, drained and diced
½ red onion, thinly sliced
1 cup packed baby spinach
½ red bell pepper, diced
1 Roma (plum) tomato, diced

½ English cucumber, quartered lengthwise and cut into ½-inch pieces
⅓ cup extra-virgin olive oil
Juice of ½ lemon
Sea salt
Freshly ground black pepper
½ cup crumbled feta cheese

1. Fill a large saucepan three-quarters full with water and bring to a boil over high heat. Add the pasta and cook according to the package directions until al dente, about 15 minutes. Drain the pasta and run it under cold water to stop the cooking process and cool. 2. While the pasta is cooking, in a large bowl, mix the chickpeas, artichoke hearts, onion, spinach, bell pepper, tomato, and cucumber. 3. Add the pasta to the bowl with the vegetables. Add the olive oil and lemon juice and season with salt and black pepper. Mix well. 4. Top the salad with the feta and serve.

Per Serving:
calories: 702 | fat: 25g | protein: 22g | carbs: 99g | fiber: 10g | sodium: 207mg

Chapter 13

Staples, Sauces, Dips, and Dressings

Creamy Grapefruit-Tarragon Dressing

Prep time: 5 minutes | Cook time: 0 minutes | Serves 4 to 6

½ cup avocado oil mayonnaise	(about 2 tablespoons juice)
2 tablespoons Dijon mustard	½ teaspoon salt
1 teaspoon dried tarragon or	¼ teaspoon freshly ground
1 tablespoon chopped fresh	black pepper
tarragon	1 to 2 tablespoons water
Zest and juice of ½ grapefruit	(optional)

1. In a large mason jar or glass measuring cup, combine the mayonnaise, Dijon, tarragon, grapefruit zest and juice, salt, and pepper and whisk well with a fork until smooth and creamy. If a thinner dressing is preferred, thin out with water.

Per Serving:

calories: 49 | fat: 4g | protein: 0g | carbs: 4g | fiber: 0g | sodium: 272mg

Tahini Dressing

Prep time: 5 minutes | Cook time: 0 minutes | Serves 8 to 10

½ cup tahini	1 garlic clove, finely minced or
¼ cup freshly squeezed lemon	½ teaspoon garlic powder
juice (about 2 to 3 lemons)	2 teaspoons salt
¼ cup extra-virgin olive oil	

1. In a glass mason jar with a lid, combine the tahini, lemon juice, olive oil, garlic, and salt. Cover and shake well until combined and creamy. Store in the refrigerator for up to 2 weeks.

Per Serving:

calories: 121 | fat: 12g | protein: 2g | carbs: 3g | fiber: 1g | sodium: 479mg

White Bean Dip with Garlic and Herbs

Prep time: 10 minutes | Cook time: 30 minutes | Serves 16

1 cup dried white beans, rinsed and drained	oregano
3 cloves garlic, peeled and crushed	1 tablespoon chopped fresh tarragon
8 cups water	1 teaspoon chopped fresh thyme leaves
¼ cup extra-virgin olive oil	1 teaspoon grated lemon zest
¼ cup chopped fresh flat-leaf parsley	¼ teaspoon salt
1 tablespoon chopped fresh	¼ teaspoon ground black pepper

1. Place beans and garlic in the Instant Pot® and stir well. Add water, close lid, set steam release to Sealing, press the Manual button, and set time to 30 minutes. 2. When the timer beeps, let pressure release naturally, about 20 minutes. Open lid and check that beans are tender. Press the Cancel button, drain off excess water, and transfer beans and garlic to a food processor with olive oil. Pulse until mixture is smooth with some small chunks. Add parsley, oregano, tarragon, thyme, lemon zest, salt, and pepper, and pulse 3–5 times to mix. Transfer to a storage container and refrigerate for 4 hours or overnight. Serve cold or at room temperature.

Per Serving:

calories: 47 | fat: 3g | protein: 1g | carbs: 3g | fiber: 1g | sodium: 38mg

Pepper Sauce

Prep time: 10 minutes | Cook time: 20 minutes | Makes 4 cups

2 red hot fresh chiles, seeded	2 garlic cloves, peeled
2 dried chiles	2 cups water
½ small yellow onion, roughly chopped	2 cups white vinegar

1. In a medium saucepan, combine the fresh and dried chiles, onion, garlic, and water. Bring to a simmer and cook for 20 minutes, or until tender. Transfer to a food processor or blender. 2. Add the vinegar and blend until smooth.

Per Serving:

1 cup: calories: 41 | fat: 0g | protein: 1g | carbs: 5g | fiber: 1g | sodium: 11mg

Seedy Crackers

Prep time: 25 minutes | Cook time: 15 minutes | Makes 24 crackers

1 cup almond flour	¼ teaspoon salt
1 tablespoon sesame seeds	Freshly ground black pepper
1 tablespoon flaxseed	1 large egg, at room
1 tablespoon chia seeds	temperature
¼ teaspoon baking soda	

1. Preheat the oven to 350ºF (180ºC). 2. In a large bowl, combine the almond flour, sesame seeds, flaxseed, chia seeds, baking soda, salt, and pepper and stir well. 3. In a small bowl, whisk the egg until well beaten. Add to the dry ingredients and stir well to combine and form the dough into a ball. 4. Place one layer of parchment paper on your counter-top and place the dough on top. Cover with a second layer of parchment and, using a rolling pin, roll the dough to ⅛-inch thickness, aiming for a rectangular shape. 5. Cut the dough into 1- to 2-inch crackers and bake on parchment until crispy and slightly golden, 10 to 15 minutes, depending on thickness. Alternatively, you can bake the large rolled dough prior to cutting and break into free-form crackers once baked and crispy. 6. Store in an airtight container in the fridge for up to 1 week.

Per Serving:

2 crackers: calories: 65 | fat: 5g | protein: 3g | carbs: 2g | fiber: 2g | sodium: 83mg

Miso-Ginger Dressing

Prep time: 10 minutes | Cook time: 0 minutes | Serves 4

1 tablespoon unseasoned rice vinegar	1 garlic clove, minced
1 tablespoon red or white miso	3 tablespoons extra-virgin olive oil
1 teaspoon grated fresh ginger	

1. In a small bowl, combine the vinegar and miso into a paste. Add the ginger and garlic, and mix well. While whisking, drizzle in the olive oil. 2. Store in the refrigerator in an airtight container for up to 1 week.

Per Serving:

calories: 100 | fat: 10g | protein: 1g | carbs: 2g | fiber: 0g | sodium: 159mg

Cucumber Yogurt Dip

Prep time: 5 minutes | Cook time: 0 minutes | Serves 2 to 3

1 cup plain, unsweetened, full-fat Greek yogurt	1 tablespoon chopped fresh mint
½ cup cucumber, peeled, seeded, and diced	1 small garlic clove, minced
1 tablespoon freshly squeezed lemon juice	Salt and freshly ground black pepper, to taste

1. In a food processor, combine the yogurt, cucumber, lemon juice, mint, and garlic. Pulse several times to combine, leaving noticeable cucumber chunks. 2. Taste and season with salt and pepper.
Per Serving:
calories: 55 | fat: 3g | protein: 3g | carbs: 5g | fiber: 0g | sodium: 38mg

Traditional Caesar Dressing

Prep time: 10 minutes | Cook time: 5 minutes | Makes 1½ cups

2 teaspoons minced garlic	1 cup extra-virgin olive oil
4 large egg yolks	¼ cup freshly squeezed lemon juice
¼ cup wine vinegar	
½ teaspoon dry mustard	Sea salt and freshly ground black pepper, to taste
Dash Worcestershire sauce	

1. To a small saucepan, add the garlic, egg yolks, vinegar, mustard, and Worcestershire sauce and place over low heat. 2. Whisking constantly, cook the mixture until it thickens and is a little bubbly, about 5 minutes. 3. Remove from saucepan from the heat and let it stand for about 10 minutes to cool. 4. Transfer the egg mixture to a large stainless steel bowl. Whisking constantly, add the olive oil in a thin stream. 5. Whisk in the lemon juice and season the dressing with salt and pepper. 6. Transfer the dressing to an airtight container and keep in the refrigerator for up to 3 days.
Per Serving:
calories: 202 | fat: 21g | protein: 2g | carbs: 2g | fiber: 0g | sodium: 14mg

Melitzanosalata (Greek Eggplant Dip)

Prep time: 10 minutes | Cook time: 3 minutes | Serves 8

1 cup water	1 tablespoon red wine vinegar
1 large eggplant, peeled and chopped	½ cup extra-virgin olive oil
1 clove garlic, peeled	2 tablespoons minced fresh parsley
½ teaspoon salt	

1. Add water to the Instant Pot®, add the rack to the pot, and place the steamer basket on the rack. 2. Place eggplant in steamer basket. Close lid, set steam release to Sealing, press the Manual button, and set time to 3 minutes. When the timer beeps, quick-release the pressure until the float valve drops. Press the Cancel button and open lid. 3. Transfer eggplant to a food processor and add garlic, salt, and vinegar. Pulse until smooth, about 20 pulses. 4. Slowly add oil to the eggplant mixture while the food processor runs continuously until oil is completely incorporated. Stir in parsley. Serve at room temperature.
Per Serving:
calories: 134 | fat: 14g | protein: 1g | carbs: 3g | fiber: 2g | sodium:

149mg

Olive Tapenade

Prep time: 10 minutes | Cook time: 0 minutes | Makes about 1 cup

¾ cup pitted brine-cured green or black olives, chopped fine	1 tablespoon capers, rinsed and minced
1 small shallot, minced	1½ teaspoons red wine vinegar
2 tablespoons extra-virgin olive oil	1 teaspoon minced fresh oregano

1. Combine all ingredients in bowl. (Tapenade can be refrigerated for up to 1 week.)
Per Serving:
¼ cup: calories: 92 | fat: 9g | protein: 0g | carbs: 2g | fiber: 1g | sodium: 236mg

Riced Cauliflower

Prep time: 5 minutes | Cook time: 10 minutes | Serves 6 to 8

1 small head cauliflower, broken into florets	1½ teaspoons salt
¼ cup extra-virgin olive oil	½ teaspoon freshly ground black pepper
2 garlic cloves, finely minced	

1. Place the florets in a food processor and pulse several times, until the cauliflower is the consistency of rice or couscous. 2. In a large skillet, heat the olive oil over medium-high heat. Add the cauliflower, garlic, salt, and pepper and sauté for 5 minutes, just to take the crunch out but not enough to let the cauliflower become soggy. 3. Remove the cauliflower from the skillet and place in a bowl until ready to use. Toss with chopped herbs and additional olive oil for a simple side, top with sautéed veggies and protein, or use in your favorite recipe.
Per Serving:
calories: 69 | fat: 7g | protein: 1g | carbs: 2g | fiber: 1g | sodium: 446mg

Roasted Harissa

Prep time: 5 minutes | Cook time: 15 minutes | Makes ¾ cup

1 red bell pepper	½ teaspoon ground cumin
2 small fresh red chiles, or more to taste	½ teaspoon ground caraway
4 garlic cloves, unpeeled	1 tablespoon fresh lemon juice
½ teaspoon ground coriander	½ teaspoon salt

1. Preheat the broiler to high. 2. Put the bell pepper, chiles, and garlic on a baking sheet and broil for 6 to 8 minutes. Turn the vegetables over and broil for 5 to 6 minutes more, until the pepper and chiles are softened and blackened. Remove from the broiler and set aside until cool enough to handle. Remove and discard the stems, skin, and seeds from the pepper and chiles. Remove and discard the papery skin from the garlic. 3. Put the flesh of the pepper and chiles with the garlic cloves in a blender or food processor. Add the coriander, cumin, caraway, lemon juice, and salt and blend until smooth. 4. This may be stored refrigerated for up to 3 days. Store in an airtight container, and cover the sauce with a ¼-inch layer of oil.
Per Serving:
calories: 28 | fat: 0g | protein: 1g | carbs: 6g | fiber: 1g | sodium: 393mg

Herbed Butter

Prep time: 10 minutes | Cook time: 0 minutes | Makes ½ cup

½ cup (1 stick) butter, at room temperature	fresh rosemary
1 garlic clove, finely minced	1 teaspoon finely chopped fresh oregano
2 teaspoons finely chopped	½ teaspoon salt

1. In a food processor, combine the butter, garlic, rosemary, oregano, and salt and pulse until the mixture is well combined, smooth, and creamy, scraping down the sides as necessary. Alternatively, you can whip the ingredients together with an electric mixer. 2. Using a spatula, scrape the butter mixture into a small bowl or glass container and cover. Store in the refrigerator for up to 1 month.

Per Serving:
⅛ cup: calories: 206 | fat: 23g | protein: 0g | carbs: 206g | fiber: 0g | sodium: 294mg

Peanut Sauce

Prep time: 5 minutes | Cook time: 0 minutes | Serves 4

⅓ cup peanut butter	Juice of 1 lime
¼ cup hot water	1 teaspoon minced fresh ginger
2 tablespoons soy sauce	1 teaspoon minced garlic
2 tablespoons rice vinegar	1 teaspoon black pepper

1. In a blender container, combine the peanut butter, hot water, soy sauce, vinegar, lime juice, ginger, garlic, and pepper. Blend until smooth. 2. Use immediately or store in an airtight container in the refrigerator for a week or more.

Per Serving:
calories: 408 | fat: 33g | protein: 16g | carbs: 18g | fiber: 5g | sodium: 2525mg

Lemon Tahini Dressing

Prep time: 5 minutes | Cook time: 0 minutes | Makes ½ cup

¼ cup tahini	¼ teaspoon pure maple syrup
3 tablespoons lemon juice	¼ teaspoon ground cumin
3 tablespoons warm water	⅛ teaspoon cayenne pepper
¼ teaspoon kosher salt	

1. In a medium bowl, whisk together the tahini, lemon juice, water, salt, maple syrup, cumin, and cayenne pepper until smooth. Place in the refrigerator until ready to serve. Store any leftovers in the refrigerator in an airtight container up to 5 days.

Per Serving:
2 tablespoons: calories: 90 | fat: 7g | protein: 3g | carbs: 5g | fiber: 1g | sodium: 80mg

Marinated Artichokes

Prep time: 10 minutes | Cook time: 0 minutes | Makes 2 cups

2 (13¾-ounce / 390-g) cans artichoke hearts, drained and quartered	leaves
	2 teaspoons chopped fresh oregano or 1 teaspoon dried oregano
¾ cup extra-virgin olive oil	
4 small garlic cloves, crushed with the back of a knife	1 teaspoon red pepper flakes (optional)
1 tablespoon fresh rosemary	1 teaspoon salt

1. In a medium bowl, combine the artichoke hearts, olive oil, garlic, rosemary, oregano, red pepper flakes (if using), and salt. Toss to combine well. 2. Store in an airtight glass container in the refrigerator and marinate for at least 24 hours before using. Store in the refrigerator for up to 2 weeks.

Per Serving:
¼ cup: calories: 228 | fat: 20g | protein: 3g | carbs: 11g | fiber: 5g | sodium: 381mg

Apple Cider Dressing

Prep time: 5 minutes | Cook time: 0 minutes | Serves 2

2 tablespoons apple cider vinegar	⅓ lemon, zested
⅓ lemon, juiced	Salt and freshly ground black pepper, to taste

1. In a jar, combine the vinegar, lemon juice, and zest. Season with salt and pepper, cover, and shake well.

Per Serving:
calories: 7 | fat: 0g | protein: 0g | carbs: 1g | fiber: 0g | sodium: 1mg

Tzatziki

Prep time: 10 minutes | Cook time: 0 minutes | Serves 4

1 large cucumber, peeled and grated (about 2 cups)	1 tablespoon fresh lemon juice
1 cup plain Greek yogurt	½ teaspoon kosher salt, or to taste
2 to 3 garlic cloves, minced	
1 tablespoon tahini (sesame paste)	Chopped fresh parsley or dill, for garnish (optional)

1. In a medium bowl, combine the cucumber, yogurt, garlic, tahini, lemon juice, and salt. Stir until well combined. Cover and chill until ready to serve. 2. Right before serving, sprinkle with chopped fresh parsley, if desired.

Per Serving:
calories: 71 | fat: 4g | protein: 3g | carbs: 6g | fiber: 1g | sodium: 325mg

White Bean Hummus

Prep time: 10 minutes | Cook time: 30 minutes | Serves 12

⅔ cup dried white beans, rinsed and drained	¼ cup olive oil
	1 tablespoon lemon juice
3 cloves garlic, peeled and crushed	½ teaspoon salt

1. Place beans and garlic in the Instant Pot® and stir well. Add enough cold water to cover ingredients. Close lid, set steam release to Sealing, press the Manual button, and set time to 30 minutes. 2. When the timer beeps, let pressure release naturally, about 20 minutes. Press the Cancel button and open lid. Use a fork to check that beans are tender. Drain off excess water and transfer beans to a food processor. 3. Add oil, lemon juice, and salt to the processor and pulse until mixture is smooth with some small chunks. Transfer to a storage container and refrigerate for at least 4 hours. Serve cold or at room temperature. Store in the refrigerator for up to one week.

Per Serving:
calories: 57 | fat: 5g | protein: 1g | carbs: 3g | fiber: 1g | sodium: 99mg

Olive Mint Vinaigrette

Prep time: 5 minutes | Cook time: 0 minutes | Makes ½ cup

¼ cup white wine vinegar
¼ teaspoon honey
¼ teaspoon kosher salt
¼ teaspoon freshly ground black pepper

¼ cup extra-virgin olive oil
¼ cup olives, pitted and minced
2 tablespoons fresh mint, minced

1. In a bowl, whisk together the vinegar, honey, salt, and black pepper. Add the olive oil and whisk well. Add the olives and mint, and mix well. Store any leftovers in the refrigerator in an airtight container for up to 5 days.

Per Serving:

2 tablespoons: calories: 135 | fat: 15g | protein: 0g | carbs: 1g | fiber: 0g | sodium: 135mg

Bagna Cauda

Prep time: 5 minutes | Cook time: 20 minutes | Serves 8 to 10

½ cup extra-virgin olive oil
4 tablespoons (½ stick) butter
8 anchovy fillets, very finely chopped

4 large garlic cloves, finely minced
½ teaspoon salt
½ teaspoon freshly ground black pepper

1. In a small saucepan, heat the olive oil and butter over medium-low heat until the butter is melted. 2. Add the anchovies and garlic and stir to combine. Add the salt and pepper and reduce the heat to low. Cook, stirring occasionally, until the anchovies are very soft and the mixture is very fragrant, about 20 minutes. 3. Serve warm, drizzled over steamed vegetables, as a dipping sauce for raw veggies or cooked artichokes, or use as a salad dressing. Store leftovers in an airtight container in the refrigerator for up to 2 weeks.

Per Serving:

calories: 145 | fat: 16g | protein: 1g | carbs: 0g | fiber: 0g | sodium: 235mg

Sweet Red Wine Vinaigrette

Prep time: 5 minutes | Cook time: 0 minutes | Serves 2

¼ cup plus 2 tablespoons extra-virgin olive oil
2 tablespoons red wine vinegar
1 tablespoon apple cider vinegar
2 teaspoons honey

2 teaspoons Dijon mustard
½ teaspoon minced garlic
⅛ teaspoon kosher salt
⅛ teaspoon freshly ground black pepper

1. In a jar, combine the olive oil, vinegars, honey, mustard, garlic, salt, and pepper and shake well.

Per Serving:

calories: 386 | fat: 41g | protein: 0g | carbs: 6g | fiber: 0g | sodium: 198mg

Appendix 1: Measurement Conversion Chart

MEASUREMENT CONVERSION CHART

VOLUME EQUIVALENTS(DRY)

US STANDARD	METRIC (APPROXIMATE)
1/8 teaspoon	0.5 mL
1/4 teaspoon	1 mL
1/2 teaspoon	2 mL
3/4 teaspoon	4 mL
1 teaspoon	5 mL
1 tablespoon	15 mL
1/4 cup	59 mL
1/2 cup	118 mL
3/4 cup	177 mL
1 cup	235 mL
2 cups	475 mL
3 cups	700 mL
4 cups	1 L

VOLUME EQUIVALENTS(LIQUID)

US STANDARD	US STANDARD (OUNCES)	METRIC (APPROXIMATE)
2 tablespoons	1 fl.oz.	30 mL
1/4 cup	2 fl.oz.	60 mL
1/2 cup	4 fl.oz.	120 mL
1 cup	8 fl.oz.	240 mL
1 1/2 cup	12 fl.oz.	355 mL
2 cups or 1 pint	16 fl.oz.	475 mL
4 cups or 1 quart	32 fl.oz.	1 L
1 gallon	128 fl.oz.	4 L

TEMPERATURES EQUIVALENTS

FAHRENHEIT(F)	CELSIUS(C) (APPROXIMATE)
225 °F	107 °C
250 °F	120 °C
275 °F	135 °C
300 °F	150 °C
325 °F	160 °C
350 °F	180 °C
375 °F	190 °C
400 °F	205 °C
425 °F	220 °C
450 °F	235 °C
475 °F	245 °C
500 °F	260 °C

WEIGHT EQUIVALENTS

US STANDARD	METRIC (APPROXIMATE)
1 ounce	28 g
2 ounces	57 g
5 ounces	142 g
10 ounces	284 g
15 ounces	425 g
16 ounces	455 g
(1 pound)	
1.5 pounds	680 g
2 pounds	907 g

Appendix 2: The Dirty Dozen and Clean Fifteen

The Dirty Dozen and Clean Fifteen

The Environmental Working Group (EWG) is a nonprofit, nonpartisan organization dedicated to protecting human health and the environment Its mission is to empower people to live healthier lives in a healthier environment. This organization publishes an annual list of the twelve kinds of produce, in sequence, that have the highest amount of pesticide residue-the Dirty Dozen-as well as a list of the fifteen kinds ofproduce that have the least amount of pesticide residue-the Clean Fifteen.

THE DIRTY DOZEN	THE CLEAN FIFTEEN
• The 2016 Dirty Dozen includes the following produce. These are considered among the year's most important produce to buy organic:	• The least critical to buy organically are the Clean Fifteen list. The following are on the 2016 list:

THE DIRTY DOZEN

Strawberries · Spinach
Apples · Tomatoes
Nectarines · Bell peppers
Peaches · Cherry tomatoes
Celery · Cucumbers
Grapes · Kale/collard greens
Cherries · Hot peppers

• *The Dirty Dozen list contains two additional itemskale/collard greens and hot peppers-because they tend to contain trace levels of highly hazardous pesticides.*

THE CLEAN FIFTEEN

Avocados · Papayas
Corn · Kiw
Pineapples · Eggplant
Cabbage · Honeydew
Sweet peas · Grapefruit
Onions · Cantaloupe
Asparagus · Cauliflower
Mangos

• *Some of the sweet corn sold in the United States are made from genetically engineered (GE) seedstock. Buy organic varieties of these crops to avoid GE produce.*

Appendix 3: Recipe Index

A

B

C

Made in United States
Troutdale, OR
01/27/2024

17213493R00060